Politics, Media and Campaign Language

ANTHEM STUDIES IN AUSTRALIAN POLITICS, ECONOMICS AND SOCIETY

This series showcases the most significant contributions to scholarship on a wide range of social science issues, dealing with the changing politics, economics and society of Australia, while not losing sight of the interplay of other regional and global forces and their influence and impact on this region. ***Anthem Studies in Australian Politics, Economics and Society*** is intended as an interdisciplinary series, at the interface of politics, law, sociology, media, policy, political economy, economics, business, criminology and anthropology. It is seeking to publish high quality research which considers issues of power, justice and democracy; and provides a critical contribution to knowledge about Australian politics, economics and society. The series especially welcomes books from emerging scholars which contribute new perspectives on social science.

Editorial Board

Series Editor-in-Chief

Sally Young – University of Melbourne, Australia

Series Editors

Timothy Marjoribanks – La Trobe Business School, Australia

Joo-Cheong Tham – Melbourne Law School, University of Melbourne, Australia

Editorial Board

Iain Campbell – Royal Melbourne Institute of Technology (RMIT), Australia

Sara Charlesworth – Royal Melbourne Institute of Technology (RMIT), Australia

Kevin Foster – Monash University, Australia

Anika Gauja – The University of Sydney, Australia

John Germov – The University of Newcastle, Australia

Michael Gilding – Swinburne University of Technology, Australia

Simon Jackman – Stanford University, USA

Carol Johnson – The University of Adelaide, Australia

Deb King – Flinders University, Australia

Jude McCulloch – Monash University, Australia

Jenny Morgan – University of Melbourne, Australia

Vanessa Ratten – La Trobe University, Australia

Ben Spies-Butcher – Macquarie University, Australia

Ariadne Vromen – The University of Sydney, Australia

John Wanna – Australian National University, Australia

George Williams – The University of New South Wales, Australia

Politics, Media and Campaign Language

Australia's Identity Anxiety

Stephanie Brookes

ANTHEM PRESS

Anthem Press
An imprint of Wimbledon Publishing Company
www.anthempress.com

This edition first published in UK and USA 2020
by ANTHEM PRESS
75–76 Blackfriars Road, London SE1 8HA, UK
or PO Box 9779, London SW19 7ZG, UK
and
244 Madison Ave #116, New York, NY 10016, USA

First published in the UK and USA by Anthem Press 2017

Copyright © Stephanie Brookes 2020

The moral right of the authors has been asserted.

All rights reserved. Without limiting the rights under copyright reserved above, no part of this publication may be reproduced, stored or introduced into a retrieval system, or transmitted, in any form or by any means (electronic, mechanical, photocopying, recording or otherwise), without the prior written permission of both the copyright owner and the above publisher of this book.

British Library Cataloguing-in-Publication Data
A catalogue record for this book is available from the British Library.

Library of Congress Cataloging-in-Publication Data
Library of Congress Control Number: 2019953378

ISBN-13: 978-1-78527-246-2 (Pbk)
ISBN-10: 1-78527-246-2 (Pbk)

This title is also available as an e-book.

Modern democratic politicians use words for two main purposes – to simplify and to mystify. They simplify because they cannot describe matters in even half their complexity and expect to be understood or listened to. They use messages: simple one or two-line message which they hope will work like semaphores as they beat their way through the tangle of political life. These messages take on a meaning independent of the complex reality, they become the currency of the debate, the story, in the end they become the reality itself; at least that is the aim.

Don Watson, *Recollections of a Bleeding Heart*, 2002

Australians and their children will increasingly live lives caught up in the phenomenon of our internationalisation and find jobs in the industry of our region. And their income growth will be guaranteed. We can enter the new century a unique country with a unique future. We can enter it prosperous and dynamic: a diverse and tolerant society, trading actively in Asia and the rest of the world; secure in our identity, the more so because we know that we have met the challenge of our times. It is the greatest challenge we have ever faced as a nation. By the year 2000 we should be able to say that we have learned to live securely, in peace and mutual prosperity among our Asian and Pacific neighbours.

Paul Keating, *ALP Policy Launch Speech*, 1996

CONTENTS

Acknowledgements		ix
1.	Introduction	1
2.	Storytelling	17
3.	Belonging	39
4.	Values	61
5.	Community	87
6.	Security	115
7.	Vision	137
8.	Hearts and Minds	159
Appendix 1.	Federal Election Dates Included in Qualitative Discourse Analysis Sample, 1901–2013	179
Appendix 2.	Australian Federal Election Dates and Results, 1901–2016	181
Appendix 3.	Major Australian Political Parties, 1901–2016	183
Appendix 4.	Changes of Government, Prime Minister and Leader, 1901–2015	185
References		189
Index		215

ACKNOWLEDGEMENTS

I completed a PhD thesis, 'A Generous, Open-Hearted People: Political Constructions of National Identity in Australian Federal Election Campaign Language, 1901–2007', in the Media and Communications Program at the University of Melbourne in 2009. This book is based on that research but is an extensively rewritten and updated piece of work.

The original research for this book was undertaken with the financial support of an Australian government Australian Postgraduate Award. I would also like to gratefully acknowledge additional financial support for research fieldwork and travel through the Research and Graduate Studies Grant received from the School of Culture and Communication, University of Melbourne, and through the Australian Research Council's Discovery Project Scheme (DP0663208).

The development of this book project was supported in its early stages by a Manuscript Sponsorship Grant from the Writing Centre for Scholars and Researchers at the University of Melbourne (now the Melbourne Engagement Lab). The advice and support provided by Sybil Nolan during this process was invaluable, and I thank her for her detailed feedback and faith in this project. Thanks also to Simon Clews and the staff at the centre for their support. The final publication of this book was supported by the Publication Support and New Appointees grants from Monash University School of Media, Film and Journalism.

The findings from my original research were presented in a number of forums and publications in the journey from PhD thesis to book. While not directly reproduced here, this book revises and updates insight and analysis from earlier articles written while this research was in development: in conference papers presented over a number of years to the Australian Political Science Association Conference and to the Politics and the Media Conference at the University of Melbourne in 2008; and in the following published articles:

- 2012. '"Secure in our Identity": Regional Threat and Opportunity in Australian Election Discourse, 1993 and 1996'. *Australian Journal of Politics and History* 58(4): 542–56.

- 2008. "Working Families" and the "Opportunity Society": Political Rhetoric in the 2007 Australian Federal Election Campaign'. *Communication, Politics and Culture* 41(2): 62–83.

I would like to gratefully acknowledge the following people and organizations for their assistance with archival access and research fieldwork: Siobhan Dee at Screensound Australia; Jenny Jeremy at the Bob Hawke Prime Ministerial Library; Lesley Wallace at the John Curtin Prime Ministerial Library; Dr Caitlin Stone at the Malcolm Fraser Collection; Jonathon Tunn at the National Press Club; Andrew Griffin at the National Archives in Melbourne, and William Edwards at the National Archives in Canberra; Marie Dudgeon in the Oral History and Folklore Department at the National Library of Australia; the staff at the Whitlam Institute, Sydney; Lisa Savage in Copyright at Channel Seven; Jenny Guion in Copyright at Channel Nine; Wai Wai Lun and Kim Mussche at the University of Queensland Library.

My deepest thanks to Sally Young, who I have been lucky enough to call supervisor, colleague and friend across my scholarly career, for her unfailing patience, mentorship and support. I would also like to thank the many other friends and colleagues who gave me support and feedback as the project developed, especially Ramaswami Harindranath for his insightful feedback on, and critical reading of, the PhD version of this research. For their help and advice in a variety of ways, thank you to Deb Anderson, Fay Anderson, Phil Chubb, Geoffrey Craig, Brett Hutchins, Carol Johnson, Mia Lindgren, David Nolan and Karen Spitz; and to colleagues past and present from the Media and Communications Program at the University of Melbourne and in the Journalism Section at Monash University.

My thanks also to Kiran Bolla, Katy Miller, Abi Pandey and the editorial staff at Anthem Press.

And finally, thank you to my wonderful family for your unfailing support, willingness to engage in political discussion, and faith in this project over many years; especially to Andrew for your invaluable advice and insight; to Georgia and Theodore; and to Katherine, Joseph, Meredith and Robert.

Chapter 1

INTRODUCTION

Two days before Australians went to the polls in the 2007 federal election, long serving Liberal Party prime minister John Howard took to the stage at the National Press Club in Canberra. He had been on the campaign trail for almost six weeks by the time he faced this room full of journalists in the nation's capital in late November. The Press Club address is one of the staples of modern Australian federal elections, bookending the earlier policy launch speech in which prime ministerial candidates open their party's campaign with an outline of policies, priorities and promises. This was Howard's final major address, at the tail end of a campaign infused with the feeling that a change was in the air. His opponent, Australian Labor Party (ALP)[1] leader Kevin Rudd, had spoken in the same place only the day before, making a case for 'new leadership' after Labor's 11 and a half years in the political wilderness. It was Howard's last chance to explain why Australians should return his government for a fifth term.

Australia, the prime minister boasted, was a 'stronger, prouder and more prosperous nation' than it had been when he was elected in March 1996. He listed his government's achievements in prosperity and productivity; defence and border security; foreign policy; social security; employment; taxes; and welfare. In all of these, Howard repeatedly emphasized that Australia was 'a nation transformed'. He then laid claim to a fundamental transformation in Australian culture:

> And finally in the area of national self-confidence this is also a nation transformed. We no longer have perpetual seminars about our national identity, we no longer agonise as to whether we're Asian or European or part-Asian or part-European or too British or not British enough, or too close to the Americans or whatever. We actually rejoice in what has always been the reality, and that is that we are gloriously and distinctively Australian. (Howard 2007f)

---

[1] The ALP changed the spelling of its party name from 'Labour' to 'Labor' in 1912; for the sake of clarity, the latter will be used throughout this book.

Howard's words are incredibly revealing, significant as much for what they say about the nature of Australian identity as for the transformation they describe. He paints an image of an Australian community that has historically 'agonized' about its identity, wondering: how will we deal with the tension between a dominant Western cultural tradition and geographical proximity to a region imagined as the Asia-Pacific? How does the problematic founding notion of *terra nullius* (or 'empty land') impact on our ability to feel ownership of, and belonging to, the national space? At the same time as he diagnosed this history, however, Howard also reassured voters that these debates were not necessary. They had *always* been 'gloriously and distinctively Australian'; what was missing was simply *confidence*. For Howard, the burst of 'self-confidence' that had transformed the nation by the end of 2007 was a direct result of the policies and actions of his government. After the critical self-reflection that had characterized the terms of his Labor predecessors, Bob Hawke and Paul Keating, Australians' faith in themselves had been restored. Howard painted a picture of progress, where a mature and newly confident national community left 'navel gazing' behind to take their rightful place as a small but prosperous player in world affairs, with a reputation for being generous and welcoming, committed to 'fairness' and 'opportunity'. However, the prime minister's reassurances betrayed deeper tensions and anxieties. Australian identity will always be in flux, contingent and unsettled; and Howard's self-congratulatory image of a nation finally 'settling' their identity questions only masked its fragile and contingent nature (and indeed, that of identity itself).

This book engages with public and political discourse to argue that the story of Australian identity is not a tale of increasing self-confidence but rather one of recurring cycles of anxiety and reassurance. Australian identity is a work of collective and individual imagination, constantly evolving and influenced by the contexts in which it is developed. The language of federal election campaigns provides a unique window into this process. Federal elections are moments of change and challenge, when citizens are called on to think beyond the local attachments of their daily lives – to friends and family, neighbourhood and community – and imagine themselves as members of a larger national collective. In every election, these voters are promised that their decision is about more than party politics; that it is vital for national development, or prosperity or security. 'My fellow Australians', new Opposition Leader Bob Hawke (1983) told voters in 1983, 'today we set out together on a task much greater than winning an election', the task 'to win the future for Australia and all Australians'.

Election campaign language is distinctive. Its goals, and its audience, differ markedly from other kinds of political language such as press releases, policy documents or the routine communications of governing. More is at stake, and there is a sense that elections are a time when it is possible to engage with those who aren't usually listening to politicians when they speak; a chance to move campaigning politicians' dialogue with their constituents to the centre of the national public stage. At the same time as the words spoken by campaigning leaders aim to attract media coverage and electoral support, they also work on a deeper level, inviting citizens to think and act as guardians of the national interest.

This book examines the way that campaigning political leaders have used their words to imagine Australian identity for voters, both now and in the past. At a time when people inside and outside politics feel alienated from the national political conversation, it reminds us of the complex and enduring relationship between political leaders and their constituents across Australian history. It asks: who are the leaders that have told the most convincing stories about Australian identity, and how have they aligned their vision and plans for the nation with the values and priorities of citizens? What were the alternative visions presented to the Australian people by prime ministerial candidates who were not successful at the ballot box? How, and why, have concerns about the economic, military and cultural security of Australian identity characterized federal election campaign language for over a century?

In addressing these questions, this book offers a detailed study of Australian political discourse, told through more than a century of election campaign language. It provides an up-to-date analysis of continuities and changes in the Australian identity stories told by campaigning leaders from Federation to the current day, and locates these political constructions of identity in a new way against an ever-changing media landscape in which understanding and responding to emerging forms of political journalism and new communication technologies is vital in appealing to voters. The chapters that follow therefore not only offer new insight into how Australian identity stories (as told by campaigning leaders) have evolved, but also illuminate the ongoing importance of spoken political language in the increasingly professional, 'mediatized' contemporary campaign. They explore the vital role of connection and emotion both in election campaigns and in the construction of individual and collective identity; both processes are about more than rational decision-making. It is for this reason that Robert Menzies, writing about the 'art' of politics in the *New York Times* magazine in 1948, argued that political speech needs to be 'made *to* [audiences], not merely in their presence'. For Menzies (1948), the 'essence' of political speech was that it 'reach the hearts and minds of [the] immediate audience'.

National Self-confidence

John Howard's words to the Press Club were underpinned by assumptions that will resonate with anyone familiar with Australian social and political history. Questions of what it means to be Australian, and the security of that identity, have been an ongoing feature of the nation's cultural, social and political life for more than a century (see Burke 2008; Walker 1999). Australians have felt isolated and insecure since their earliest days as a nation, acutely aware of potential threats to their way of life: the regional immigrants who seem to represent a 'Yellow Peril'; the unfamiliar ideologies that might take hold in national space imagined as *ours*; the asylum seekers whose arrival seems to breach secure national borders; and the danger of being irrelevant on the global stage. In his incisive 2003 study *Against Paranoid Nationalism*, Australian social theorist and anthropologist Ghassan Hage (2003, 3) argued that during the Howard years, 'a culture of caring' about the nation eroded, replaced by 'the institutionalisation of a culture of *worrying*'. Hage (2003, 3) characterizes this as inherently narcissistic: 'you worry about the nation', he argues, 'only when *you* feel threatened' and, 'ultimately, you are only worrying about yourself'. This is driven by long-held feelings of insecurity about the nation and our relationship to it – 'a White paranoia' that has 'structured Australian nationalism from the time of its birth' (Hage 2003, 47).

The project to more clearly define Australian identity (which historian Richard White [1981, viii] has described as a 'national obsession') operates in this context. It has been a project aimed at providing Australians with what I refer to in this book as *identity security* – the feeling that their way of life, and the space in which it plays out, is free from threat. Narratives of identity security work through the twin reassurance mechanisms of definition and protection, which have been as consistent in Australian history as the state of anxiety they address. The first is a form of diagnosis that attempts to define both the national community itself, and the potential threats that might cause concern: whether uncontrolled immigration; unfamiliar religions or ideologies; changing global social and economic circumstances; war; or terrorism. The second offers treatment for the symptoms, a reassurance through empowerment, and the promise that we are in control of (and able to protect) both the national way of life and also the national space in which it is lived. This takes both positive and negative forms, manifesting in the inspirational language of nation building as well as the defensive discourse of exclusion.

This distinctive discourse of *identity security* echoes throughout Australian social and cultural history. It emerges in public and political debates about who we are and where we belong; what makes us unique as a people; whether our way of life is secure against military, economic, cultural and ideological threat; and whether we are able to influence our own future. Seeing concern over, and attempts to provide, a secure sense of identity as *cyclical* offers a new insight into the nature of Australian identity, and the narratives through which it is constructed and understood. While the specific causes of concern change as social, political and economic contexts in Australia and globally impact on cultural dialogue and public debate, the fundamental underlying condition of *insecurity* is remarkably consistent.

Australian identity is characterized by these cycles. In many ways, Australians have been having the same conversations for more than a century. A particular (real or perceived) threat bubbles to the surface, causing a crisis of confidence that requires reassurance. When the crisis passes, the underlying condition – a sense of insecurity – persists. As a national community, we continue to react to this underlying feeling in the same way, seeking treatment in the face of a scary new symptom (or an old one appearing in a new guise). For example, while the perceived threat posed by uncontrolled immigration in Australia has flared up, in different forms, since Federation, the language that has been used to name this threat has changed dramatically. The most striking shift occurred as explicitly race-based language became inappropriate in the latter half of the twentieth century. Australian political leaders therefore worked to exclude those immigrants defined as undesirable from the national space and identity in different ways. In the 1906 election, Prime Minister Alfred Deakin (1906) used his policy launch speech to identify and number the 'kanaka' labourers working in the Queensland sugar plantations, promising to return them to 'the land of their birth' in line with the White Australia Policy. While this kind of language would be out of place today, the construction of threat and accompanying promise to manage the nation's borders resonates. It finds its clearest legacy in language used by both sides of politics to promise, at the start of the twenty-first century, to manage those who come to Australian shores seeking asylum. In these more recent elections, these immigrants are defined by their 'illegal' method of entry or 'incompatible' culture rather than by references to their race, and promises are made to implement offshore processing of arrivals to ensure 'stronger protection of our borders' (see, for example, Gillard 2010a) or to simply 'stop the boats' (Abbott 2010a; 2010b; 2013g; Turnbull 2016d).

However, these defensive reactions are not the only responses that develop from Australia's underlying identity insecurity. Other mechanisms of reassurance lead to identity narratives that are more positive, with the same feeling of insecurity motivating a positive articulation of values and a story Australians can feel proud to be associated with. Anxiety can therefore be harnessed to propel Australians forward as a nation, with the discourse of *identity security* manifesting in nation-building language that provides inspiration to strive for progress, and calls on Australians to *do* and *be* better. The defensive and inspirational outcomes of these cycles of insecurity and reassurance are closely linked. For example, accompanying the exclusive discourses of immigration management discussed above have been elements of the national story that have asked Australians to be welcoming and tolerant, more open in their definitions of who belongs to the national collective and what 'Australianness' looks like. In the language of leaders like Joseph 'Ben' Chifley, Malcolm Fraser and Bob Hawke, Australians have been asked to see themselves as a diverse, multicultural community that accommodates cultural, religious and other differences and welcomes immigrants into the national identity.

The Australian national story is therefore constructed from things that make voters feel good about themselves as well as those that seem to threaten the security of their valuable identity. This has been one of the most powerful and consistent elements in Australia's national political conversation. The lack of confidence that pervades Australian identity is revealed in a new way in this book, through close attention to the identity stories told by campaigning leaders during election campaigns.

I'm Talking to You

The language of campaigning political leaders offers a unique window into the national mood. Campaign speech crystallizes something of what the nation is and who it contains, offering an insight into narratives of identity as they play out in the political realm. The most significant moments in Australian political history are inextricable from the political language that framed them: Andrew Fisher's 1914 campaign pledge of Australian support for Britain in World War I to 'the last man and the last shilling'; Ben Chifley's 1949 description of Labor as the 'light on the hill'; Gough Whitlam's 1972 conviction that *It's Time* for a change; and John Howard's 2001 assertion that 'we will decide who comes to this country and the circumstances under which they come'.

The particular relationship between politicians and the people that they represent lends a distinctive dimension to these Australian identity stories. Political leaders are conditioned by and immersed in the same shared histories, values and culture that they work to define once in office. As a result, they are shaped by the same underlying national hopes and anxieties as the rest of the population, members of the same national collective that they hope to rework in line with their own personal and political vision for the future. Political leadership is as much about this desire to change the nation, to make a difference, as it is about specific policy outcomes. Understanding this makes clear how political discourse operates to connect the individual to the national, evoking the collective 'we' in a way that invites citizens to imagine themselves as part of it.

In this book, I am interested in the stories of Australian identity expressed by the leaders of major political parties in federal election campaigns since Federation. Engaging with the language of these campaigns – from words spoken in the heat of campaign battle to those carefully drafted and focus group tested – I demonstrate that political leaders play a key role in helping to define a secure sense of shared identity for Australians. In their campaign appeals, political leaders have drawn on long-held myths of national values, priorities, hopes and fears. As they have worked to capture the votes of the Australian public, they have also told the nation's identity stories, reinvigorating and reworking these to suit both the times and their own political personas.

Campaigning leaders' attempts to engage and shape a constituency have been characterized by a series of questions about Australian identity that recur in elections from Federation. These mirror the persistent concerns of the discourse of *identity security*. They are questions about who we are and where we fit into the world; who belongs to the national collective; how we will identify and neutralize potential threats; and what our future will look like. The politicians who have explicitly wrestled with these questions are often remembered as our greatest leaders and their answers become, for a time, a dominant national narrative. They define official discourse, guide policy decisions and can come to characterize an era, but must also speak to pre-existing ideas and concerns and compete with other narratives. The stories of Australian identity told by political leaders during campaigns (and then in government or opposition) are powerful but not absolute. They are open to challenge, and must work within a diffuse network of social discourse and representation if they are to become a definitive strand in a broader tapestry. Political leaders negotiate the diverse ideas and debates of the communities in which they work and to whom they appeal for electoral support. More deeply, they must also appeal to the fundamental need of any group of people – especially in a young nation like Australia – for a narrative of shared history and culture that offers membership in a stable collective identity. When leaders ask voters to invest in the Australian national collective, the image they present is predominantly that of a pre-existing natural entity (John Howard's 'glorious and distinctive' Australian identity that had 'always been the reality') to which birthplace and kinship, and later citizenship or the embrace of the Australian way of life, provides membership. While the criteria shift according to changing political and historical contexts, political leaders' language consistently offers voters a sense of who they are, and where they fit into the world, within the (often unspoken) framework of a naturally existing nation.

However, this very act of speaking about the nation as natural and self-evident highlights the power of political language. In doing so, political leaders themselves become part of the project of imagining Australian identity for citizens. Invoking shared understandings and then reinforcing or challenging them, they imbue what Benedict Anderson (1983) has famously called the 'imagined community' of the nation with its sense of shared history. This does not mean that this history is fabricated, but rather that leaders employ stories of Australian history and identity to appeal to voters in particular ways and at particular moments. To explore this, it is important to look not only at the formal rhetoric of political campaigns but also think about the role of empathy, instinct and sincerity in making meaningful political connections. These connections matter not only in terms of short-term political success, but also because they have engendered a real sense of investment among so-called ordinary voters in the national story.

In order to convince citizens to vote for a policy or party, campaigning leaders need to communicate a sense that their political personality and promises are genuine, and that their plans are in the best interests of the nation. Leaders tap into the themes and issues voters care about, speaking to the concerns of the electorate in language designed to both reflect and help shape the nation's values and priorities. Through this, voters are asked to feel a sense of recognition when listening to a political speech or hearing the response to an interviewer's question; to feel that this policy or proposal is *about me* and relevant to my life. This is attempted through language, using the media to talk about yourself, your candidacy and your vision of the nation in a way that makes sense to as many of 'the people' as possible. As Australian elections become increasingly presidential, it is the role of the party leader to develop this across the nation.

In our most idealistic notions of democracy, we hold in our minds the image of a well-informed, rational voting public weighing up policy proposals before casting their ballot. But voting is a more complex proposition than this, and the decisions voters make rely on a range of influences. Certainly media coverage of the campaign (both in traditional and emerging social and digital news spaces) and the parties' policy promises play a role, but so too do conversations with family, friends and colleagues, our perceptions about the performance of previous governments or the integrity of the opposition and our long-held partisan preferences. With all of this in mind, we make decisions based on intellect, instinct and emotion about the leader most likely to represent us well and make decisions in line with our own ideas about what is best for the nation.

The ability to harness this complexity is one of the characteristics by which political leaders are measured. We judge who is cutting through and who is losing touch based on an ability to reflect voters' personal and collective values. In this way, leaders are remembered, and their success as politicians evaluated, according to their oratorical skill: from Alfred Deakin's nation-building vision and Robert Menzies's fame as a master of the spoken word; to Bob Hawke's use of the Australian colloquial and Paul Keating's outbursts of parliamentary invective.

Effective political speech doesn't need to be grand or lofty. At its most powerful, it connects a political leader to voters, engaging with their experiences and aspirations. Don Watson (2002, 56–57), one of Australia's best-known political speechwriters, has written that a good speech is like 'a lover's embrace, or a brother's, father's, friend's, or mother's, depending on the circumstances'. For Watson, a political speech should make you feel that the speaker understands you. It should remind you of everything you have in common: 'your love of trees or cows, the sacrifice of soldiers, your loathing of tariffs or welfare' (Watson 2002, 56–57). John Howard, whose 2007 National Press Club speech opened this chapter, exemplifies this. While not remembered as a master orator, his electoral success was partly attributed to his ability to connect with the middle-class Australians who came to be called 'Howard's battlers'.

In his Press Club speech, Howard imagined the nation in a particular way, using both implicit and explicit narratives of Australian history to develop a familiar, secure idea of that identity and then connecting it with his own party and policies. It is in this way that campaigning political leaders provide the materials through which citizens imagine themselves as part of a collective, along with writers, artists, historians, journalists and others. There is a cultural power in their role, and paying attention to their campaign language (as this book will do) offers a valuable perspective on the themes that have characterized Australian identity stories across more than a century of Australian history; and through these a window into Australian identity itself.

This process occurs primarily through the media. The majority of voters will never hear their political leaders speak or meet them in person, but they might develop an intimate knowledge of the prime minister's voice by watching the nightly news or videos uploaded to Facebook. In the same way, they might come to recognize the opposition leader's favourite attack lines when listening to talkback radio or reading tweets or blog posts. Election campaigns are about politics *and* communication. They are a dialogue between candidates and voters conducted through mass media and, increasingly, digital and social media. As American political communication researchers Judith Trent and Robert Friedenberg (2004, 15) argue, communication 'serves as the bridge between the dreams and hopes of the voter and the actions of the candidate'. Over time, political leaders have adapted this bridge to the evolving media landscape whose technologies form the central battleground of election campaigns: from the newspaper advertising and town hall meetings of the pre-television era; and the broadcast ads, interviews and debates of the mid- to late-twentieth century; to the 24-hour news, social networking and video-sharing technologies of the twenty-first century. These elements make up the modern professional campaign in which media coverage increasingly focuses on the leader and substance vies for airtime with spin. It is in this dynamic landscape that campaign battles play out.

Despite these developments, however, the essence of Australian election campaign speech has changed very little since Federation: it is, at its core, about politicians connecting with voters in order to secure their support at the ballot box. The leaders of Australia's political parties vie for power with their *words*, which invite voters to identify with them and engage actively with their vision of and for the nation. To pull this off, campaigning leaders must make clear that they understand the concerns and priorities of the electorate; and they must use the dominant media of their time to reach as many voters as possible.

Five key questions about Australian identity have resonated in federal election campaign language since Federation:

What is Australia's place in the world?
Who is an Australian?
What are Australian values?
Is Australia's 'way of life' secure?
What is our vision of Australia's future?

These questions will be addressed in each of the chapters that follow, after a discussion of the book's methodological approach (below) and theoretical foundations (Chapter 2). These chapters will not only introduce the political leaders who battled over the answers but also explore the context in which they worked and the communication strategies they employed. Successful campaign language is firmly of its time, using the medium of the day and speaking to current concerns; but it manages also to be timeless, addressing long-held anxieties and voters' need to feel part of a secure and familiar national collective. In Australian federal elections since Federation, political leaders have vied to tell resonant identity stories that paint positive images of Australianness, identify sources of worry and reassure voters about the security of an imagined national way of life. It is those leaders who tap into the enduring concerns of the Australian electorate, and whose policies connect both to their own personality and that of their constituents, who are remembered in political folklore as playing a key role in imagining a secure identity for Australian voters in the face of persistent threat.

Notes on Methodology and Approach

The insights and analysis undertaken in this book are based on a large-scale longitudinal language analysis that was the foundation of my PhD thesis research, undertaken in the Media and Communications program at the University of Melbourne from 2006 to 2009. That project undertook a mixed methods approach. First, a content analysis was employed to identify and quantify broad patterns of language use across federal elections in Australia 1901–2007. Then a discourse analysis was used to undertake a more nuanced, contextualized examination of political leaders' election campaign language. While the quantitative results of the content analysis undertaken for my PhD research are not included here, they operated as a guide for the key themes and patterns of language use that are the focus of this book's discursive analysis.

Content analysis

The systematic content analysis of Australian political language was undertaken to allow a comparative examination of how political language has developed and changed across campaign history. These quantitative results were an invaluable starting point for identifying key themes and patterns in the spoken language Australian political leaders have used to construct national identity and belonging. They helped reveal how these have changed across more than a century, as well as providing a guide for further analysis. Content analysis is a popular method for analysing political speech, particularly in North American research[2]; in Australia it has been employed to examine direct political speech (McAllister and Moore 1991; Kabanoff et al. 2001) although research of this kind has been rare. Content analysis was chosen for its value in 'offering hard evidence about topics about which we often have quite firm but unfounded opinions' (McKee 2002, 67). It can deal with both historical and current texts and is particularly useful in the 'systematic analysis of vast quantities of data' (Krippendorf 2004, 40–42; Bertrand and Hughes 2005, 184) either in its manual or computer-assisted variations. However, the analysis was undertaken with a keen awareness of its limitations: issues of sampling and category definition, the assumption of concrete 'meanings' in a text and the study of language outside of its production and reception contexts (Berger 2000, 185; Bertrand and Hughes 2005, 184).

The results of this content analysis guide the more detailed qualitative analysis of the construction of Australian identity in political leaders' election campaign

---

[2] Here, quantitative approaches have been applied to election campaign debates (Hart and Jarvis 1997; Benoit 2003; Airne and Benoit 2005; Banwart and McKinney 2005); speeches and political broadcasts (Johnston 1991; Hart and Johnson 1999; Hart and Childers 2005; West et al. 2005).

language undertaken here, an analysis that has been updated to include in the sample items from the two most recent federal election campaigns complete at the time of writing, 2010 and 2013 (Appendix 1; Appendix 2). While not included in the formal sample, insights from the 2016 election campaign (held at the time of writing) are also included where relevant. A close discursive analysis of a smaller, select sample of material allows for the study of political language use in context.

Discourse analysis

A number of scholarly approaches to discourse analysis (such as mediatized political discourse and critical discourse analysis, discussed below)[3] guided the development of the grounded approach to studying Australian election campaign language used in this book. Discourse analysis is an interdisciplinary approach to the study of language, both in its foundations and application. It developed as a research method in the early 1970s, across disciplines including anthropology, linguistics, semiotics, psychology, sociology and mass communications (van Dijk 1985, xi). Its aim is to set language within its social context, to highlight 'systematic links between texts, discourse practices and socio-cultural practices' (Fairclough 1995, 16–17); to highlight how the 'cognitive, social, historical or political cultures of language use […] impinge on the structures and strategies of text and dialogue', and vice-versa (van Dijk 1991, 45). The method's interdisciplinary nature was a key attraction for this work, as it allows researchers to draw together aspects of previous work and integrate insight from other disciplines (e.g. see Macdonald 2003, 304). While often overlooked in Australian political science approaches[4], Carol Johnson (2002, 1) has argued that discursive analyses allow 'important and fruitful areas of research' that can complement other strands of work, helping to develop understandings of Australian identity that are 'complex' and 'plural'. This book does so with an understanding that political discourse operates, in Bourdieu's terms, as the 'clearest illustration of the constitutive power of discourse', as it both reflects and alters the social world by 'reproducing or changing people's representation of it' and the classification principles that underlie those representations (Fairclough 1995, 182).

The chapters that follow analyse political discourse from the theoretical position that spoken political language should be understood as 'mediatized', following Simon Cottle (2006, 3–4) in using the term to 'deliberately capture

---

[3] For more detail on the study of mediatized political discourse, see Fairclough (1995, 176–77); and on the concept of mediatization, see Cottle (2004; 2006).

[4] While rare, there are exceptions – see, for example, Johnson's own work, or Gleeson's (2014) analysis of 'War on Terror' discourse in Australia, which applies critical discourse analysis to political language.

something of the more complex, active and performative ways' that the media are implicated in 'reporting' on election campaigns. While Cottle's use of the term refers to media conflict, the positioning of spoken campaign language as mediatized political discourse underlies the perspective taken in this book. It signals that media coverage is not simply about transmitting the words of politicians directly to the public, but rather 'actively "doing something" over and above disseminating ideas, images and information' (Cottle 2006, 3–4). This is a performative role played out in the dynamic relationship between political actors and the media that shapes and influences what politicians say, as well and how and when they say it (a trend exaggerated during election campaigns). Contemporary political language is written and spoken with an awareness of this mediatization and is shaped by the demands of ever-evolving genres, formats and technologies in political journalism: from newspapers, radio or television broadcasting to the emerging array of digital and social media platforms. Political candidates, and their professional staff, increasingly pre-plan campaign communications to function as part of a dynamic, interconnected campaign designed to appeal to the demands of political journalism and to the electorate themselves. Election communications must fit into, but also seek to shape, the broader narrative of the campaign. They will be experienced by the electorate in their roles as citizens and *audience members*; politicians therefore will undertake a range of activities designed to garner direct and coverage. They:

> debate, appear on television, answer call-in questions on radio and television talk shows, prepare and present messages for media commercials, take part in parades and rallies, wear funny hats, submit to media interviews, write letters and position papers, and speak at all forms of public gatherings. They kiss babies, shake hands at factory gates and supermarkets, prepare and distribute videotapes and email newsletters, wear campaign buttons, and establish phone banks to solicit money, workers and votes. (Trent and Friedenberg 2004, 15)

This exhaustive map of campaign activity, missing only politicians' engagement in the social networking, microblogging and video-sharing technologies developed after it was written, brings vividly to life why political language cannot, therefore, usefully be studied without first understanding it as a *mediatized* discourse form. In doing so, it is vital to ask how politicians 'reconcile their traditions with the shifting demands of media practices and genres' (Fairclough 1995, 191).

This understanding will inform the analysis undertaken in this book, as will the broader concerns of critical discourse analysis (CDA), which seeks to 'make explicit power relationships which are frequently hidden' (Meyer 2001, 15; see also Caldas-Coulthard and Coulthard 1996, xi) through close attention to structures of power and inequality in language used. However, the tendency of some CDA research to rely on the 'rules' of formal linguistics in an overly prescriptive approach will be avoided as this can render analyses inaccessible to those without a strong knowledge of classical linguistics and can produce results that lose sight of broader questions. To counter this, the approach taken in this book draws on the political and media discourse analysis traditions, which have been less methodologically rigid (see, for example, Fairclough 1995, 182; Wilson 2001, 401–10).[5] This hybrid approach makes possible an examination of why representations of the key themes of belonging, values, community, security and vision in election campaign language remain such powerful and necessary ways of constructing individual and collective identity for some groups in Australian society. What lends them their ongoing power in campaign discourse?

The sample

To address this question, this book understands spoken political language during election campaigns as mediatized political discourse, drawing on a large sample of texts from federal election campaigns across Australian political history. It includes eight major Australian political parties (Appendix 3), whose relevance to this study is that they have provided a prime minister or opposition leader in an election campaign or have been capable of forming government. The sample for the formal content and discourse analysis limits itself to the words spoken 'out loud' by the incumbent prime minister and challenging opposition leader during formal election campaigns[6], and excludes other genres of political communication (press releases, political advertisements, policy documents, party pamphlets, direct mail, social media and microblogging) and political coverage, although these will be referred to where relevant.

The original content analysis was performed on a sample which included items of direct, spoken language by the prime minister and opposition leader

---

[5] For examples of political discourse analysis, see Wodak (2002); Brett (1992, 2003, 2005); Curran (2006); Johnson (1998, 2000, 2005). For more detail on media discourse analysis, see Garrett and Bell (1998, 6–17); Fairclough (1995, 2).

[6] Identifying the start and end point of formal election campaigns is not simple in the era of the 'permanent campaign' (Blumenthal 1980, 7). To allow continuity across the sample, the material included is dated from the issuing of the writs (with the exception of the campaigns where policy launch speeches or announcement press conferences were given before this) until the victory or concession speeches, whether delivered on polling night or later. On occasions where the election result was unknown on polling day (such as 1923 or 2016), the post-election speeches made by the candidates on election night were included as the final date (see Appendices 1, 2).

from 42 Australian federal elections, 1901–2007, totalling 741 examples of direct election campaign speech across ten genres: election, policy launch, victory, concession and post-election speeches; radio, television and doorstop interviews; press conferences and election debates. The sample was coded according to a schedule developed by the author to identify the presence of themes of identity and belonging in campaign language and to map shift and change across more than a century, in consultation with a critical review of literature.[7] With the results as a guide, the discourse analysis explored language use in more detail; however the limitations of time and scale make it impractical to apply this close qualitative analysis to such a large sample. Therefore, a form of *purposive sampling* was employed that focused the discourse analysis on the most powerful and pertinent examples in the texts (identified through grounded, systematic and repeated reading of the sample) in order to identify contrasts and continuities in historical and contemporary campaign language, and to explore social and political contexts more deeply. While there are a number of thematic strands that could have been chosen for analysis (for example, the perspectives of class and the economy, gender and sexuality would provide valuable insights) it was the discourse of *identity security* that was the most significant, consistent and evocative in the sample. As a result the book is structured around the interconnected and overlapping themes through which this construction of Australian identity plays out.

In the writing of this book, the original sample was updated to include an additional 402 items from the 2010 and 2013 election campaigns in the discourse analysis.[8] It draws on passages from leaders' direct spoken language as the basis of both *example* and *analysis*, linking 'particular, micro-analysis' of texts with what is 'typical and patterned in the discourse' (Georgakopolou and Goutsos 2004, 185). The balance of examples chosen for the discourse analysis

---

[7] All 741 items in the sample were coded for identifying details (e.g. election year, speaker, party, genre) and then for the presence and frequency of use of 78 language terms or groups of terms, arranged into: references to *nation* and national characteristics; *politics*, parties and leaders; *immigration*, unity and diversity; *threat*, war and conflict; and the nation's place in the world and *international relationships*. Full details including descriptions of pilot studies, coding schedules and codebooks and the quantitative results themselves, are available from the author.

[8] The balance in items across historical campaigns – 741 items from 1901–2007, 402 from 2010 and 2013 – reflects both the dramatic increase in the volume of campaign communications in the contemporary era and the increasing ease of access facilitated by campaign websites and website archiving projects such as the National Library of Australia's PANDORA archive. Some early material has been digitized in collections, such as the Malcolm Fraser Collection at the University of Melbourne, prime ministerial libraries, such as the Bob Hawke Prime Ministerial Library at the University of South Australia and archives and libraries such as the National Library of Australia and National Archives of Australia. Other material has been accessed through contemporaneous newspaper reports in microfiche or digitized form. However much remains undigitized and scattered and was collected by the author in person; while in other cases, the material simply no longer exists as some Australian political leaders left few records behind.

come from policy launch speeches as these are both the most consistent and the most visible genre in Australian campaign communication. Speechwriter Graham Freudenberg (2005, 35) has described them as 'a unique Australian institution – a working document and solemn ritual that combined statements of high endeavour and pork barrelling'. With this combined quantitative and qualitative analysis as its foundation, the book examines how Australian political leaders have constructed notions of Australian identity and *identity security* in their spoken language during federal election campaigns, asking how language use has changed or remained constant over time; and exploring how this language has been mobilized to link into, and help construct, broader structures of identity and belonging in Australian society.

Chapter 2

STORYTELLING

Australian Identity, Leadership and Political Language

Australian identity stories have been a key feature of campaign language since Federation, a defining discursive theme of election appeals through which political leaders have sought to articulate shared experience and collective values. Political iterations of these identity stories are not definitive reflections of the nation's true essence. Rather, they give citizens options from which to create both individual and collective notions of belonging. These political narratives do not provide the sole inspiration for identity formation. They are part of, and compete with, other elements of the 'media culture' that, Douglas Kellner (1995, 1) has argued, helps 'produce the fabric of everyday life' and provides 'the materials out of which people forge their very identities'. They must also engage and align with, reconceptualize or challenge a wide range of lived experiences and the myriad other social and cultural cues for what it means to be, and to *feel*, Australian. Why might an Australian who has never personally visited the Great Barrier Reef, Uluru or the Sydney Opera House recognize images of them as home? Why might someone living in the suburbs of Melbourne feel a stronger connection to the experiences of those in Perth than in Auckland? While the boundaries of the political nation-state provide some insight, they are not the whole answer. There is a much more powerful process of definition and identity formation underway, in which the need to *belong*, and to be both part and proud of a distinctive community, operates as a fundamental element of the human experience.

This process of identity formation is a fundamental aspect of why election campaigns capture public attention and call on citizens to engage and respond, and it plays out in the narratives that political leaders tell about themselves, voters and the nation. Stephen Coleman (2015, 168–69), in his argument for conceptualizing elections as 'storytelling contests', highlights that:

> Democracies need periods of political performance in which stories are told about who we are, what we think we deserve, who we think politicians are, and who we think they think we are. Elections are storytelling contests in which the *demos* comes to be represented by identifying with competing and contested narratives about itself.

Coleman's (2015, 169) identification of the importance of storytelling and narrative in election campaigns[1] is useful in two ways. First, it highlights the way that leaders tell political stories – about themselves, their political values and aspirations and about voters – because 'they want to appear to be close to us [...] to seem to know us and be known'. Second, it foregrounds the way that these 'narratives compete for public attention and approval'. The stories that political leaders tell about themselves and their values must be linked to something broader, a strategy characteristic of US presidential elections (Gupta-Carlson 2016, 71) and exemplified in the political discourse of Barack Obama during both his campaigns and time in office (e.g. Dickerson 2009; Diaz 2010). This is because, as Gupta-Carlson (2016, 71) highlights, they 'gain narrative energy through their paralleling of their stories of the nation', positioning 'the candidate-as-protagonist as a metaphor for the nation-in-making'.

This paralleling lies at the heart of appeals to collective identity and national values in election campaign language, a discursive strategy that has endured across more than a century of campaigns. On 4 August 2013, Labor prime minister Kevin Rudd opened his campaign at Parliament House in Canberra flanked by the Australian flags that have become customary for prime ministerial press conferences. This first press conference is an opportunity to set the tone of the campaign. Framed by mundane, 'banal' (Billig 1995) signifiers of national identity, the newly reinstated prime minister relied on two key discursive strategies. First, he sought to align himself with a vision of Australian collective identity that would resonate with voters. Second, he painted his opponent as untrustworthy, negative and a direct threat to that identity. These strategies came together in his key message. Australians should, he argued, vote for the candidate who could best safeguard their shared values:

> Ours is a truly great country [...] Around the world we are seen as one of the best countries on the planet. Blessed with a strong economy, a hardworking, talented and creative people and a people who will never surrender their deep sense of a fair go for all. These are the values which have steered our nation through the first century of its federation. And I believe they are the values which will guide us into the future as well. (Rudd 2013a)

---

[1] For more on 'storytelling' in political language and communication, see Vromen and Coleman (2013) on storytelling strategies used by online campaigning organizations, and Papacharissi (2016) on social media, affective publics and storytelling. For a narrative analysis of political leadership, see Hanska (2012) on Ronald Reagan's use of storytelling and narrative to contruct a 'mythical America'.

Rudd consistently mobilized the discourse of collective identity when addressing the electorate, constructed in his language as the *Australian people* or the *great Australian family*. He asked them to connect their inherent nature as 'a positive, practical people who believe in nation building' to the 'values, ideas and policies' his party would deliver for the nation's future. Rudd's construction of, and appeal to, a particular narrative of Australian identity highlights that the nation is not fixed or static; nor is it a naturally occurring, pre-existing entity. Rather, it operates as an 'imagined political community' (Anderson 1983, 6) within which members are asked to believe that they share values, rituals and characteristics with their fellow members (most of whom, Anderson points out, they will never meet). It evolves over time, in response to changing domestic and international social, political, economic and cultural contexts. This book understands national identity as both imagined and evolving in this way. It therefore does not undertake a search for the truth of Australian identity or ask which political leaders have come closest to that truth. Rather, it asks what British social psychologist Michael Billig (1995, 70) has called the 'crucial question relating to national identity': 'how the national "we" is constructed, and what is meant by such a construction'.

These questions remain salient despite the changes brought about by an era of increasingly global politics and pressure. The question of Australian identity endures for many of the same reasons it might otherwise be seen to be breaking down in an interdependent world: the border-crossing impacts of climate change; the spread of infectious diseases like SARS, avian flu, ebola or zika virus; financial crises experienced as global; the movements of refugees and the displaced; and the seemingly ever-present threat of globalized terror. However, it is often these very pressures that lead to a renewed emphasis on the comfort provided by clear boundaries between nations, between those who belong and those who do not. Anthony Moran (2005, 9), in an insightful study of Australian society and identity in the global age, notes that while 'many theorists of globalization argue that national identity is becoming [...] less salient for people as the world becomes more global', this is 'not the case for Australians'. Rather, he argues that 'intensifying globalisation stimulates new forms of Australian national identity, just as it challenges older forms' (Moran 2005, 9).

This chapter will clarify how the term 'Australian identity' will be used in those that follow, and will make clear the role that Australian political leaders play in helping to construct that identity. Arguing that leaders have a powerful, although not absolute, ability to shape the debates though which members of a national community imagine themselves, it engages with examples from across Australian political history and with scholarship. It considers the relationship between politicians and political professionals, speechwriters and the electorate, locating this within the media landscape to argue that mediatized election campaign language is a unique and invaluable basis from which to map and understand constructions of Australian identity.

A Site of Contest and Struggle

The Australian project to articulate, protect and reimagine a national collective identity predates Federation, and has been one of the characterizing strands of public and political dialogue. More recently, James Curran and Stuart Ward (2010, 16) argue, it has operated as 'a seemingly endless round of ponderous musings about the elusive national spirit'. These conversations about Australian identity and nationalism have their own histories, and have been the subject of extensive scholarly attention. Definitions of Australian identity have been analysed in film, art and literature, sport, tourism, newspapers and popular culture (White 1981; Wills 1993; Nicoll 2001; Tsokhas 2001; Cashman 2002; Warren 2004; Ward 2010; White 2011; Winter 2011). Graeme Turner's (1986, 1994) insightful work analyses film, literature, news media and popular culture to trace the narratives that Australians have told about themselves; narratives that 'generate meanings, take on significances, and assume forms that are *articulations* of the values, beliefs – ideology – of the culture' (Turner 1986, 1; see also Elder 2007).

Studies of Australian identity have run parallel to explorations of nationalism in Australia (e.g. Alomes 1988; Alomes and Jones 1991), and traced its historical development (McLachlan 1989) or compared it with similar nations (like New Zealand; McLean 2003). Seminal early works such as Donald Horne's (1964) *The Lucky Country*, Russel Ward's (1967) *The Australian Legend* and Richard White's (1981) *Imagining Australia* have been influential both in mapping and contributing to scholarly and popular understandings of the Australian identity. These explorations have often been misread as a search for the true national character; more contemporary work has called for an approach that 'emphasise[s] the extent to which *multiple identities* have been available to Australians' (Hudson and Bolton 1997, 1). While not discounting the contribution of early attempts to define and understand Australian identity, critiques have focused on the singular, 'stereotypical' or 'exclusivist' (Archer 1997, 29) nature of some of these conceptions. Introducing their edited collection *Creating Australia*, Wayne Hudson and Geoffrey Bolton (1997, 3) positioned Australian identity in more challenging terms as a 'site of contest and struggle', an admission which means 'undermining monolithic notions of what we mean by "Australia"'. Their collection, and others (Day 1998a; Stokes 1997; Curran and Ward 2010) emphasizes the plural and contested nature of collective identity narratives in Australia, as well as the foundations of these images in broader understandings of race, class, gender, colonialism, indigenous identity, Empire and globalization. In the chapters that follow, this book explores familiar themes and tropes of Australian identity in a unique way: analysing how campaigning political leaders have both drawn on and helped to construct Australian identity for voters since Federation.

Heroic Achievement, Democratic Innovation and the Fair Go

Australian political party leaders have been powerful, although not singular, players in this dynamic, contested discourse of Australian identity. As highly visible figures with significant cultural capital, they play a central role in directing and defining the parameters of national imaginations of self. Historian Richard White (1997, 20) has argued that there are some people in society who 'of necessity think more about being Australian' than most other people; who have more reason 'to imagine Australia as a community'. In this category, he placed journalists, writers, historians, intellectuals, manufacturers in the national market and federal politicians, who must 'construct national politics to appeal to a national interest'. These people, White argues, operate in 'the most powerful imagined community of all', and their words reach beyond local and state borders to construct and mobilize a shared sense of identity. Some political leaders do this more self-consciously than others. While the very act of campaigning for the prime ministership brings with it an opportunity to intervene in public dialogue about the nation's priorities and vision for the future, some leaders rely on consistent and explicit discussion of Australian identity. Liberal Party founder Robert Menzies, for example, was instrumental both in his redevelopment of tropes of British-nationalism and in his recognition (and construction) of the 'forgotten people' of Australia's middle classes (Brett 1992). Liberal prime minister John Gorton was associated with the 'new nationalism' that, according to Curran and Ward (2010, 6), was an 'attempt to set out a new, more distinctively Australian self-image' in the context of declining British loyalties. Labor prime minister Bob Hawke is often remembered as a master of 'Australian popular nationalism', pioneering the use of flags in his advertisements and speeches and offering citizens a sense of Australian identity based on the comforting themes of 'contemporary life and TV politics' (Alomes 1988, 273, 285).

In the same way, some elections are remembered in political history as battles over Australian identity and history; for example, 1996 is seen as a turning point in debates about, and understandings of, identity. In this campaign the political battle between Labor prime minister Paul Keating and Liberal opposition leader John Howard was fought, to a significant degree, over conceptions of the nation's identity. It is remembered as marking a dramatic shift in the 'cuewords of public discourse', from Keating's Big Picture to Pauline Hanson's Asian Invasion, and from Labor speechwriter Don Watson's emphasis on tolerance to John Howard's 'assault on the black armband view of history' (Hudson and Bolton 1997, ix). Keating had relied on 'familiar episodes' in the nation's history to tell a story of 'a people who had triumphed over their tribulations and prejudices' in order to 'embrace diversity with an egalitarian honesty', which Howard countered with a story of 'heroic achievement, of democratic innovation, of the fair go' (Hudson and Bolton 1997, x).

These examples signal both the richness of political language and the importance of appreciating political leaders' role in telling Australian identity stories, a task this book will undertake. Australian identity is constructed, and contested, by political leaders within and against powerful discourses that locate nationalist understandings of self within broader social, economic and political contexts. Their language speaks to those at home and abroad, signalling the boundaries of the national collective and constructing secure discursive borders around the Australian way of life. As outlined in the previous chapter, this project has been characterized by an anxiety about potential *threats* to the Australian identity, and a concern to provide a sense of *security* from these threats. In this context, political leaders have both contributed and responded to an Australian culture that is:

> Grappling intellectually with the nature of the place and its borders, with the idea of nation and globalisation, with our Indigenous past and continuing immigration from the ends of the earth, with ourselves and our destinies. (Cope and Kalantzis 2000, 120)

These conversations come to the fore at moments of change, contest and celebration. Whether at local, state or federal level, campaigns are such moments and they feature complex negotiations between candidates and citizens about who *we* are and what *we* value, played out through the dominant media platforms of the day. As Elihu Katz and Yael Warshel (2001, 10) argue, election campaigns are 'opportune moments for observing the workings of "imagined communities"'. At a time when experiences of nation and identity 'are being altered by both individualism and globalism', they position elections as offering an insight into 'the extent and ways in which political ritual bolsters national identity' (Katz and Warshel 2001, 10). This book understands federal election campaigns in this way, as conversations that reflect and contribute to broader debates about how the character of the national collective is constructed, experienced and understood. These campaigns are a powerful symbolic time when collective identity and values are negotiated through political and public dialogue. As such, they provide a window into how Australians are invited to make sense of their place in the nation, and their nation's place in the world, by campaigning political leaders who provide opportunities for citizens to fit themselves into narratives of nation. These narratives are as significant for their silences, for the stories of Australianness that they do not tell, as they are for those that they do.

The Concerns of Indigenous Australians

One of the most significant silences in Australian campaign language – one of the stories least often told – is that of the colonial and post-Federation community's problematic relationship with the nation's indigenous population. This is a story of physical and symbolic violence; of displacement and dispossession; of the vast social and economic disparities that are the product of these processes; and of conflicted attempts in mainstream political language to acknowledge, reconcile and move forward. For the most part, the diverse and distinct nations of Australia's original inhabitants, whose civilization and culture was erased in the colonial imagination of *terra nullius* and the political and policy decisions this concept of 'empty land' made possible, are simply absent from the campaign language of political leaders. The powerful political speeches that Australians may remember addressing indigenous issues have mostly occurred outside of the arena of campaigns: whether Gough Whitlam's (1975) remarks at the handover of Northern Territory lands to the traditional owners of the Gurindji nation; Paul Keating's 1992 'Redfern Park' address at the opening of the United Nations' International Year of the World's Indigenous Peoples; or Kevin Rudd's 2008 Apology to Australia's Indigenous Peoples, delivered in Parliament House in Canberra. These are moments of vision and clarity, where political leaders have attempted to take seriously the historical and contemporary role of race in Australian identity stories. They have asked voters to do the same; to consider the complex impacts that a history of symbolic and tangible exclusion continue to have on the lived experiences of the indigenous population.

In election campaigns, however, political discourses of this nature are rare and indigenous Australians have often been either sidelined or invisible. This will be highlighted where relevant in the chapters that follow (with significant exceptions analysed). Where issues relevant or specific to the indigenous community *do* appear, these are traditionally presented as separate from the concerns and values of those voters imagined as the mainstream. In campaigns, these are either relegated to addresses to indigenous community members on areas that specifically concern them or listed along with other so-called special interest groups whose needs must be addressed by the mainstream. In the first instance, this discursive strategy locates members of the indigenous community outside the (often unspoken) shared space of Australian collective identity. For example, campaigning leaders often speak or are questioned about indigenous issues only while campaigning in the Northern Territory, or in relation to policies that will impact directly on that region. In 2013 Prime Minister Kevin Rudd was asked, at a doorstop in Darwin on 15 August, whether he was working with 'Aboriginal organizations' in his proposed expansion of the Ord river irrigation scheme, and whether he could guarantee that 'the Aboriginal people [...] will benefit from the expansion?' His response covered the 'concerns of Indigenous Australians' in relation to native title issues and his government's desire to be 'entirely mindful of those sensitivities', while also expressing the importance of the project for Australia more broadly in tapping into our 'enormous export potential for Asia and beyond, particularly in food and food processing industries' (Rudd 2013d). In the second instance, this discourse allows those Australians who see themselves as part of the governing mainstream to feel that they are taking the needs of the indigenous community seriously, while retaining power over the imagined centre of collective identity. In 1975, for example, Malcolm Fraser (1975) included indigenous issues as part of a broader discussion about 'meeting the needs of the disadvantaged in society' in his policy speech. It is also important to note that the invisibility of Australia's indigenous population in campaign language is exemplified in other more subtle ways. For example, the enduring history of promises and policies aimed at 'developing' and 'populating' Australia's north highlights the way in which that region that continues to be imagined in Australian political language as both remote and empty (Rudd 2013g) despite its indigenous history.

How Is an Electorate Invited to Understand Itself?

The approach taken in this book moves away from traditional (and often contradictory) research that locates the value and meaning of political campaigns in whether and how they are able to influence how citizens vote, leading to an emphasis on effects and an interest in campaign outcomes. It advocates a reorientation, leaving to the side 'reductionist research questions' (Norris et al. 1999, 172; Brady and Johnston 2006, 12) in order to extend understandings of the ways in which campaigns 'matter' beyond electoral outcomes (Holbrook 1996, 18). This allows for an alternative approach that examines how election campaigns, as a period of heightened political and media activity around issues key to Australian identity, are significant in a broader sense. It reflects the approach taken by American communications scholar Roderick Hart (1994, 10), who has criticized the 'positivist' methods that have 'hijacked so much of campaign studies'. Hart and colleagues (2005, 108) have argued that the electorate is not a pre-existing 'ontological entity' but rather is constructed periodically by 'political actors who define it in order to control it'. Analysing speeches in the US House of Representatives during the Clinton impeachment proceedings and after 11 September, Hart and colleagues (2005, 109) asked 'who the American people are, or better, who they have been invited to become' through political rhetoric. This question – 'how is an electorate invited to understand itself, and what results from those understandings?' – will be explored in the chapters that follow across more than a century of campaigning leaders' language.

Hope for the Future

In Australian political science research, and the much more extensive North American field, the focus on electoral 'outcomes' has led to a dominant interest in the numbers and machinations of national politics rather than the wider implications discursive political activity might have for society. In order to explore how political discourse invites Australians-as-voters to understand their role and place in the national collective in specific ways, as this book seeks to do, the work of Belgian political theorist Chantal Mouffe is particularly valuable. Mouffe (2005, 25) argues that voting cannot simply be understood as a decision to defend one's own interests or driven by a 'rational' weighing up of policies. In emphasizing these elements, she argues, we overlook the 'important affective dimension' of voting, where what is at stake is a 'question of identification'. This notion – that there is deeper *feeling* at play both in campaign communications and voting decisions – asks us to understand something vital about political language:

> In order to act politically, people need to be able to identify with a collective identity which provides an idea of themselves they can valorise. Political discourse has to offer not only policies but also identities which can help people make sense of what they are experiencing as well as giving them hope for the future. (Mouffe 2005, 25)

Mouffe's description of the political identity 'provided' for citizens fails to emphasize the negotiated mechanisms through which collective identity is formed through political dialogue. However, her foregrounding of this 'affective' dimension of voting is invaluable, as it compels us to connect political discourse to processes of identification. Carol Johnson's (2015, 35) articulation of the role of *emotion* in politics, and 'at election time in particular', similarly calls for a recognition that politics is a 'battle for hearts *and* minds' (emphasis added), in which politicians 'evoke emotions such as fear and anxiety' but also 'feelings of hope to foster support for the vision of the future enshrined in party policies'.

In the late 1970s, political theorist and communications scholar Paul Corcoran (1979) argued that identification had become the central aim of political language in the broadcast era. Blaming changes in media technology and campaign strategy, he was concerned that political language no longer employed tools of classical rhetoric (logic, persuasion, evaluation of information). Instead, the speaker 'invokes symbolic commonplaces' in order to 'associate himself [...] and his proposals (if any) with images, ideals and values which are [...] uncontroversial within the dominant culture' (Corcoran 1979, 169). This process of identification, where political actors appeal to citizens though shared cultural understandings, undoubtedly remains a central feature of political language. However, the idea that persuasion has been replaced in political language overlooks the way that political speech, especially in election campaigns, has always sought to persuade *through* identification.

In the contemporary political environment, campaign communication operates within a dynamic and fractured media landscape. In this context, campaigns can be viewed through Simon Cottle's (2004, 31) conceptual lens as 'mediatized public rituals':

> Exceptional and performative media phenomena that serve to sustain and/or mobilise collective sentiments and solidarities on the basis of symbolisation and a subjunctive orientation to what should or ought to be.

These rituals are characterized by processes of identification. Cottle (2004, 47) notes that 'affective, emotional and symbolic appeals are an inextricable part of mediatised rituals and lend them much of their affect (and effects)'. The term *mediatized* is used deliberately in preference to more neutral terms such as mediated, and helps to guide this analysis; for Cottle (2006, 3) the term works to 'capture something of the more complex, active, and performative ways' that the media operate. He argues that the term signals that the media 'are actively "doing something" over and above disseminating ideas, images and information' (Cottle 2006, 3).

Whether on stage or online, political speeches, announcements, interviews and debates form the basis for the many of the stereotypes and images circulated in legacy and emerging media coverage and discussion. Election campaigns are *conscious* attempts at attracting voters, and campaign language operates as a mechanism of both persuasion and identification, using 'vivid phrases which condense a range of historical and contemporary meanings' and so acting as 'a focus for people's political identifications' (Brett 1994, 151). Political language has a profound influence on how citizens see themselves as belonging to a nation, and how they understand the characteristics and values of that nation. The chapters that follow explore this language and analyse the narratives of Australian identity that voters are called to identify with, the subject positions they are invited to take on and the identities and positions that are excluded.

It is important, when taking an analytical position like this, to be aware of the danger of seeing election campaigns as a direct microcosm of issues and debates in Australian society more broadly. It is also vital not to assume that voters pay as much attention to campaigns as a political scientist or media analyst might; or that all citizens are equally engaged or interested in political language or journalism (Young 2011, 27–32). This book provides an analysis of political language; not of election outcomes, voting preferences or citizen engagement and response. It doesn't propose to explain how citizens understand or interpret the political language they experience through the media, nor will it make broad statements about the 'intentions' of politicians and political professionals. These would be different projects and would require in-depth focus group research or interviews with citizens, politicians and advisers. Rather, this book draws out and interprets constructions of Australian identity in campaign language, and points to some of the dominant, powerful and problematic aspects of identity discourses in this political speech. This is why the term *invited* is used in the chapters that follow, to signal something of the power dynamic active on all sides of the campaign communication relationship: engaged and persuasive intent on the part of the speaker; the goals and values inscribed in active and performative political coverage, related to professional journalistic notions of fairness and balance in reporting; and the agency retained by the citizens addressed by political speech. While power is dynamic and contested here, there is rarely an equal distribution. For example, the considerable social capital of leaders in campaigns can be seen in their ability to influence the parameters of public debate, media coverage and digital and social media dialogue, and shape broader social assumptions and ideas (McCombs and Shaw 1993; Ward 1995; McQuail 2000).

A consideration of processes of subject formation is a valuable basis for understanding the ways that citizens are invited to make sense of Australian identity and locate themselves within that collective during election campaigns. French Marxist philosopher Louis Althusser's (1970) theory of 'interpellation' provides insight into the relationship between speaker, discourse, and audience member (or voter). Althusser (1970, 128) follows Marx in defining ideology as 'the system of ideas and representations which dominate the mind of a man or a social group', and argues that ideology functions by *interpellating* individuals as subjects. In this process, the discourse 'hails' the addressee, who becomes a subject through the process of acknowledging that the 'hail' was addressed to him or her and responding accordingly. This is a concept that has been much debated since its conception, and in the last few decades has 'fallen from favour' as part of a broader academic turn against structuralism (Purvis and Hunt 1993, 482). However, Althusser's concept of interpellation remains valuable when asking questions about the process of identification, and can illuminate for us the process through which political leaders 'hail' voters to recognize themselves as members of a collective national identity, and see that identity reflected in certain privileged tropes and constructions. Judith Butler (1995, 6), the American gender theorist and poststructuralist philosopher, has argued that the doctrine of interpellation 'continues to structure contemporary debate on subject formation', offering a way to 'account for how a subject comes into being after language'. Interpellation can therefore offer an account not only of the process of hailing, but also the 'process of recognition by the interpellated subject' (Purvis and Hunt 1993, 482), situating subjects within specific discursive contexts. Althusser's conception also allows us to see the links between interpellation and discourse that will be vital in the approach taken in the chapters that follow. For sociologist and cultural theorist Stuart Hall (1983, 64), Althusser's work allowed for a 'more discursive or "linguistic" conception of ideology', making possible a recognition of the role that discourse plays in the constitution of social subjects. This re-reading of Althusser, proposed by Trevor Purvis and Alan Hunt (1993, 483–84) is particularly helpful here, as it allows for a consideration of the positional identifications voters are invited to take on by political leaders' campaign language; as it is 'through discourse that individuals are interpellated as subjects'.

Questions of emotional connection and identification recur in public and media conversations about the relationship between political leaders and their constituents. These manifest in concerns about the 'professionalisation', 'presidentialisation' or 'personalisation' (McAllister 2015) of Australian politics; the interrelated impacts of digitization, changing media technologies and the evolving art of voter research and grassroots mobilization often critiqued as 'astroturfing'[2]; in concerns about the performance of political and press gallery journalism; and in discussions about the role of transparency and authenticity in political language and election campaigns. These concerns came together in public discourse in the lead up to, and during, the 2010 election campaign, which saw both Opposition Leader Tony Abbott and newly installed Labor prime minister Julia Gillard struggle to effectively communicate their vision of Australian identity, and plans and policies for the nation's future.

---

[2] For an insightful analysis of these critiques, see James Hay's (2011) discussion of the emergence of a 'new political populism' in the United States.

Gospel Truth

Two months before Julia Gillard called the 2010 election, Tony Abbott sat across from Kerry O'Brien in the Australian Broadcasting Corporation's (ABC's) television studios. *The 7:30 Report* was one of the country's toughest political interviews, and Abbott had been perched on the edge of his seat from the beginning. Facing him, O'Brien (in ABC 2010) peered over his wire-rimmed glasses and began gently, testing Abbott's knowledge of the policy detail outlined in his Budget Reply Speech four days earlier. This was not the first time Abbott had sparred with the formidable broadcaster and journalist. He had been a member of federal parliament for more than a decade, and a high-profile minister in the Howard government. He was prepared for most of the questions that came his way, and his responses were peppered with the careful hedging of a practised politician: 'my understanding is', 'I think people would understand' and 'to get back to the fundamental point'. But his adversary wasn't about to let things tick along at a measured pace. A 45-year veteran of his craft, O'Brien was renowned for his razor-sharp instincts, and he was brimming with confidence after scoring a journalistic coup a month before: an exclusive interview with US President Barack Obama, filmed from the White House. O'Brien let Abbott finish an attack on the Rudd government's mining taxation plans and then moved smoothly into a different kind of question. Abbott had been successful in painting the prime minister, Kevin Rudd, as untrustworthy, calling attention to a disconnect between his persona in the 2007 election campaign and his actions in office. But on what basis, O'Brien (in ABC 2010) asked, should the public trust Abbott?

The stakes were high in this interview. Abbott had only been opposition leader for six months, and in that time his party's political prospects had risen dramatically. His opponent at the time of the interview, Rudd, once had polling approval numbers that placed him alongside Bob Hawke as Australia's most popular prime minister (Coorey 2009). But by 17 May 2010, when Abbott gave this interview, the political landscape had shifted. Labor's poll numbers had fallen, caucus was rumbling and leadership tensions had emerged. An opposition that had seemed doomed to regroup in the political wilderness was suddenly in with a chance, with Abbott at the helm. A tough competitor, the former Rhodes scholar and champion boxer didn't want to get this wrong.

Abbott deflected O'Brien's question about trust by emphasizing that the public would make their own judgements. He argued that, over time, voters would see him 'growing into' the job of opposition leader. O'Brien pressed again, and this time used a change in Abbott's policy promises to make his point. In February Abbott had promised not to introduce new taxes to fund policy promises, and a month later he'd said that a tax on big companies would be used to fund a paid parental leave scheme. O'Brien (in ABC 2010) asked, 'I'm not quite sure how you justify such a fundamental U-turn in such a short time?' He let Abbott address the question of the paid parental leave scheme, then pulled him back to the initial focus of his query. Policy detail aside, he asked, could the opposition leader explain the complete change in his views within the space of a month? O'Brien leaned back in his chair, and threw up his hands in an expression of apparent confusion. But his knowing look alerted the viewer that there was something amiss: a politician playing the game, staying on message rather than answering the question.

Abbott began to reiterate his line about voters making their own judgements, but O'Brien (in ABC 2010) interrupted: 'No, but I'd like you to explain it [...]'. Abbott (in ABC 2010) responded instinctively, without rhythm or grace, as he pieced together an answer that would lead the next day's news and open up a national debate about truth and trust in political office that would colour the election campaign to come:

> Well, again Kerry, I know politicians are gonna be judged on everything they say, but sometimes, in the heat of discussion, you go a little bit further than you would if it was an absolutely calm, considered, prepared, scripted remark, which is one of the reasons why the statements that need to be taken absolutely as gospel truth is those carefully prepared scripted remarks.

Tony Abbott's honesty exposed a thinly veiled truth about the relationship between politics, the public and the news media. The notion that a political leader might go beyond the 'gospel truth' in order to win an argument, a day's news cycle or an election was no great revelation. An opposition leader drawing attention to this on national television, at a time when preparation and scripting are positioned as the opposite of sincerity and believability in politics, placed these questions firmly in the spotlight.

The 'Real' Julia

Abbott's admission that there is a difference between prepared remarks and words spoken in the heat of the campaign sheds light on a key area of concern about the role of political language and the relationship between politicians and citizens in public debate. The desire for emotive sincerity in political speech, and political life, speaks to an essential aspect of campaign communication: the ability to connect with an audience. Whether speaking to a single voter or the nation, whether face-to-face, broadcast, webcast or tweeted, political leaders need to engage voters if their identity stories are to resonate.

So during election campaigns, they attempt to make this connection with their words: relying on the content but also the style, tone, timing and location of delivery of those words. The most successful do so by engaging voters on the issues they care most about, concerns about the nation's values, priorities, security and future.

In the 2010 campaign, only two months after Abbott's 'gospel truth' comment, the new Labor prime minister, Julia Gillard (in Hudson 2010), implored voters to believe she had abandoned the script and would 'discard all of that campaign advice and professional or common wisdom' to make sure that 'the real Julia is well and truly on display'. This concept dogged her campaign, just as the perception that Tony Abbott's usually fiery personality was being kept under wraps followed the Liberal leader. The election had played out as a contest between two experienced parliamentarians who were both inexperienced as leaders, and appealed to the electorate on the grounds of what they 'would do' in office rather than their track records. As the campaign moved into full swing, Gillard was quickly characterized as cautious to the point of being dull. Jennifer Hewett's (2010) depiction in *The Australian* was typical, describing the prime minister as a 'hesitant, over-rehearsed political robot'. The 'real Julia' was a response to these critiques, a way for the prime minister to reassure those in the electorate who 'worry that modern campaigning is too managed and too tightly scripted' and promise that she would take 'more direct control of the campaign' in its final weeks (Hudson 2010).

The preoccupation with the 'real Julia' also led to a search for the 'real Tony'. During a breakfast television interview on 9 August, *Today* host Karl Stefanovic (2010) chastised the opposition leader for being 'on message', demanding 'I want to see the real Tony Abbott'.[3] Media coverage characterized Abbott's campaign as 'restrained', 'deliberately controlled', 'careful and disciplined' and 'low-risk' (e.g. Keane 2010; Ewart 2010; Berkovic 2010). Tony Wright (2010a), in the *Age*, dismissed both leaders as being 'as packaged as plastic-wrapped cheese', with careful marketing to ensure they were just as 'bland'. This became the conventional wisdom about the 2010 election campaign. Journalists, political commentators and academics bemoaned the decline of political language and the lack of a genuine national conversation that engaged with significant issues and dissected policy positions. Evidence of this decline seemingly abounded in the campaign's lacklustre key events (even the televised leaders' debate was outrated by the final episode of the popular reality program *Masterchef* [Bodey 2010]) as well as its gaffes and

---

[3] These questions followed Abbott into the 2013 campaign; in an interview in the first days of the campaign, *Sunrise* host David Koch (2013) complained that contemporary campaigns were 'stage managed to the point where it becomes a reality show', challenging Abbott: 'We don't actually get to see the real you.'

missteps. In critiques that emerged after the election, both former Labor MP Lindsay Tanner (2011) and journalist and author George Megalogenis (2010a) observed that the state of public debate and political language in Australian election campaigns pointed to a deep disconnect between the business of professional politics and citizens' expectations of prime ministerial candidates.

Banal, Deadening Chaff

This concern was not new to the 2010 election. There has been a tendency in media, academic and professional analyses of modern political language (intensifying from the 1970s onwards) to see the professional, mediatized election campaign as signalling the decline of political language. Here, when compared with the elections of an imagined historical 'golden age' – where men of wisdom conducted public debates on issues of substance – modern political language was seen as 'dull stuff, intended to make tarnished ideas or no ideas at all seem bright and glossy' (Hudson 1978, 16). In this conception, political language works to 'inflate its author's reputation, to score points off an opponent, or simply to deceive' the public. Contemporary Australian political speech is often critiqued along these lines: 'banal, deadening chaff' overtaken by corporate language (Ramsey in Glover 2007, 148), doing little more than providing the 'soundbites' demanded by the evening news (Young 2008). Journalists and political professionals are implicated in this critique, as politicians are groomed by their staff, carefully 'marketed' (Scammell 1995; Kavanagh 1995), 'packaged' (Franklin 2004) and positioned to appeal to citizens whose voting and other preferences are meticulously researched and documented through focus group, polling, social media and other data collection methods. This process of professionalization (Norris 2000; Scammell 1995) has impacted directly on the conduct of campaigns. Graham Freudenberg (2005, xvi), for example, has argued in this vein that the demise of the public meeting (where politicians would address, and interact directly with, voters) is not because of the rise of television or the unwillingness of voters to attend but rather:

> because it suits the convenience and the self interests of the governments, politicians, party officials, the staff apparatus [...] the media commentators, the radio jocks, the advertising agencies and the security industry, not to hold them.

Here, the twin processes of professionalization and mediatization are drivers of an unprecedented level of rehearsal and stage-managing in campaigns (Shea 1996; Schultz 2004; Stockwell 2005), which are seen as contributing to the demise of political speech.

While there remains a common-sense notion that the days of great orators and inspiring political speeches have been overtaken by poll driven, pre-rehearsed soundbites and appealing images, former Labor speechwriter Dennis Glover (2007, 156) instead connects changes in public language to the evolving global political landscape, arguing that political speech has 'become more vicious and violent' to reflect an era of insecurity:

> The themes of successful politicians [...] are the more aggressive and depressing ones concerned with low-level war: leadership, weakness, and internal enemies [...] Big speeches today may not always sing and inspire; they may very well parrot and bore; they certainly deceive; but most importantly, they threaten and scare. They inspire fear [...].

For Glover, changes in political rhetoric are not a symptom of a broader decline of political language but rather the decline of post–World War II optimism, which allowed politicians to instinctively turn to an ethos of democratic citizenship and notions of collective responsibility to evoke emotional response from citizens. While contemporary campaign language routinely locates its identification appeals in positive images of Australian identity and values, it can and does also operate to divide the electorate, excluding those who do not see their own identity reflected in the national histories and futures constructed during campaigns. In contemporary political discourse, Glover (2007, 157) argues, language is used not only to inspire but also to 'arouse dark passions'. This is not a recent development: even in the idealized 'golden age' there was an awareness of the power of propaganda, the potential for political language to be wielded 'by the demagogue to divide and rule' (Glover 2007, 157). Effective political language has always worked in this way, designed 'with a complex understanding of the audience, their social norms, values and fears' and working to include some groups and exclude others in representations of collective identity (Lillker 2006, 183).

While many of these discussions of the relationship between leaders and their constituents may seem pessimistic – either marking the decline of 'quality' political speech, or bemoaning its use for divisive purposes – others have taken a more positive approach. Former Labor speechwriter Don Watson (1995, xiv) argued more than two decades ago that a move beyond cynical, world-weary attitudes was possible. For Watson (1995, xiv) a return to appreciating the positive power of political language would mean rhetoric could again be employed to:

> make people cry and laugh. Rhetoric to reassure and inspire. Rhetoric to lever open our minds, to throw light in the valleys and roads through them. Rhetoric which makes them think, and thinking easier.

In this conception, political language is capable of simultaneously drawing on shared identity myths and assumed common values *and* proposing and explaining substantive policies. It can build consensus by 'binding people around ideas and issues' (Lilleker 2006, 183) rather than simply presenting them with stereotypes and style. When citizens are invited to see themselves in images of Australian identity projected in political speech, they are asked to feel that they belong to a community of shared vision and values (although some will be able to feel this more easily than others). This is not lost to an imagined golden era of campaigns and communication, but has the potential to be increasingly relevant in the contemporary global landscape (Glover 2007, 157).

Both concerns about the dull, divisive or exclusive nature of political language, and attempts to rehabilitate it, signal the ongoing importance of political speech in Australian political, media and public debates about the health of the national conversation. This is evident in the publication and popularity of memoirs of political speechwriters, advisers and insiders (c.g. Freudenberg 1977; 2005; Watson 2002; Gurr 2006; Button 2012; Deane 2015) and collections of 'significant' political and other speeches (e.g. Cathcart and Darian-Smith 2004; Kemp and Stanton 2004; Warhaft 2004; Fulilove 2014; Lewis 2014). It is also reflected in the popularity of fictionalized behind-the-scenes accounts of politics such as in television series *The West Wing, Veep, House of Cards, The Thick of It, Yes, Minister, Secret City* and *The Hollowmen*. Across popular culture, political journalism and other areas, attention is being paid to political speech: to the relationships and connections that it forges between leaders and citizens; to its vital role in the process of building a constituency; and to the search for political 'authenticity' in response both to political professionalization and an increasingly fragmented digital and social media landscape.

The Anonymous John Smith

In 2010, these issues came to the fore in coverage of the ALP's policy launch. The search for the 'real Julia' recommenced in earnest when Fairfax newspapers published images on their website, taken by *Sydney Morning Herald* photographer Andrew Meares, of what columnist Tony Wright (2010b) described as a 'thick sheaf of typed papers' on her lectern, put in place before the speech by a Labor staffer. Using written notes for a lengthy speech is not unusual. However, the prime minister's advisers had told journalists in an earlier media briefing that she would deliver her speech without autocue or scripting, and early coverage repeated this (Grattan 2010; Wright 2010c). After the images emerged, media commentators, more irked than outraged, questioned why Gillard's staffers had felt the need to paint the 45-minute-long address as off-the-cuff rather than written in advance by Gillard and her team (Rehn 2010; Wright 2010b). More importantly, why had the prime minister herself played into this perception by describing her speech as 'from the heart'? What was it about the image of a prime minister outlining her plans for the nation without scripting or rehearsal that was so seen to be so appealing to voters?

Gillard's privileging of spontaneous political speech both accorded with her return to the 'real Julia' and tapped into a long history of interest in, and concern about, the role of speechwriters, media advisers, press secretaries and other political staff in Australian campaigns. It played into debates about the professionalization of politics, and perspectives that position the true values and positions of politicians as undermined when their language stays carefully 'on message'. Australian political speechwriters have traditionally kept a lower profile than their North American counterparts, such as Theodore Sorensen (for John F Kennedy: 2005; 1965) and Peggy Noonan (for Ronald Reagan: 1990). This has, perhaps, been a result of the 'unwritten contract' of anonymity that has existed in Australia between speechwriter and politician (Freudenberg 2005, viii). Political speechwriters have become more active and better known publicly as the media and speaking commitments of prime ministers have increased. In his memoirs, Robert Menzies (1970, 9) reflected that the rise of the 'institution of speechwriter' was related to the growing number of speeches a prime minister was expected to make in a year. This meant that a dedicated speechwriter was required in addition to the job of press secretary or media adviser. Despite the general rule of anonymity, a number of politician-speechwriter relationships stand out in Australian political history. Among the earliest was Don Rodgers's work for Prime Minister Ben Chifley, in a role formally described as press secretary from the mid-1940s. David Day (2001, 447) writes in his biography of Chifley that Rodgers found the prime minister difficult to work with in comparison to his predecessor, John Curtin. While Rodgers tried to project a public image of Chifley as a 'humble, hard-working and genial' prime minister, Chifley was unpredictable and volatile, often 'tossing aside Rodgers' carefully prepared speeches or otherwise refusing to cooperate' with strategy. More recently, Graham Freudenberg's speechwriting for Labor prime minister Gough Whitlam, and Don Watson's for Paul Keating, have become part of Australian political folklore.[4] Watson (2002) and Freudenberg (2005)'s memoirs provide valuable insights into the role of

---

[4] Freudenberg had previously worked for Labor leader Arthur Calwell and also wrote for Bob Hawke, Neville Wran, Bob Carr, Barrie Unsworth and Simon Crean; Watson had previously been a speechwriter for Victorian premier John Cain.

political speechwriters, although it is important to note that both had unusually close relationships with their respective prime ministers. A very different picture is painted, for example, by James Button's (2012) account of his role in the Rudd government. Useful insights into the political speechwriting process have also been provided (usually after their retirement) by well-known press secretaries, media advisors and speechwriters Bob Ellis, Dennis Glover (for Labor), Tony Eggleton, Alan Jones and David Kemp (for the Liberal Party).[5]

Speechwriters have played an important role in the development of campaign communications in Australia, and an understanding of the evolving process of speechwriting provides a useful starting point for the analysis of political language this book will undertake. The following chapters will analyse closely the words through which political leaders seek to construct, maintain and represent a constituency. While these words can and should be taken as representative of the political ideas and vision of the speaker, it is important to also acknowledge the lengthy, often collaborative process of writing a political speech. For example, policy launch speeches – perhaps the most high-profile speech a campaigning leader will give during an election campaign – are written 'by a committee through the medium of a speechwriter' (Watson 2002, 327). This is not a new development; Graham Freudenberg's meticulous and detailed files, housed in the National Archives, demonstrate the range of contributions and suggestions from ministers, party heavyweights, lobbyists and interest groups that are synthesized into a final policy launch speech.[6] The speechwriting process also varies according to the temperaments of both speechwriter and political leader. For example, Cecil Edwards (1956, 115), who travelled with Stanley Bruce as a press officer in the 1925 campaign, found him 'courteous', 'painstaking and careful'; a 'quick study' who could 'take a final draft of a speech an hour before a meeting and follow it perfectly'. This stands in contrast to Donald Horne's (2000, 170) description of the preparation of a major speech for Billy Hughes:

> His staff would draft, and redraft, sometimes for a month or more. He would tear up the drafts, throw the pieces on the floor, demand that they be put together again; he would never say what he wanted, merely reject everything that was offered; in the last moments of hysteria before a speech was made he might still be altering drafts, perhaps restoring some of his most trusted clichés.

---

[5] Masters (2006, 121–24), in his biography of Jones (better known for his later career as a controversial talkback radio host), questions the extent of Jones' speechwriting for Malcolm Fraser. He paints the relationship as brief, and limited by Jones' inability to move beyond eloquent 'motivational' rhetoric to language with more depth and substance.

[6] Freudenberg's files run from 1 January 1961 to 31 December 1973; they are housed in the NAA Sydney Office, Series #M156.

Other Australian prime ministers have been unwilling to use speechwriters at all. John Curtin worked on his speeches and articles himself 'on trains or in railway refreshment rooms' as he travelled the country during the 1937 campaign (Ross 1996, 171). Menzies (1970, 9), remembered as one of the most skilled orators in Australian political history, has famously claimed to have 'never employed a speechwriter' for two reasons:

> Partly because I had an obstinate objection to have other people's words put in my mouth, and partly because, except for formal lectures and statements on foreign affairs made by me to Parliament, my practice has been to speak from brief notes, allowing the language to come spontaneously as the actual speech developed.

Words written by speechwriters, for Menzies (1970, 10), cheated both the audience, hoping to be 'roused and stimulated' by a passionate human being speaking in their own voice, and the 'future historian' hoping to 'perceive a man through his words' in the years to come and instead encountering 'the anonymous John Smith and not the statesman'. Menzies (1967, 295) claimed to have written his policy launch speeches himself after consultation with party colleagues; although Freudenberg (1977, 295) has noted Menzies 'failed to acknowledge' his heavy reliance on drafts prepared by departmental staff and ministers. What is vital, here, is not the historical fact of Menzies's contributions, but the value attached in these accounts to writing your own speeches or speaking off-the-cuff. Liberal prime minister John Howard, in his four terms in office, famously 'shunned professional wordsmiths' (Jean 2008), a claim that became a point of pride in an otherwise tightly controlled political environment. In his memoir, Howard (2010, 18) ponders whether it was his 'chronological memory' or 'love of debating' that made him uncomfortable reading prepared speeches. While he acknowledges the 'necessity' of doing so in senior levels of authority, he nevertheless says that he read less than 10 per cent of his speeches from prepared texts while prime minister:

> I feel that I always give my best speeches when, having thought about what I will say, I then eyeball the audience and speak directly to the people in it. Never in my life have I used an autocue or teleprompter. I hold them in contempt as rhetorical crutches. (Howard 2010, 18)

This same unwillingness to work with a speechwriter became an issue for his successor Kevin Rudd, who in his first year in office developed such a reputation for being a workaholic and 'control freak', he was dubbed 'Kevin 24/7' (a play on his 2007 campaign moniker, Kevin07). This, combined with media criticism of his bureaucratic 'Ruddspeak' and public urging from former Labor prime minister Bob Hawke (Jean 2008), led to the hiring of Fairfax journalist (and son of Hawke government minister John Button) James Button as full time speechwriter in late 2008 (Atkins 2008; Grattan 2008).

Whatever the level of their involvement, Don Watson (2002, 57) has stressed that while speechwriters write political speeches, 'politicians own them':

> If a speech sinks, the politician sinks with it. If it bores people, fails to inspire, if the jokes don't work, if it misjudges the audience, if the figures or anything else are wrong in fact, the politician suffers the consequences. A political leader *chooses* from the words the speechwriter has chosen […] the speech is his, and never the writer's. This is as it should be.

It is perhaps ironic that Watson was at the centre of the most high-profile recent battle over the roles of politician and speechwriter: an ongoing clash with former Labor prime minister Paul Keating over the ownership of his famous 'Redfern Park' speech, which was reignited by the National Film and Sound Archive's addition of the video and audio of the speech to its library in August 2010 (see Glover 2010; Keating 2010; West 2010; Clark 2013). This debate, which saw Keating (2010) respond passionately to what he perceived to be Watson's suggestion that the prime minister should be credited for *delivering* but not *authoring* the speech, reveals some of the emotive power afforded to political speech. Here, the privileging of political speech that appears to be authentic or off-the-cuff emerges as a mechanism of successful storytelling, through which political leaders can work to construct and maintain a connection to a constituency whose borders are imagined as analogous to the contours of Australian identity.

Chapter 3

BELONGING

The European inhabitants of *terra Australis* have grappled with an enduring sense of geographic and cultural isolation since the earliest of days of their settlement. In its earliest manifestation, this was driven by a perception of themselves as white-British pioneers inhabiting a far-distant outpost of Empire surrounded by unfamiliar (and potentially aggressive) nations. These anxieties about culture and belonging, geography and isolation have endured. They resonate deeply, playing out in art and culture; in media and public debate; and in the language of foreign policy and economic development in the private and public sectors. Throughout Australian history, political leaders have worked in this context to provide answers to the question 'where do we belong?' and employed various mechanisms to invite Australians to locate themselves securely in the world.

This chapter engages with the campaign language of three leaders who provided complex, multilayered answers to the fundamental question 'what is Australia's place in the world?' at key periods in the nation's history: the decade following Federation; the time of upheaval between World War II and the end of the Cold War; and the strategic repositioning that followed the economic restructuring of the mid- to late-1980s. George Houstoun Reid, Robert Menzies and Paul Keating all provided voters with a vision of Australian belonging that was *both* a comfort and a challenge, familiar and unsettling. The shifting and dynamic nature of Australian belonging comes into focus here, as these leaders grappled with uncertainty in ways that were often surprising: calling on Australians to think in new ways about their place in the world. All three, despite their vastly different levels of success at the ballot box and length of time in office, had a deep and enduring impact on the discourse of national belonging in Australian politics. The legacy of their language both echoed in the campaign battles to come and also fundamentally influenced the shape of Australian identity stories.

Rather than proposing radical shifts, these leaders claimed to be the guardians of Australia's traditional place in the world, using this as the basis to extend voters' understandings of where they belonged. All three aligned Australia with the 'peoples' with whom they felt an affinity – in the Empire, the Commonwealth or the 'Anglosphere' of Western nations – while at the same time encouraging engagement with, or differentiating themselves from, others. In campaign battles they clashed over the balance Australia needed to strike between allegiance and independence: between international relationships with those imagined as great and powerful friends and the development of a unique Australian voice in world affairs. In providing answers, they evoked Australian history to appeal to both traditional and emerging understandings of national identity.

The specific content of the political discourse of belonging has changed markedly over more than a century in response to changes in the global political, economic and strategic landscape and in the Australian electorate. Despite these changes, careful definitional work has been required throughout Australia's political history to provide voters with a stable sense of belonging in the world. This develops a sense of national independence while at the same time emphasizing the vital need for strong alignments and allegiances.

This discourse is partly shaped by the specific relationship between political leaders and their constituents; however, it is also part of the broader identity security discourse through which Australians have addressed their fundamental anxiety about the national story. In its most familiar form this is the story of Australia's emergence from British colony through a number of stages: a Commonwealth partner; a small nation 'looking to America'; a dynamic and engaged leader in the Asia-Pacific region; a middle power that 'punches above its weight'. However, this straightforward arc masks that Australian discourses of belonging have always been multiple, complex and fluid. While elements of the story have been dominant at different times in the nation's history, our political leaders have grappled for more than a century with competing, at times contradictory strands when attempting to provide a secure sense of belonging for voters. Their discourse has relied on a promise of control offered to those who were able to see themselves as part of the Australian mainstream, neutralizing anxieties about the nation's ability to operate comfortably in the world. This was expressed in the language of Empire and Alliance, family and friendship; in promises of unfailing support for allies in trade or conflict; and in assurances that Australians could feel at home in the region. In this way, Australian political leaders called on voters to imagine themselves as part of a network beyond the national shores, connected to a larger history and offering both a deep sense of belonging *and* control over their own destiny.

Mother Country

Australia's changing relationship with Britain has been of concern throughout electoral discourse, reflecting and helping to construct similar themes in Australian history more broadly. The patriotism of British belonging that formed the foundation for identity development in the immediate post-Federation period was 'at once national and imperial', with feelings of attachment based on the 'sentiment of shared blood, traditions and ideas' as well as a 'shrewd calculation of self-interest' (Macintyre and Clark 2004, 35). In the first decades following Federation, Imperial attachment provided a sense of cultural and defensive security for a new nation: 'shared Britishness' (Partington 1994) was central to Australians' understandings of their own identity, which in the emerging political culture was connected to the experience of white-British settlers making a new life far from home. In Australia's colonial and immediate postcolonial era, the discourse of 'British belonging' provided a seemingly solid foundation for both individual and collective identity, drawing the often-parochial colonies together. It also operated to place Australians in the world, offering a way to grapple with the question of where their new nation belonged in the global landscape.

In the political realm, these were key concerns addressed by Australia's first politicians operating at the federal level, figures familiar from their pre-Federation roles (in the legal system, or in colonial politics as members of parliament) and involvement in the Federation movement. These years were a time of relative instability in Australian federal politics. They were characterized by a multiparty system in which three parties, loosely formed along economic policy lines, vied for office: Labor, the Protectionists and the Free Traders. Governments rarely won electoral majorities and were often defeated in parliament without serving full three-year terms.[1]

Australia's first two prime ministers were Protectionist party leaders Edmund Barton and Alfred Deakin. Barton tends to be remembered fondly, if indistinctly, as the nation's founding father while Deakin is recalled as a visionary leader. Their chief political opponent, opposition leader by default in Australia's first three federal elections, was George Houstoun Reid of the Free Trade Party. Reid became Australia's fourth prime minister in August 1904 when Labor's John Watson lost support in the parliament after only four months in the job. Although his term as prime minister was short lived (less than a year), Reid was an influential voice in early Australian politics. As premier of New South Wales in the early 1890s, he was seen as a man of the people who 'would speak his mind honestly, and who appreciated the real problems faced by ordinary people' (Hogan 2006, 196). Reid's reputation in his day was as a witty and engaging speaker, progressive thinker

---

[1] By 1910, this had settled into what was essentially a two-party system, with the Australian Labor Party and the Commonwealth Liberal Party (formed by a fusion of conservative parties) the dominant electoral forces. For more information, see Jaensch (1994).

and 'consummate politician'. When he is remembered now, however, it is for his large moustache and physique, and even larger personality. Mungo MacCallum (2013, 31) attributes this unflattering memory to the notion that 'history is written by the winners':

> In this case the winner was Alfred Deakin, who loathed our fourth prime minister, undermined his career, crippled his brief time in office, and eventually hounded him out of politics altogether.

The caricatures of those who disliked Reid live on in Australian political folklore. Deakin (in MacCallum 2013, 31) mocked his rival's 'immense, unwieldy, jelly-like stomach, always threatening to break his waistband'; his 'thick neck rising behind his ears to his many-folded chin'; and his 'air of insolent juvenility' granted by an 'infantile breadth of baldness'. These colourful descriptions mask the key role that Reid played in the development of Australian political discourses of identity. In his campaign speeches he presented a clear and dynamic vision of a new nation that could balance its own independence with familial and strategic ties. Reid's Australia would be actively engaged in the world while maintaining the fundamental purity of its white-British identity. Although unsuccessful with voters, his image of Australia's place in the world had a vital impact on the developing discourse of belonging that continues to be a key (although not always explicit) concern of federal elections. His progressive vision asked Australians, at a very early stage in the development of their collective identity, to embrace a nuanced and sophisticated image of a world in which Australia would *both* be securely 'British' and also engaged more broadly in global affairs. This language, which developed Australian independence from a stable foundation of British belonging, was symbolic of the shape Australian self-perception would take in the decades to come, despite the nation-building rhetoric and protectionist economic policies of Reid's opponents resonating more deeply with voters at the time.

Reid asked Australian voters to think of themselves, for the first time, as members of a nation rather than individual British colonies. In Australia's first federal election, he and Barton 'criss-crossed the nation, excepting Western Australia, speaking at every opportunity' (Jaensch and Manning 2001, 103). It was an intense campaign where candidates 'kept up heavy schedules of daily meetings' (Simms 2001, 10) in town halls and public spaces. Speaking at the Richmond Town Hall in January, Reid (1901) appealed to his audience to think of themselves in this new national capacity:

> Now I have not come here to address the electors of Victoria; I have come to address the electors of Australia. One of the boons of the Australian union is that we are to cease calling each other aliens.

Reid went on to grapple with the question of the new nation's position in the world, a task he continued in all three campaigns he contested as opposition leader. The election battles of 1903 and 1906, in which Reid locked horns with his political rival, the Protectionist prime minister Alfred Deakin, are particularly relevant here. In these campaigns, the discourse of British belonging implicitly structured discussions of the central issue: the parties' competing economic policies that offered differing solutions to the choice between free trade and protectionism and question of preferential trade with Britain. However the two leaders used the language of kinship in different ways and in service of two very different visions of the nation's place in the world. Importantly, Reid extended this language to other areas when outlining his policies for voters.

In his campaign speeches, Reid consistently drew on the language of blood ties and kinship to imagine Australia as naturally and irrefutably part of a family of nations. Often, this language emphasized Australia's junior role in the relationship. For example, in a critique of the government's immigration policy Reid (1903) worried that 'the current of honest immigration from the mother country to this daughter land has been absolutely stopped'. This language pervaded Reid's discussions of immigration: if Britain was the 'mother' of the Imperial family then the citizens of other member-nations were our 'kith and kin' (Reid 1903). For example, Reid (1906) used kinship language when arguing that 'white agricultural labourers' should be privileged in Australian immigration policy:

> The Contract Immigrations Act makes things worse for the best kind of immigrants – those who come out, not as adventurers, but under engagement to do work waiting for them. Thanks to Mr Dugald Thompson, not the Government, a provision was inserted relieving our kinsmen in England, Scotland, and Ireland from some of the odious conditions still attaching to other nations.

This emphasis on Australia's familial ties to Empire was a common element of political discourse on both sides of politics in the early decades following Federation. Reid also described Australia's Imperial membership in biological terms, with Britain imagined as the heart of the Imperial body. Campaigning in Australia's first federal election, Reid (1901) imagined the free flow of labour within the Empire as equivalent to the circulation of blood in the body:

> If the population of England became too redundant, it circulates to the extremities of the Empire, so that the more over-crowded England becomes, the more magnificent is the flow of vigour and manhood to the furthest part of its dominions.

This corporeal construction drew on a familiar central feature of nationalist discourse: the language of blood and race. It is linked to primordialist theories of nationalism that see national identity as based upon the natural ties of blood and kinship, on 'claims of common origin' (Puri 2004, 44). Reid's use of primordialist language established a discourse that resonated in later campaigns. For example, more than a decade later, conservative prime minister Joseph Cook (1913) again constructed immigration within the Empire as 'the promotion of the circulation of its Imperial life blood', while in defence he implored voters not to 'leave the Dominions in danger of dismemberment by one swift blow at the centre of the Empire'. This kind of language was unremarkable at the time; news coverage focused instead on logistical issues such as the 'great trouble' Cook had taken with the speech that he read from notes to a large, attentive crowd (*Sydney Morning Herald* 1913, 6).

The familial language of British belonging was most prominent, however, in discussions of the economic issues that were at the heart of the 1903 and 1906 campaigns. For the most part, Reid and Deakin used this discourse to argue that their own economic policy positions would allow Australia to maintain a healthy relationship with the mother country and to accuse each other of championing policies that would put this familial relationship at risk. In 1903, Reid argued that the principles of 'protectionism' meant that for the past three decades there had been 'a wall [...] against the mother country', which 'shut out our fellow countrymen from Australian commerce' and treated them as if they were the same as 'the Germans and Yankees and coloured races'. He positioned these policies as 'unneighbourly' and 'disloyal' (in addition to their restricting the volume of raw materials that Australia was able to export to Britain). Reid also accused the government of selfishness in their recent change of heart on these issues; while they had started to 'feel ashamed of the policy' and were now 'making overtures to the motherland', they still refused to grant preferential trade without something in return. Reid (1903) characterized Deakin's government as separating the Australian interest from what was best for the Empire. This was an enduring critique; in the following election, he accused Deakin of making a 'sham offer' of preferential trade to Britain in which 'not a single duty was reduced in favour of Great Britain' (Reid 1906).[2]

---

[2] Reid (1906) also argued that Deakin had refused to remove a controversial amendment to the bill on preferential trade, introduced by the Labor Party, which required that crew members on British ships carrying goods covered by the bill must be 'white seamen' in line with the conditions of the White Australia policy. This amendment, he argued, would make 'acceptance of that bill by the British Government impossible' (Reid 1906).

In contrast, Reid (1906) positioned his own party as supporting an 'unconditional preference, offered by Australia to the mother country'. The language of loyalty was a vital element of his discourse. For Reid (1903), Australia had an *obligation* to preference the mother country in economic and trade policies, to 'act fairly by the mother country' and be 'straightforward' in dealings with her. He extended this language to other policy areas; for example, when speaking about defence in his 1906 policy speech, Reid argued:

> We owe to the Empire, as well as to ourselves, the duty of laying the foundation of an efficient system of port and naval defences, an 'inner line' of naval defence which is at present sadly neglected.

Loyalty is vital here, and Reid consistently located Australia in the world by highlighting her responsibilities to the Empire in key policy areas of defence, trade and immigration. As part of the British family of nations, Australia had certain obligations to fulfill; and in exchange Australians were able to feel part of a community that stretched well beyond the shores of a continent perceived as vast and unpopulated, helping overcome feelings of geographic isolation from the mother country. It is important to note that this is an enduring construction of the Australian continent; in early political speech it was a common discursive device which both erased the history and presence of the indigenous population and made invisible the problematic nature of white colonial settlement. As noted in Chapter 2, the silence in regard to these stories in early campaign narratives of Australian identity is a stark reminder of the power of language to construct identities, both in what is said and what is left unsaid.

Deakin fiercely contested Reid's claim to ownership of Australia's familial connection to the mother country, using similar strategies to position himself and his Protectionist government as the true guardians of Australia's British belonging. Characterizing the free traders as 'foreign traders', he argued that their policies betrayed a lack of 'affection' for the mother country and 'their own kith and kin', instead 'treating her only as the rest of the world' (Deakin 1903). Defending the Protectionist position in 1903, Deakin argued in pragmatic terms that his party's policies were in the national interest, allowing Australia to 'accept preferential trade with the mother country and our sister dominions to our great mutual gain':

> We are told by the foreign trader that to speak of self-development in parts of the Empire is a doctrine which is selfishly Australian […] A protectionist tariff is essential to Australia, but there is nothing in that antagonistic to close trade relations with the mother country. It is true patriotism which trades with its kindred and prefers its own productions.

Three years later, he again employed familial language to suggest that those who opposed his government's fiscal policies therefore also opposed 'the policy of bounties of preference, and closer relations with the mother country, and of other measures for the benefit of Australia' (Deakin 1906). This last phrase points to a key difference in Reid and Deakin's use of the discourse of belonging. While the familial language of white-British belonging was apparent in their battles over preferential trade, Deakin's speeches were dominated by domestic issues, such as a concern with the enforcement of the White Australia policy, the establishment of the Federal ministry and departments, the high court and electoral system and choice of a site for the federal capital (earning him the reputation for nation-building rhetoric discussed in Chapter 5). In contrast, Reid's language explicitly developed a complex image of Australian belonging that presented the nation's allegiances and commitments as multiple and dynamic.

For Reid, the task of positioning the new Australian nation in the world went beyond connections to the mother country. Rather, the construction of Australia as part of an Imperial family afforded the new nation a stable basis from which relationships to other parts of the world (including its geographical neighbours) could be established. In Reid's speeches, exclusionary language, in which Australia's international allegiances and its very identity were based on the ties of blood, was combined with an interest in establishing international and regional links. Reid's 1906 policy launch speech, at the Independent Order of Odd Fellows Temple in Sydney, expressed this as a tension between maintaining the 'purity' of the national identity and the desirability of interaction with our closest neighbours:

> Without sacrificing the vital principle of racial integrity, we should set ourselves to develop the friendliest possible relations, not only with the islands of the Pacific, but with all nations.

This language balances concerns about the 'racial purity' required for continued white-British belonging with a broader interest in regional exchange and relationships with other nations. Here, it is only if Australians are comfortable with, and able to protect, their place in the world that they can establish 'friendly' relations with others without threat to their own developing identity. The language of shared biological origin therefore reassured those who felt isolated from their familiar (experienced or imagined) homeland that their connection to this could not be challenged or disrupted. This a feature of what Ghassan Hage (2003, 48) has described as the 'paranoid nationalism' that characterizes colonial-settler societies. Here, distance from the mother country led those early settlers with 'the power to shape the identity and culture' of the new nation to construct Australia as 'an isolated White British colony in the heart of a non-European (read also uncivilized) Asia-Pacific region'. References to race and family afforded Australians who could imagine themselves as 'White' and 'British' an image of the nation whose borders lay not at the shores of the wide and empty continent but in the far reaches of the Empire. This enabled leaders to construct a discursive promise of identity security for voters. From this position, Australia could be active in the region; for example, developing 'friendly relations' with other nations, or managing her 'obligations' to New Guinea, which Reid (1906) imagined as a 'vast and populous' territory. Here Australia, acting as an arm of Empire, had a duty to 'promote and encourage white enterprise' while also protecting 'a vast black and defenceless population committed to our care'.[3]

The unquestioned discourse of white-British Australian belonging became less prominent, however, in campaign language following World War II. As David Goldsworthy (2002, 1) notes, a central theme of twentieth century Australian history and nationalism is 'the journey out of Britishness'. Where family and kinship had provided a comforting basis for national identity immediately following Federation, it was new international connections based on culture that would offer a basis for Australians to locate themselves in a rapidly changing world. These shifting discourses are exemplified in the campaign language of long-serving prime minister and Liberal Party founder, Robert Gordon Menzies.

Great and Powerful Friends

In election campaigns during two crucial periods of upheaval, World War II and the Cold War, Robert Menzies offered Australians a sense of stability through the relationships (familial, cultural and strategic) that anchored them in the global landscape. Menzies looms large in Australian political folklore. He was Member for Kooyong for more than three decades (from September 1934 until February 1966), founded the Liberal Party of Australia and served two separate terms as prime minister. The last to retire on his own terms, he remains Australia's longest serving prime minister. Political mythology positions him as formidable campaigner, keeping Labor in the electoral wilderness for more than two decades; a peerless public

---

[3] The use of terms like 'vast' and 'populous' are again significant here, as they mobilize the Yellow Peril fears (prevalent in Australian political discourse well before Federation) that Gavin Souter (2000, 96) has argued lie 'at the root of Australian nationalism'. This discourse betrays Australians' perception of the inhabitants of Asian and Pacific nations as 'surrounding' and always potentially threatening Australia. The development of Australia's ties to a white-British Anglosphere was therefore a vital line of defence in light of the (often explicit) fear that might at any moment these populations imagined as vast may move south and seek to overwhelm the sparsely populated continent.

speaker and master of the witty comeback; a politician with a unique connection to his constituency, the 'forgotten people' he spoke to in his radio addresses of the 1940s (Brett 1992). Menzies' communication skills evolved over his decades in office in response to changing media technology: he gave campaign speeches in town halls, exploited the intimacy of radio and, in his later years, was a 'superb television performer' (Freudenberg 2005, 25; 209).

Robert Menzies is often associated with a particular kind of Australian identity that proudly located itself first and foremost as a white and British. However, this obscures the key role he played in asking Australians to think differently about their allegiances, particularly during his second term in office. Close engagement with Menzies' campaign language demonstrates how his discourse developed a complex, nuanced image of Australian belonging throughout his time in politics.

Menzies fought only one election during his first stint as prime minister, in September 1940. Australia had joined World War II in support of Britain a year earlier, and a sense of unease and upheaval pervaded the campaign language both of Menzies and his opponent, Labor's John Curtin. Throughout this election Menzies located Australia in the world by echoing the reassuring discourse of familial belonging voters recognized from earlier campaigns, and from their daily immersion in broader political, cultural and social expressions of identity. In the campaign, Menzies established connection with voters and called for loyalty in the context of the perceived wartime threat to the security of a nation imagined as incorporating not only Australian territory but also the British Empire as a whole. His 1940 policy launch speech, reported at the time as 'the most forceful and dramatic of his career' (*Melbourne Herald* 1940b, 8), constructed the Empire as a 'family of nations', and Britain as the 'vital centre of that family':

> We must, realising that we are not only politically but morally, spiritually and materially, an integral part of the great British family of nations, make the highest possible contribution to the war effort of Great Britain, the vital centre of that family, wherever and whenever that contribution can be made. (Menzies 1940)

This speech exemplifies the two central features of the discourse of British belonging discussed above: first, the language of kinship or 'blood' ties; and second, the emphasis on loyalty and tradition in strengthening those racial bonds. The language of family offered voters a stable image of Australia's place in the British Empire. In this construction, Australia was threatened when any other member of her family was under attack; and in this case, the very heart of that family required assistance. Menzies provided a particularly eloquent expression of the language of blood ties and kinship; however, there was a clear shift in his campaign discourse across his time in office. Familial language was increasingly replaced by references to friendships, partnerships and alliances.

As the discourse of Empire and Britishness faded from use in the 1950s and 1960s, the US Alliance became the dominant 'Western' international relationship referred to in Australian campaign speech. Australian political leaders have been mentioning the United States since Federation; however, these references rose sharply in the 1930s and 1940s during World War II. The dominant explanation for this shift, in Australian political history and nationalism literature, is that references to Australia as a racially pure Imperial outpost became unsustainable in the face of dramatic changes in the global social and political landscape in the mid-twentieth century (Day 1998b, 86; see also Alomes 1988). Britain's gradual abandonment of their aggressive Imperial policy, the shift to discourses of Commonwealth rather than Empire and their withdrawal from the Pacific during and after World War II – combined with changing perspectives towards Europe and the project to join the European Economic Community – were seen as undermining Australians' ability to rely on familial ties to an increasingly distracted mother country as the basis for a stable sense of belonging in the global landscape. Political leaders responded in their campaign communications, reassuring an electorate faced with rapid and destabilizing change about their connections to the Western world.

Menzies' language exemplifies this shift. Characterized as pro-Empire in both academic literature and popular culture (e.g. Brett 1992; Curran 2006), close analysis of his campaign speech reveals his instrumental role in developing Alliance rhetoric in the many elections he fought, particularly from the mid-1950s to his retirement. In the post–World War II environment, Menzies linked international tensions and conflicts to Australia's need for the US Alliance from a discursive position where his well-established Imperial links softened the confronting nature of strategic realignment. This was informed by the domestic issues through which Cold War politics played out in Australia: Menzies' failed 1951 attempt to ban the Communist Party (Goot and Scalmer 2013); the sensational Petrov Affair and Royal Commission into espionage in Australia (announced by Menzies as Parliament was dissolved before the 1954 election) (Menzies 1970, 154–97; Daly 1984, 122–24); the 1954 Labor split; and formation of the Democratic Labor Party in 1955. These coloured the political battles between Menzies and Labor leader H. V. Evatt. In 1955, for example, the campaign was dominated by media coverage of the Petrov defection, the dangers of communism and security threats (Daly 1984, 123). In this context, Menzies' speeches emphasized the importance of Australia's 'powerful friends' and the ANZUS treaty to national security. Three years later, Menzies delivered his 1958 policy launch speech at Canterbury Memorial Hall in Melbourne to a crowd of over 9,000 and to a nation-wide radio audience. Struggling to be heard above hecklers who maintained 'a fire of interruption and interjection' (Cox 1958, 7), he again placed Australia's traditional relationships in a defensive framework:

> Why powerful friends? Does anyone suppose that we could in our own strength defend against a major aggressor? [...] That's why a truly Australian foreign policy requires the cultivation of friendships, and in particular a close alignment with the Commonwealth and the United States of America. (Menzies 1958)

Australia's developing strategic relationship with the Unites States received largely bipartisan support in campaigns by the 1950s, with Evatt (1954) presenting a similar image of the nation as 'integrally' associated with the British Commonwealth but also 'associated very specially with the United States'. This shift has traditionally been seen as an attempt to replace the Empire as the basis for Australian security, and there is clear continuity in the move from one powerful Western protector to another. However, images of the Alliance were not simply a direct replacement for Australian-British identity. Rather than continuing to present Australia as a member of a family of nations, Menzies's language exemplifies a discursive shift to talk of *friendships* with the world's great Western powers. This reflects a growing sense that the Alliance presented a chance for Australia to have a more independent voice in world affairs, operating as partner rather than junior family member.

The increasing visibility of the American Alliance in political discourse provided an opportunity to fill the gap left by the decline of unproblematic membership of a white-British global community as a basis for belonging. However, the language of Alliance was neither an immediate nor complete replacement for the traditional narrative. In the period of relative insecurity about Australia's place in the world from the 1960s onwards, leaders struggled to make the Alliance friendship speak deeply to belonging as familial Imperial ties had done. The less unsettling security aspect of the Australian-US relationship was initially more prominent in these representations, and both Menzies and his immediate political successors positioned the American Alliance as about strategic alignment rather than a fundamental change to the nation's deeper identity.

In the mid-1960s, during the Vietnam War, Liberal prime minister Harold Holt's campaign language echoed the shift in the foundations of Australian belonging developed by Menzies, and continued to emphasize a strategic allegiance that carried less emotive force than the Imperial relationship. From being part of a natural family of British nations, Australia was now presented as having 'long allied ourselves with Britain and the United States' (Holt 1966). This placed the two strategic relationships on equal footing and constructed Australia's defence interests in the framework of that pragmatic connection. This language echoed over the successive decades, where leaders from both parties used the language of friendship to implicitly construct Australia and the United States as sharing both cultural perspectives and economic interests: speaking of 'close links' (McMahon 1972); 'trading partners' (Whitlam 1974); 'close cooperation' (Fraser 1980); and 'mutually beneficial involvement' (Peacock 1990). This re-imagining of Australian security as based on friendship was not a complete break from the discourse of British belonging; it echoed the earlier rhetoric of leaders such as Reid and Menzies. However, in Alliance discourse it was cultural and historical ties, rather than the familial bonds of race, that would provide depth to this security relationship.[4] This discursive construction endures. It was explicit in the campaign language of John Howard, who positioned ever-closer ties to the US as an important chapter in the history of Australia's engagement in the world across the elections he fought as prime minister (2001d; 2007f).

In contrast Labor leader Kevin Rudd, Howard's opponent in 2007, realigned these traditional relationships. Speaking at a press conference at the Lavarck Barracks in Townsville, he argued:

> Our Defence policy is based on three pillars: our alliance with the United States, our membership in the United Nations, and of course our policy of comprehensive engagement in East Asia and in the wider Asia Pacific region. These are the three pillars which underpin our approach to national security policy. (Rudd 2007b)

This construction placed the American Alliance on equal footing with Australia's relationships in the region and wider international community (through the United Nations). Striking, here, is the clear echo of Menzies' realignment of Australia's international connections. When outlining his government's defence policy in 1955, Menzies pointed to four 'main principles'

---

[4] It is important to note that this shift was by no means uncontroversial or undertaken without broader debate, particularly over concerns about Australia shifting from a subordinate role in the Empire to being dominated by American policy and culture; see, for example, the discussions from Ashbolt (1966) and Blainey (1967) in *Meanjin*'s 1966–67 Godzone series.

(the United Nations charter, British Commonwealth defence, the ANZUS treaty, and the SEATO treaty) as providing the stable allegiances that would guarantee Australian security. However, Rudd's evocation of a 'policy of comprehensive engagement' in the region draws more deeply on the campaign language of his Labor predecessors Bob Hawke and Paul Keating, who in the campaigns of the 1980s and 1990s grappled explicitly with the questions of Australian belonging in the region that, as we have seen, have been part of broader conversations about the nation's place in the world since Federation.

Our Natural Place to Be

Election campaigns do not take place in a vacuum. The dominant issues are influenced by broader social and economic contexts and ongoing public and media debates. In the 1980s and 1990s, there was sharp rise in campaign discussions of Australia's place in the region, corresponding to a time when politicians, policy-makers and the population were adapting to the increasingly visible changes resulting from globalization and the emerging importance of Asian trade markets to the national economy. As leaders like Labor's Bob Hawke and Paul Keating pursued reform agendas that saw the Australian economy 'opening up' to the world (through deregulation and other processes), election language aimed to help voters make sense of these shifts by connecting policy proposals with their experience of a rapidly changing world. These external factors do not mean that the personal and political agendas of those involved had no influence on campaign language. For example, Paul Keating's agenda can be seen as driving both sides of politics to increasingly consider Australia's role in the region in the mid-1990s. However, it is also important to acknowledge the role that 'preexisting ideational structures play' in these campaign debates, and in wider foreign policy approaches to regional engagement (Burke 2010, 78). Policy debates about 'Australia's regional relations have always been imbued with a domestic political significance' and therefore have 'deep resonances for the self-perception of Australian identity' (Griffiths and Wesley 2010, 18). Here, discussions about Australia's place in the region and world reflect and rework elements of a broader public and political debate about the shape of Australian identity, in which both 'through the post-colonial era and more recently'

> civilisational constructs of identity have both influenced national foreign policy and shaped a broader mix of cooperation and confrontation between an Australia self-identified as "Western" and an Asia imagined in anti-Western terms as culturally and politically unique. (Burke 2010, 78)

Burke (2010, 78) argues that 'barely disguised racism' runs beneath both constructs; these conceptions of race, identity and civilization have informed the ambivalent discourses of regional threat and opportunity Australian leaders have offered to voters across campaign history.[5]

Paul Keating is a study in personal and political contrasts. He was capable of wit and eloquence while wielding an instinctive command of the Australian colloquial; a 'boy from Bankstown' who developed a love of antique clocks, Mahler and expensive suits; a compelling parliamentary performer who struggled to communicate his vision on the campaign trail. Michael Gawenda (1996, 1), writing in the *Age* during the 1996 election, noted that it was 'a mystery' that this 'matchless parliamentary debater, a man whose language is so startling and sharp' could be 'reduced, by a written speech, to a cardboard cut-out of himself'. Keating is remembered for his 'big picture' political program; as a leader whose vision for the nation challenged Australians to see themselves, and their place in the world, in a new way. He developed a language of regional engagement that continues to resonate in Australian public discourse[6]; however close analysis demonstrates that Keating's language was in many ways less radical, and more sophisticated, than political memory records.

In the two elections he fought as prime minister, Keating asked voters to see their nation as moving towards closer engagement with those he imagined as neighbours in the Asia-Pacific region. This redefinition sought to locate Australia's *identity*, as well as its economic and military, security within the region. In 1996, Keating was battling an unexpectedly formidable opponent in second-time Liberal Party leader John Howard. Howard had struggled with an image of 'outdated conservatism' since his unsuccessful tilt at the prime ministership in 1987 (Williams 1997, 60), and his political resurrection relied on redefining this image as putting him in touch with the values of those imagined as ordinary Australians. This was a group he 'spoke to, never down to' in a 'flat accent' designed to emphasize that there 'was no essential distance between leader and led' (Kane 2014, 4). To do so he mounted a clear and consistent challenge to the discursive construction of the nation associated with Keating's big picture politics. In their campaign battle, the central discursive contours of the search for Australian

---

[5] I have written about the development of these ambivalent discourses of regional engagement in more detail elsewhere; see Brookes (2012).
[6] This is something that Keating himself sees as one of the key parts of his political legacy. At the conclusion of a four-part interview with veteran political journalist Kerry O'Brien (which aired in late 2013) Keating positioned the continuing discussion of how Australia locates itself in the world, and the role it will play, as one of the most important impacts he'd had on Australia's political discourse (see Australian Broadcasting Corporation 2013).

belonging that would define the next two decades were established, echoing and extending those of previous campaigns.[7]

Keating presented his 1996 policy speech from a 'starkly lit stage' at Melbourne's World Congress Centre, before a background emblazoned with the word *Leadership* (Williams 1997, 264). He asked voters to think creatively about their nation; to be bold when imagining its place in the world as their own lives, and those of their children, would be 'caught up in the phenomenon of internationalization'. Australians would need to adapt in order to 'find jobs in the industry of our region', Keating argued. He presented a hopeful image of an Australian future:

> We can enter the new century a unique country with a unique future. We can enter it prosperous and dynamic: a diverse and tolerant society, trading actively in Asia and the rest of the world; secure in our identity, the more so because we know that we have met the challenge of our times [...] By the year 2000 we should be able to say that we have learned to live securely, in peace and mutual prosperity among our Asian and Pacific neighbours. (Keating 1996a; see also 1993)

Keating is dealing directly with issues of *belonging* and *identity security* here: challenging voters to embrace 'internationalization' and engagement as a means of ensuring that Australians remain 'secure in our identity'. Voting Labor, it is implied, would allow Keating to guide citizens into this new era where Australia was connected in new ways to the world beyond its borders. This was a project reliant on Labor's political success as only Keating, known for his close personal relationships with regional leaders and frequent visits to Australia's neighbours, could deliver on its promises. His image of Australian belonging in the region was a challenging re-imagining that called on voters to embrace the 'porous boundaries' of cosmopolitan identity (Calhoun 2004, 231; see also Himmelfarb 2002; Nussbaum 2002). All that was needed was trust that regional engagement could co-exist with Western connections:

> We will not be cut off from our British and European cultures and traditions or from those economies. On the contrary, the more engaged we are economically and politically with the region around us, the more value and relevance we bring to those old relationships. Far from putting our identity at risk, our relationships with the region will energise it. (Keating 1996a)

---

[7] For a detailed analysis of the key issues and themes of the 1996 election campaign, see Pamela Williams' (1997) excellent behind-the-scenes account *The Victory*.

This was a sophisticated image of Australian belonging, and it called on voters to take a risk by extending their feelings of belonging beyond familiar boundaries (Benhabib 2002, 185) and adapting with confidence to the changing global landscape. Keating's big picture vision of regional engagement (combined with other elements of his social and cultural reform agenda) echoes in political memory as a direct challenge to familiar narratives of Australian identity. What is often overlooked, in these assessments, is that Keating's language invited voters to feel at home in the region rather than asking them to replace their traditional sense of Anglosphere belonging with a radically new conception. References to the Asia-Pacific as a 'community of nations' (Keating 1996b) encouraged voters to find security in regional belonging, which Keating (1996a) presented as a necessary precondition for guaranteeing economic opportunities:

> We will only succeed in the region around us if we truly want to be there. If we regard it as our natural place to be, with the people around us as real and genuine neighbours.

However, Keating's reconceptualization of Australian belonging made 'no passionate appeal to Labor's heartland' (Williams 1997, 265), and was unsettling for many voters, especially in the context of changing global economic conditions.[8] In the space left unfilled by Keating, his opponent was able to mount a 'sustained pitch' for those who felt left behind (Williams 1997, 256). This group came to be known as 'Howard's battlers'. Both the opposition and new political groups, like the One Nation Party (led by the controversial MP Pauline Hanson), worked to tap into the perceived groundswell of resistance sparked by Keating's political agenda.[9] As these fiery political, public and media debates played out, the Liberal leader offered voters a safe (albeit nostalgic) alternative. Howard successfully distanced himself from the Labor government's vision of Australian belonging. Despite positioning 'good relations with the region' as a 'bipartisan constant of Australian politics', Howard

---

[8] The dangers of leaving so-called ordinary voters behind were not lost on Keating's staff, who worried before the 1996 election that the prime minister was 'identified almost exclusively with the concerns of special interest groups', without being seen to feel the pain of 'mainstream' Australia (Williams 1997, 172; also Macintyre and Clark 2004, 125–28). Adviser Don Russell and speechwriter Don Watson were concerned that the public image of Keating as passionately committed to reforming the traditional institutions of Australian identity (an image Watson helped create) was causing 'widespread resentment' (Williams 1997, 172). The two pushed for a return to focusing on the economic concerns of 'middle Australia' before the election, but eventually agreed this sudden change would not play well in the media or with the electorate.

[9] For a closer look at the rise and impact of the One Nation phenomenon at that time, see Gray and Winter (1997); Johnson (1998); Kingston (1999).

(1996b) emphasized that the Keating agenda was a threat to Australia's standing in the global political, economic and cultural landscape. In his National Press Club Address, two days before the election, he was 'relaxed' when presenting an 'unscripted and articulate, if predictable', speech (Firth 1996, 11). In response to questioning from journalists about regional engagement, Howard (1996b) tapped into long-held concerns about geographical isolation and more recent anxieties opened up by the uncertain fluidity of globalization:

> The only point of departure with myself and the government on this issue is that when you hear them, the language used is often code for saying that in some way our associations with Europe and America are a liability rather than an advantage. I mean, to me, the great opportunity for Australia is that we are, we have this remarkable intersection of our history and our geography and we can be seen as the link between Europe and North America and our part of the region.

Here, Australian belonging remains firmly anchored to its Anglosphere origins, and Australians can take advantage of the region's economic opportunities without forfeiting their familiar image of the world around them. In the same way that Labor's agenda was connected to Keating's personal values and goals, Howard worked with the advantage (and liability) of voters' assumed memory of his controversial 1988 critique of Asian immigration levels (Jupp 2007, 106–7). From this position, he was able to present himself, and his party, as the guardians of Australia's identity security by arguing that his opponent's vision of regional belonging moved Australianness away from 'its purely European roots towards a more cosmopolitan Asian identity' (Wesley 2007, 10).

Reassuring those discomfited by Keating's vision of an Australia at home in the region, Howard's campaign language focused instead on domestic policy: for example, a one billion dollar family tax package that brought cheers from the crowd when it was announced (Williams 1997, 252). This was particularly effective in appealing to those in the electorate for whom the lived experience of working class decline and the disintegration of traditional sources of community did not align with Keating's construction of a dynamic, confident Australia. Howard instead promised voters a 'relaxed and comfortable' image of national belonging, successfully challenging his opponent's location of identity security in the region. Through this close consideration of the language of Keating and his opponent we gain a vital new perspective on the much-analysed 1996 campaign, which highlights that this was predominantly a battle over whose narrative of belonging was more reassuring for voters experiencing the disruptions of globalization.

I Want Australia to Lead

Campaign discussion of Australia's place in the world faded considerably once the Howard government came to power in 1996, committed to leaving explicit attempts to relocate Australian belonging behind (Wesley 2007, 9). Both conservative and progressive leaders, perhaps with the impression that Keating's defeat signalled an electorate reluctant to engage on big picture issues, shied away from detailed discussion of the nation's place in the world. With the election of Kevin Rudd to the Labor leadership in December 2006, some of these issues re-emerged in political discourse. On one hand, Rudd's close personal connection with China (as a former diplomat fluent in Mandarin) exemplified an 'emotional regionalism' (Wesley 2007, 153) from which he addressed questions of Australian belonging in his political speech. On the other, however, his campaign discussions of Asia and the Pacific exemplified the ambivalence characteristic of Australian political leaders' discursive constructions of the region (Brookes 2012). Carol Johnson and colleagues (2010, 67) have noted 'that "Asia" is not always a totally positive sign for Rudd', and that his arguments for his own ability to guide Australian engagement in the region were reliant on 'a fear that Australia could be left behind and/or become a Chinese and Indian mine, rather than a developed 21st century economy'.

In the 2007 election, for example, Rudd (2007g) was concerned that the region's economic and social development would mean Australia was left behind. In this scenario, the white-Western leadership of the Asia-Pacific that cemented the nation's broader place in the world would be threatened:

> If elected, I also want to ensure that Australia once again has its own voice in the affairs of the world. I want Australia to lead, and not just follow, in dealing with the international challenges of the future. I want Australia to be a leader in the global fight against poverty, disease and underdevelopment – starting right here in our own region, our own neighbourhood, our own backyard. And I want Australia to be a leader in the global negotiations on climate change – rather than Australia being excluded from the negotiating table.

Rudd's focus is on economic competition. His discursive construction draws on earlier frameworks of opportunity, echoing Keating's concerns about the swift movement needed to embrace regional engagement. In areas such as education policy, climate change and broadband, Rudd (2007g) argued that Australia had been 'falling behind' nations such as China, Singapore, Japan and South Korea, constructing them as competitor *economies* whose developing prosperity and stability (and 'Westernization') might upset the natural hierarchy of the region and the world. Hage (1998, 220) has identified these kinds of concerns as replacing older negative characterizations of the Asian 'lack of rationality'. Rather, newer constructions worry about 'superhuman' characteristics: 'they're powerful, work harder at school, get better jobs' and have taken *control* (Hage 1998, 221). Hage's (1998, 225) insights illuminate that Rudd's discourse of regional competitiveness operates as a 'neurotic discourse'. For Rudd, here, new forms of cultural defence were required to protect Australia's role as a regional leader and place it afforded the nation globally.

A Neurotic Discourse

The consistent preoccupation with defining where Australia belongs in the world, and protecting this through the maintenance of a network of friends and allies, is based on the notion that the ties of 'race' or 'culture' provide Australians with an irrefutable means of security. Kinship or values-based belonging was presented to voters as deeply held and self-evident. However, political leaders' campaign language reveals a consistent, and seemingly contradictory, anxiety about the maintenance of those ties.

Narratives of Australian belonging recurred in campaign discussions of policy areas like defence, immigration and the economy. Ostensibly taken-for-granted connections to the Empire or to those imagined as great and powerful friends were restated and re-emphasized in the face of new challenges or when old threats re-emerged. The ongoing process of reassurance about these connections betrayed a deep, persistent anxiety about where 'we' belong. Far from being comfortable as British subjects or an outpost of Western civilization in the southern seas, Australians were invited to worry about the nation's place in the world by their leaders through reassurances that they had nothing to worry about. In the face of fears of isolation or abandonment, party leaders promised control: national agency operating as a mechanism to ensure the maintenance of the Imperial and Alliance ties or regional belonging that could provide Australia's guarantee of military and cultural security.

This challenges traditional narratives of Australian political history that position the reliance on so-called great and powerful friends as stifling the formation of an independent identity, with Australian nationalist movements working in spite of, or directly against, Imperial, Alliance or Western belonging. Rather, it was those very ties that allowed the fledgling nation the symbolic security and discursive space to develop a distinctive identity. The Australian national myth of belonging has evolved; however, the discursive space within which leaders define and contest this national vision has always been dependent on a basic level of secure belonging. The emphasis on Australia's international relationships, and the project to find new protectors when previous alliances faded, must therefore be seen as providing a comforting foundation for the nation's developing sense of self. For example, Menzies's reassuring rhetoric of British belonging helped him grapple with complex questions of international engagement, easing the transition to a reliance on the US Alliance as Australia's primary means of locating itself in the world. Rudd's language approached the same challenge in a different way, echoing what David Walker (2010, 47) has described as an enduring belief, since before Federation, that 'knowing Asia would prove critical to Australia's future'. This was informed both by anxiety that 'aggressive Asia might overrun "empty" Australia', but also by the notion that we 'had something to learn from Asia' and that isolation was not in the nation's best interest (Walker 2010, 47). In various forms, therefore, leaders' descriptions of the nation as naturally belonging to a wider global network worked to provide a secure location for Australians in the world. These constructions were always presented in contrast to a (real or perceived, implicit or explicit) threat. The discourse of racial and cultural identity separated the spaces where Australians belonged from those where they did not, connecting to voters' lived experiences to grant these discourses a powerful and ongoing resonance. The next chapter explores how from a foundation of belonging political leaders developed discourses of Australian values as a mechanism for establishing, and claiming ownership of, a distinctive story of Australian identity.

Chapter 4

VALUES

One of the most powerful ways that campaigning political leaders forge a connection with voters is by talking about Australian identity in positive terms. This is a discursive strategy that pervades political speech beyond election campaigns. It seeks to use explicit discussions of the Australian people and the things they care about as a foundation to allow leaders to align themselves, their parties and their promises with what is imagined as the Australian way of life. This strategy can be incredibly effective, helping citizens feel as though they are part of a community that is valuable and worth protecting, a community within which their dreams for the future and personal ideals will be respected. It seeks to construct for voters a positive story of their own individual identity, and then connect this to an image of Australian identity that aligns their sense of self, if not wholly then in the ways that are seen to *matter*, with the values and priorities of those around them.

Political leaders who provide positive articulations of individual and collective Australian identity do so with a keen partisan eye, ensuring that they develop for themselves a political persona aligned with these articulations. If a party leader can claim what they present as the positive story of Australian values for their side of politics, using the Labor or Liberal tradition as a stand-in for national history more broadly, then they can cast themselves both as personifying these values and as their staunchest defender. While this discursive strategy runs throughout Australian political history, some leaders have worked explicitly in their campaign speeches, interviews, debates and press conferences to bring Australian values to life. Through mythologized descriptions of the national character, historical reimagining and storytelling, and personal anecdotes, they have used this discourse to pledge to govern in the spirit of the carefully constructed Australian way of life that these shared values make possible. The challenge for leaders is to ensure that their mobilization of these discourses seems sincere. Aligning yourself with Australian values or the national character can backfire unless it is seen to accord with a deeply held personal belief about, and shared lived experience of, the priorities and concerns of the electorate. Labor prime minister Kevin Rudd, for example, became known for his awkward attempts to insert the Australian colloquial into his speech. During a *Sky News* television interview in June 2009 he used the phrase 'fair shake of the sauce bottle' three times, prompting the opposition to characterize it as a 'desperate' attempt to connect with voters (AAP 2009; Kenny 2009). Political commentator Bernard Keane (2009) noted that Rudd had used this colloquial innovation previously, and that the basis of his 'forced attempts to sound ocker' could be attributed to the complex influences that informed his political speech: his rural childhood; public school education; career spent in the 'specialised enclave' of the public service; and significant periods of time living overseas. For Keane (2009) it is vital to pay attention to the way that our political leaders speak, both because it is 'fundamental to political success' but also because it can illuminate 'important and ignored' issues like class. Here, socio-economic background, education and other factors can significantly impact a political leader's ability to connect with those imagined as ordinary Australians. This does not mean that leaders are powerless in the face of their upbringing and experience, but that these will inform the ways in which they use language to connect with voters.

This chapter introduces two prime ministers who have effectively mobilized positive discourses of Australian identity in their campaign language: Bob Hawke and John Howard. Although representing different political parties, both talked explicitly and consistently about Australian values and the national way of life in their campaigns, going some way towards filling in the spaces often left blank in the discourse of shared national characteristics and preoccupations. The specific detail of these constructions evolved across their careers; Hawke and Howard won four election campaigns each, dominating the political landscape of their era. Both are remembered as having a particularly strong connection with the electorate. Hawke's time in office is commonly referred to as a 'love affair with the Australian people', while Howard is mythologized for having a deep and personal understanding of the Australians at the heart of his constituency. This chapter explores two central strategies used by these leaders to mobilize the discourse of Australian values in the election: the positioning of their own personal and party traditions as aligned with *true* Australian values; and the valorization of the Anzac myth as the most powerful embodiment of these values.

The True Heart and Soul of Australia

Across the four elections he fought as opposition leader and prime minister, Bob Hawke used explicit discussions of Australian values to position the national way of life as a central campaign battleground. Hawke mobilized this language into the routine discourse of campaigning in which each election is positioned as a moment that represents either great opportunity or deep crisis depending on the choices voters make on election day. Voting for *us*, in this construction, will mean safeguarding Australian values and ensuring that citizens can continue to live, or return to living, according to those values.

This success of this strategy was reliant on Hawke's particular political persona, and made possible by the common-sense perception of his skills as storyteller, negotiator and facilitator of consensus. Bob Hawke was a master of political mythmaking. From the identity stories he told Australians about themselves and their history to the painstaking construction of his own complex political persona, Hawke's connection to the electorate was founded on his ability to cast his plans and policies in political narratives that made sense to voters' lived experiences. In doing so, he successfully navigated one of the most difficult challenges of political leadership: communicating to constituents an ability to understand their concerns and values as 'one of the people', while simultaneously developing the notion that he was exceptional in the way that national leaders must be. Journalists Robert Haupt and Michelle Grattan (1983, 14), in their account of the 1983 election *31 Days to Power*, refer to Bob Hawke as 'the most thoroughly psychoanalysed man in Australian politics', but note that Hawke himself has been 'a gleeful participant' in the process. They paint a picture of Hawke as driven and intelligent, but with a healthy self-esteem which allowed him to see himself as 'one of the giants of his time, a man of destiny' (Haupt and Grattan 1983, 14). Graham Little (1997b, 17), writing on narcissism in Australian politics, argues that the term itself was 'defined for Australians by Bob Hawke', who believed:

> He had a calling, a destiny, and he was the Messiah. His vanity was legendary, attaching to his hair, his sexuality, his drinking, his stamina, his intelligence and, feeding on itself, the love the people had for him […] Hawke did not like to be alone. His recreations were gambling, tennis and sport […] He claimed his greatest skills were negotiation and managing a team. He 'pressed the flesh' in shopping malls and clubs. He could never resist television.

It was this carefully constructed mixture of the ordinary and the exceptional that gave Hawke a platform from which to express his vision of Australian values and identity at a time of global change and uncertainty. A key element of this was the notion of his *authentic* Australianness, which at times leaned towards caricature: based as much on his colourful, colloquial speaking style as on his love of sport and proficiency with a yard glass.[1] These elements, and

---

[1] Hawke has become associated in Australian popular memory with the yard glass, a tall thin glass used in pub games to challenge participants to drink almost 1.5 litres of beer as quickly as possible. The legend has a number of elements: most prominently, Hawke's stint as world record holder

the legacy of his time as Australian Council of Trade Unions (ACTU) leader, meant that a particular 'perception of Bob Hawke flowed through the electorate' that was immune, in Bob Ellis's (1983, 54) recollection, to media or elite counter-narratives: 'that Bob was a) his own man and b) on our side'.

Hawke's reliance on this perception was apparent from his first campaign as opposition leader in 1983, a campaign he successfully contested with the slogan *Bringing Australia Together*. This was a campaign unusual in Australian politics, rivalled perhaps only by 1975 in the drama that preceded it. On 3 February the prime minister, Malcolm Fraser, called a snap double dissolution election designed to catch the opposition unprepared and take advantage of Labor leader Bill Hayden's dwindling support in this own party and in the electorate (Haupt and Grattan 1983, vii-ix). On the same day, as powerful allegiances shifted, a series of meetings ensured Hayden's resignation and Hawke's ascension to the leadership (Haupt and Grattan 1983, ix-xi). Hawke's rise had seemed almost inevitable from his entry into federal politics as member for the Victorian seat of Wills in 1980, a natural extension of his swift upward movement within the ACTU to spend a decade as its highly visible and popular president. Bob Ellis (1983, 4), in his 'election journal' *Things We Did Last Summer*, reflected that 'ordinary people had prophesied and wanted' Hawke's rise to political power 'long before the experts', in no small part due to his time as ACTU president. In this role, according to Haupt and Grattan (1983, 18), Hawke had become:

> A national figure, cast as the defender of the poor against the privileged, the righter of wrongs, the knight defending the working class against the incursions of the bosses.

Hawke spoke with an Australian accent and used Australian expressions; he addressed the values, and seemed to personify the lived experience, of those imagined as ordinary Australians. This translated to his campaigning style. In 1983 he 'talked the language of the man of the street' (Daly 1984, 296) in his interviews and speeches, in clear contrast to Fraser's more formal patrician style. His language explicitly invited Australians to see the campaign as the beginning of a national conversation that would continue if Labor were elected, an invitation that went as far as newspaper advertisements asking

---

after managing the feat in less than 12 seconds while a Rhodes Scholar at Oxford in 1953; and an infamous and often reproduced (see Pilger 2014) black-and-white image of Hawke drinking from a yard glass in Melbourne in 1972, with Gough Whitlam looking on. This reputation was reinforced, many years later in 2012, when a widely circulated video showed Hawke, then 82 years old, 'skolling' (drinking without pause) a beer while attending a cricket game at the Sydney Cricket Ground (e.g. Lion 2012).

members of the public to attend his policy launch at the Sydney Opera House (a strategy far removed from the exclusive invitation-only launches of twenty-first century campaigns).

Hawke's 1983 policy speech was written by veteran Graham Freudenberg, and designed to elevate the opposition leader's language above the colloquial. It was so carefully tailored to his 'love affair with the television audience' that it actually failed to connect with the expectant crowd at the Opera House (Ellis 1983, 61). The same 'restraint' that made the speech seem 'lacklustre' to those listening in person came across, in lounge rooms across the country, as demonstrating Hawke's 'calm resolve' (Haupt and Grattan 1983, 90–91; see also Ellis 1983, 60–61). Hawke's facility with television provided a significant contrast with his opponent. The Fraser campaign had little understanding of, and was ill prepared for, the 'voracious demands' for 'action, drama, [and] emotion' made by television news (Haupt and Grattan 1983, 41). Haupt and Grattan (1983, 36–37) note that members of the press gallery tried to warn the prime minister that the lack of forethought about the needs of television and limited information provided to the press meant that 'Hawke was dominating the airwaves by default'. Hawke's campaign, on the other hand, fostered warmer relations with the press gallery by paying attention to details and making sure that the candidate was constantly available to, and cooperative with, the media (Lloyd 1993, 122). In addition, they had an even greater advantage in the candidate himself, as Hawke was a skilled television performer who 'filled the cameras with his full, almost baroque array of signals, gestures, grimaces, frowns, smiles, laughs and stares' when on the air, (Haupt and Grattan 1983, 41–42).

Hawke's 1983 policy speech set out the contours of the construction of Australian values he would go on to develop not only in this campaign, but also in the three that followed. From the outset, he placed Labor on the side of *true* Australian values and the security of the national way of life in the campaign battle, which was constructed as:

> A fight for the future of Australia, for the true heart and soul of Australia. For we are asking, on the fifth of March, for a decision from the Australian people which will declare to the world that the politics of division, the politics of confrontation – the deliberate setting of Australian against Australian – which have debased the national leadership and disfigured the national life for so long, have no part in the true Australian way. (Hawke 1983)

Hawke, here, undertakes the task of empowering Australians and promising them a return to their true selves, aligning with his campaign theme of 'national reconciliation'. This was a reconciliation between 'business and labour', an element of the broader need to 'establish a consensus' that was one of 'the defining features of his government' (Johnson 2009, 5; 3). The election, in this construction, was therefore an opportunity for voters to work together to support what Hawke (1983) presented as the 'one great goal' of his government (if elected): to 'reunite this great community of ours', and in doing so 'bring out the best we are truly capable of, together'. Asking voters to opt in to the process, in this way, is a powerful discursive strategy that casts constituents themselves as vital to the maintenance and security of the national way of life, and the safeguarding of the values at its core. Hawke (1983) warned voters that there were sacrifices to be made, and that 'all sections of the Australian community' would be asked to 'share the common burden for the common national purpose'. The development of this broad consensus was both reliant on 'the skills he had developed as a negotiator during his many years with the ACTU' (Johnson 2009, 4) but also positioned as vital to reverse the effects of 'Fraserism', which he listed as including high unemployment and inflation rates; high taxation and interest rates; and declining home ownership levels and living standards. These, he argued, were exacerbated by the government's own internal problems: broken promises, instability, 'Cabinet turmoil' and public scandal. His opponent, in his own policy launch the day before, had argued in contrast that only his government offered 'the certainty of recovery', based on a track record in which their policies had 'done much to rebuild Australia' and ensured that 'Australia was one of the last countries to be hit by the world recession' (Fraser 1983). For Fraser, voters were posed with a clear and important choice. Labor's 'divisiveness and irrelevance' would put this positive progress at risk, and it was 'only the Liberal Party' that could 'work to fulfil the hopes of all Australians' (Fraser 1983). In contrast, Hawke (1983) asked voters to understand the election as about more than who would govern or economic security, and to see it instead as a decision about the values and priorities of the nation itself:

> It is nothing less than a judgement about the very nature of Australia – the kind of Australia you want for yourselves and the children of Australia.

Voters could be reassured, here, that what Labor was asking of them was no more than to be 'true to ourselves as Australians', and to act in accordance with the 'true Australian way' (Hawke 1983). This was to work constructively together so that the nation's identity and future could be salvaged. Once elected, this would translate into an attempt to create common ground through 'a process of negotiation and compromise' that would lead to economic stability and social harmony (Johnson 2009, 5–10). This manifested, in the first months of the Hawke government, in the facilitation of the 1983 National Economic Summit and subsequent negotiation of what is referred to as 'the Accord', an agreement with trade unions which Pocock (2009, 188–89) has described as 'the defining industrial relations initiative of the early Hawke years'. The Accord came to represent the search for consensus through discussion and engagement with stakeholders that was more broadly characteristic of Hawke's approach to governing (Laing and McCaffrie 2013, 93). While its legacy and impact on subsequent decades of social and economic policy has since been subject to analysis (see Archer 1988; Johnson 2009; Pocock 2009), it became a touchstone measure of what Australians *could* achieve that Hawke referred to in subsequent campaigns.[2]

The discursive positioning of election campaigns as battles over Australian values was developed and extended by Hawke across the elections that followed. With each successive victory Hawke reminded voters that it was through their own electoral choices and willingness to work together, with the guidance and vision of his own leadership, that they had overcome past challenges to the national way of life. In *this* election, all they needed was to do so again. In 1984, Hawke returned to this theme when he faced off against Liberal opposition leader Andrew Peacock in Australia's first modern-style televised leaders' debate.[3] The debate was hosted by the National Press Club in Canberra and moderated by its chair Ken Randall, and the leaders faced questions from a panel of six journalists. In his opening statement, Hawke (1984) reminded voters that by working together, they had 'eliminated much of the confrontation and bitterness that was tearing our society apart' before his government had taken office. Together, he told them, 'we've provided the basis for Australians to regain their pride and optimism in the nation's achievements' (Hawke 1984). *We* is used as a powerful and effective mechanism to appeal to voters here: while it can be read, in the first instance, as referring to Hawke and his government it is also specifically deployed to include voters themselves, as it is only by working together that the task of building a nation 'with greater opportunities of all Australians' can be continued.

---

[2] It is interesting to note that despite mixed assessments of its legacy, Hawke (2012) himself continues to defend both the Accord and the Summit as the source of 'virtually all of the […] economic success' brought about by his government.

[3] Australia's first televised election debate was actually held in 1958; however, it was significantly different from the leaders' debates that have become a set-piece event of the contemporary mediatized campaign. The debate was chaired by the editor of the *Sydney Morning Herald*, Angus Meade, and was broadcast on ATN 7. Prime Minister Robert Menzies declined the invitation to participate, so the Labor Opposition Leader H. V. Evatt and Deputy Leader Arthur Calwell faced off against Liberal Treasurer Harold Holt and Primary Industry Minister Billy McMahon. The participants sat around a table before a fixed camera, and the *Canberra Times* (1958) reported that it revealed 'sharply conflicting views' between the two parties 'on major issues'.

One of the most sustained, explicit discussions of Australian values in Hawke's campaign language (and indeed, across Australian campaign history) is found in his 1987 policy launch speech. In this campaign, Hawke's opponent was John Howard, who had been in the role since Andrew Peacock's unsuccessful attempt to unseat Hawke in 1984. Howard was a familiar, if not popular, figure in Australian politics but in 1987 was out-campaigned by a confident prime minister. The Labor launch was held at the Sydney Opera House on 23 June. Much of Hawke's (1987) address was dedicated to reinforcing the significance of the choice voters would make at the ballot box on 11 July: a 'fundamental decision for yourselves, your families, your children' about 'what kind of country you want Australia to be'. This, then, was more than a decision about policy or political alignment; rather it would determine 'what kind of a people we are' and 'what kind of a nation we are going to be' (Hawke 1987). What is unusual in Hawke's speech is both the amount of time he dedicates to this discussion and the specific nature of the discourse of Australian values he employs. While this construction is often left empty, to be filled in by voters with content that reflects their own lived experience, Hawke (1987) both lists some of these values in this section of the speech ('a strong, united, stable, confident, forward-looking people'; 'the great ideals of fairness and justice') but also returns to the question of Australian values when wrapping up his address. Here, the prime minister argued that for his government, economic policy is about more than financial outcomes. He told voters: 'we have never believed that the only values in life […] are the ones with the dollar tag on them' (Hawke 1987). Instead, he lists others as defining Australian identity: 'the matchless beauty of our land'; the 'enrichment of the arts and culture'; the fostering of 'leisure opportunities'; a 'generous and open Australia'. This is an explicitly positive discursive construction of Australian values, an aspirational vision of a national community imagined as:

> A free, proud, independent, intensely individualistic, uniquely diverse people, yet a united people – a people who want a fair go for themselves and their families, but just as much, a fair go for all their fellow citizens, for all their fellow Australians […] This is the promise of Australia. This is the Australian vision. This is the reality of the Australian dream. (Hawke 1987)

While Hawke appealed to a glittering 'Australian dream', his opponent located himself as the champion of 'middle Australia' and the 'average Australian family' (Howard 1987). In his address to the National Press Club, three days before polling day, he spoke of a 'growing grassroots surge' of support for his party, coming from voters disenchanted with a Labor campaign he constructed as indicating 'just how out of touch with middle

Australia' the government had become (Howard 1987). He sought to provide a positive counter-vision of Australian values for voters, speaking of a nation where power rested with the people rather than with government; where 'individual effort is rewarded'; the 'family is recognised as the cornerstone of society'; 'understanding, compassion and care' for those less fortunate 'is paramount'; and value is placed on 'creativity, innovation, productivity and achievement' (Howard 1987). Howard's 'Liberal vision' did not resonate with voters as strongly as Hawke's in 1987, and the Labor government was returned for a third term. However, it would be John Howard, almost a decade later, who would provide a strong counter-discourse to the Hawke/Keating story of Australian values, developing a successful challenge to the narrative of Australian identity that had characterized Labor's 13 years in office.

Mr Reasonable

On the day John Howard returned to the Liberal leadership in 1995, a front page *Canberra Times* headline read 'Mr Reasonable has his day' (Cole-Adams 1995, 1). This gives an insight into the persona that the opposition leader hoped would elevate him, and his party, into government. Howard's 'reasonableness' would, it was hoped, allow him to undertake an explicit project to construct and connect to a constituency asked to respond to the nostalgic repositioning of familiar white, Anglo-Celtic values at the centre of the national way of life. Political historian Judith Brett (2005, 32) has argued that Howard was effective in constructing and maintaining this constituency because rather than speaking 'to' the nation, he spoke 'from' it, giving voice to Australians' shared beliefs and their 'commonsense understandings of themselves'. For Brett (2004, 74), Howard was 'the most creative political leader' the Liberals have had since Menzies: adapting and updating traditional party values and positions to respond both to changes in the Australian social and political landscape and the changing nature of the opposition. Howard's ability to do this came not just from his close study of Australian political history, but because he was 'steeped […] in the experiences of those he speaks to', a constituency Brett (2004, 73–74) identifies as:

> Families and small-business owners whose lives centre on work and neighbourhood and are bounded by a relatively taken-for-granted nationalism […] like Menzies before him, he has been able to adapt the language and thinking of his party's political traditions to the circumstances of his political present.

This image of Howard is the outcome of his own careful construction of a political persona whose central features were a distinctive ordinariness and instinctive understanding of the nation and its values. For Marion Maddox (2005, 106), in her insightful study of the rise of conservative religious politics in Australia *God Under Howard*, Howard developed a 'mainstream persona' whose familiar features were that he was 'cricket-loving, suburban [and] Methodist'. It was this persona, which 'pictures him as the grey-suited paladin of an imagined, endangered ordinariness', which would come into play to lend authenticity to his sophisticated campaign constructions of Australian values and the national way of life.

Howard's rise to the prime ministership was anything but meteoric. Rather, it is a tale of 'persistence' and 'tenacity' (MacCallum 2013, 187). The title of his 2010 autobiography, *Lazarus Rising*, refers to a quip Howard made when, after being removed as Liberal leader in May 1989, he was asked about his chances of returning to the leadership: 'like Lazarus with a triple bypass' (Howard 2010, 180). He was first elected to parliament in 1974, representing the Sydney electorate of Bennelong; became treasurer in 1977 and was voted in as leader after Andrew Peacock's failure to beat Hawke in 1984. However, he too was unsuccessful against Hawke in the campaign that followed, and by 1989 (after a period in which he made a series of controversial policy interventions questioning the government's policies on indigenous reconciliation, Asian immigration and multiculturalism [see Gulmanelli 2014, 582]), he was ousted by the man he had replaced. Maddox (2005, 34) attributes Howard's unsuccessful first stint as opposition leader to a 'lack of subtlety'. She argues that while he had mastered 'the technique of playing down the scary hard right economic policy' with the 'mask' of a 'comfortable and relaxed' social policy, he and his supporters:

> had not yet prepared Australia for explicitly voiced anti-Asian racism or his overtly back-to-the-fifties vision. It involved tying social conservatism to the 'inevitable' economic agenda [...] It involved skilfully fostering the impression of 'mainstream' support for his views. (Maddox 2005, 34)

One of the innovative ways that Howard learned to foster the impression of this support, a tool that would prove effective both in office and in campaigns, was through his use of talkback radio. As argued in Chapter 2, effective political speech needs to be both timeless and contemporary: it evokes and updates deeply held shared narratives of the nation's history and identity, but at the same time must speak to the issues of the day and meet the requirements of its dominant communication media. Some leaders are remembered for their particular affinity with a technology or genre: Robert Menzies's use of the intimacy of radio addresses, or Kevin Rudd's embrace of the various elements of what is referred to as celebrity media (combining FM radio and late-night television interviews, social media presence and an affinity for 'selfies'). John Howard's exploration of the political possibilities of talkback radio was a defining characteristic of his communication strategy in campaigns and in office. It demonstrated an awareness of the performative role of spaces for political communication and journalism in the mediatized campaign and allowed him to present himself as both willing and eager to speak *directly* to the voters he constructed as ordinary Australians.

Talkback radio had emerged in the late 1960s (Ward 2002; Griffen-Foley 2007), allowing the question and answer interview format between politicians and presenter to be varied, with the addition of a segment where listeners call in and speak directly to the politician. The format was used across radio genres, and its rising influence in political interviews has often been linked to Howard, who has described it as a 'great Australian phenomenon' (2006) 'tremendously important' in 'determining the outcome of elections' (2002). Talkback has a number of attractions for a campaigning leader. It allows candidates to bypass 'traditional' or 'serious' journalists; 'ignore difficult questions and focus on matters [they] want to raise' (Bennett 1996, 118); and 'speak "directly" to the people' (Warhaft 2004, xviii). Ward (2002, 23) highlighted these benefits in arguing that there were clear strategic reasons for Howard's fondness for the genre, as it allowed him to avoid close scrutiny from Press Gallery journalists, 'play to his own strengths as a political communicator' and access the predominantly older conservative citizens that formed the backbone of his early electoral support.

The Very Values We Hold Dear

A key element of Howard's positive construction of Australian identity was the repositioning of the mainstream as defined by a shared set of (implicitly Western, Judeo-Christian) values or distinctive way of life. The development of this discourse of cultural identity can be seen as a response to the reworking of Australian identity and belonging that had emerged in the Keating era (discussed in Chapter 3), and evoked rather than erased historical discourses of racial identity in its appeal to voters. Howard's campaign language positioned the group who could identify with his construction of Australian values in the centre, and then promised to govern on their behalf. In 1996, Howard fought his first election after returning to the Liberal leadership. He'd been elected unopposed when the previous leader, Alexander Downer, stepped down, and was acutely aware that a new style and message was required to avoid repeating the experience of 1987. In 1996, Howard promised to govern *For*

All Australians, a slogan that would echo in less explicit terms in the campaigns that followed (Johnson 2000, 18). This aimed to create a distinction, Johnson (2000, 18) argues, between the Labor government who represented sectional interests (although Howard was vague about who those interests were) and his own party, who would govern for all. Cope and Kalantzis (2000, 244) have elucidated these 'sectional interests' in their analysis of Howard's political language, arguing that it created a 'series of great divides': with united, patriotic, mainstream Australians on one side and 'the politics of difference', multiculturalism, indigenous rights campaigners and 'noisy interest groups' on the other. This latter group, which included those who supported Keating's big-picture agenda, were constructed as separate from the 'true Australians' that were the focus of Howard's appeals. Howard's use of this positioning as opposition leader in 1996 has become part of Australian political folklore, and he continued to privilege 'the central role of Anglo-Celtic heritage in Australian identity' once in office (Johnson 2006, 2; see also Gulmanelli 2014, 585).

From this position, Howard made particularly effective use of the Australian-US relationship in his campaign language over 11 years in office, using it to present voters with an image of Australian values as simultaneously distinctive *and* strongly connected to those of its friends in the Western world. In doing so, he relocated Australian values as linked to Australia's historical allegiances with the so-called great and powerful friends that located Australia *culturally* in the 'West' despite its geographical location. These relationships were about more than military protection for Howard: they were a result of deeply felt and long-running resonances between our values and those of our allies. In 2001, for example, when justifying his government's decision to join the American-led 'Coalition of the Willing' in the 'War on Terror', Howard (2001c) drew explicitly on the shared memory of this important historical and cultural relationship to argue that voters needed to 'think about the values we hold in common with the American people' when considering how to respond to 11 September. Kathleen Gleeson (2014, 76), in her analysis of war on terror discourse in Australia, illuminates the discursive strategy employed here. She argues that Howard, working from a position in which he held a 'high degree of autonomy in structuring Australia's response to key security issues', used 'pre-existing, familiar representations of identity and threat' as a means of justifying Australian involvement, while also mobilizing 'war on terror discourse as a vehicle for furthering his own deeply held views about society' (Gleeson 2014, 76).

Howard (2001c) positioned 11 September as 'an attack on Australia as much as it was an attack on the United States' because it 'assaulted the very values that we hold dear'. It is for this reason, he argued, that Australia needed to pledge its military support, as well as because the relationship was 'the one guarantee we have of the future survival of the way of life that we believe in', as it had been during World War II (Howard 2001c). This representation asked voters to recall the sense of abandonment and betrayal that followed Britain's withdrawal from the Pacific in World War II, evoking familiar race-based fears about 'the expansionist plans of Japan' (linked to long-held fears of the Yellow Peril). For Howard, the very survival of Australia's *way of life*, which he places in the central position once held by the ties of race and kinship in the campaigns of the early twentieth century, relied on the strength of the American Alliance. In this way Howard (2007d) was able to argue for the importance of these traditional cultural ties, locating his conception of the national way of life in a 'broadly Anglo West' (Johnson 2006, 6). Brett (2003, 70) has argued that Howard worked to 're-create a convincing language of unity' for the Liberals by appealing to a sense of parochial nationalism in the electorate. In this passage, Howard employed the language of values to present Australia's relationship with the United States as based on shared cultural history; not so close as a familial relationship, but harder to shake than a strategic practicality. A sense of obligation is also apparent, in the same way that Prime Minister Andrew Fisher (1914) pledged during World War I that Australia would stand by the Empire to the 'last man and [the] last shilling'; the price for belonging to the worldwide network of Western allies is Australia's military involvement when one of those allies is threatened.

To make this argument, Howard also relied on an assumption of voters' knowledge of his close personal friendship with US president George W. Bush. This was deepened through media coverage of Howard's visits to the United States and meetings with Bush throughout his time in office; for example, coverage of the president dubbing Howard a 'man of steel' in May of 2003 (*Sydney Morning Herald* 2003) and emphasis on Howard's presence in Washington D.C. on 11 September, 2001. This coverage continued after Howard's defeat in the 2007 federal election, with Bush praising his friend in language littered with Australian colloquialisms in a personal video message to Howard's 7 May 2008 farewell dinner ('You're a digger who is simple, direct and tough, and you have never let this cobber down' [Bush in ABC Radio National 2008]) and awarding Howard the prestigious Presidential Medal of Freedom as one of his own last acts in office in January 2009 (*Australian* 2009). Through consistent reinforcement of Australia's traditional alliances in the face of threat and change, Howard countered both his opponents' challenging picture of Australian identity and the 'increasingly multiracial and multicultural nature of Australian society' by attempting to 'reinforce and privilege Anglo-Celtic identity and cultural values' (Johnson 2005, 40). He tapped into the enduring themes of conservative political rhetoric, and offered voters a sense of identity security as stable as that once afforded by the ties of blood and common origin.

We Will Decide Who Comes to this Country

Howard's positive articulation of Australian values was a pervasive element of his campaign language, colouring debates about other policy areas. For example, it is an often-overlooked, but vital, element of perhaps his most famous campaign utterance: the much-analysed and critiqued assertion, made in the 2001 election campaign, that 'we will decide who comes to this country and the circumstances in which they come' (Howard 2001c). Howard was speaking in defence of the government's newly implemented Pacific Solution[4] and in the context of the controversial 'Tampa' and 'children overboard'[5] affairs, as well in the shadow of 11 September and the newly urgent spectre of international terrorism. The line played 'perfectly with the middle-aged, middle-class, middle-Australia audience' of Howard's policy speech (Charlton 2002, 105). David Marr and Marian Wilkinson (2003, 246) reflect that, by the end of the speech, Howard had 'a crowd of prosperous, white Australians baying for border protection'. The Liberals were onto a winner, and the line resonated throughout the campaign, used in party advertising and other communications. What is often missing in analyses of this line is that its effectiveness is reliant on the passage that comes before, in which Howard offered voters a positive articulation of Australia's inclusive approach towards immigrants. Here, he justified the nation's stance on national security, which he characterized being as much about a 'proper response to terrorism' as it was about:

> Having an uncompromising view about the fundamental right of this country to protect its borders. It's about this nation saying to the world that we are a generous, open-hearted people taking more refugees on a per capita basis than any nation except Canada, we have a proud record of welcoming people from 140 different nations. But we will decide who comes to this country and the circumstances in which they come. (Howard 2001c)

---

[4] The 'Pacific Solution' refers to the Howard Coalition government policy of transporting asylum seekers to two Australian-funded camps on small Pacific islands, Nauru and Manus Island, for detention and processing. The laws enacting this policy were passed in September 2001 and were seen as a response to the controversial Tampa affair a month earlier, when the Australian government refused to allow the *MV Tampa* (a Norwegian ship that had rescued more than 400 asylum seekers) into Australian waters. The newly elected Labor government ended the policy in February 2008, but it was reinstated in the guise of 'offshore processing' by Rudd's successor, Julia Gillard in 2012 and is still, at the time of writing, Australian policy for dealing with immigration arrivals deemed to have entered illegally.

[5] For a detailed account of the highly controversial 'children overboard' affair, in which Howard government ministers repeatedly claimed that asylum seekers on board the SIEV 4 had thrown their children into the sea to ensure rescue by the Australian *HMAS Adelaide*, see David Marr and Marian Wilkinson's *Dark Victory* (2003).

Howard reassures voters here that support for restrictive border control measures did not compromise their basic Australian values: the generosity and open-heartedness, the willingness to offer a 'warm welcome' that he positions as distinctively Australian. His construction of a typical Australian response to immigrants that can be valorized gives voters permission to see their desire to 'protect' the national borders as a legitimate response to the threats posed by so-called illegal immigration. This construction, which draws together discourses of Australian generosity and control, echoes the earlier language of political leaders concerned about the impact of immigration on the Australian identity but also anxious to paint themselves and the Australian people as open to accepting newcomers. For example, when presenting Labor's immigration policy in 1966 Opposition Leader Arthur Calwell (1966) spoke of the need to 'strengthen and protect Australia's national and economic security' and avoid the social and economic challenges which would arise from 'an influx of people having different standards of living, traditions and culture'. At the same time, however, he reassured voters that the Labor Party (and by extension they themselves) 'gives and always has given, a warm welcome to migrants from other lands'.

Howard's 2001 campaign language must be understood within this legacy. The prime minister and his Labor opponent, Kim Beazley – described as 'two conservative leaders chasing the same very conservative voters' (Marr and Wilkinson 2002, 90) – repeatedly invited Australians to connect with a positive image of themselves as 'open' to new arrivals. In an environment where public and media debate centred on Australia's new anti-terror and border security laws and increasingly tough stance on asylum seekers, both leaders sought to reassure voters that their support for these policies (and the policies themselves) was not racist or discriminatory. To do this both explicitly and repeatedly linked the generosity of Australia's refugee program and Australia's reputation as a good international citizen (Beazley 2001; Howard 2001c) to the *true* values of the Australian people. Howard reassured voters that they were 'generous', 'open-hearted' and 'tolerant' (2001c; see also 2001b), assurances that were most often expressed in broadcast interviews or press conferences in response to questions about border protection. Only days before the election, for example, Howard faced veteran broadcaster Tony Jones on ABC Television's *Lateline* program. Jones referred to the controversial debates about border security that had played out during the campaign when asking Howard: '[w]hoever wins this election, will there be a need for healing on the question of race?' Howard's (2001d) defensive response to this question took offence on behalf of 'the Australian people', whose motives he felt were being called into question:

> That question is based on the inference that what we are doing on asylum seekers is racially based. I want to reject that. It's not racially based. The reason that we are adopting our policy on asylum seekers is that people seek to come here illegally. We're not saying that we'll allow some people to come of a particular race and we'll reject others. If that were the case, then you would be perfectly entitled to allege or infer that it's based on race […] People who seek to come here illegally would all be treated the same way. It is not based on race. And I reject completely the inference that the whole policy is racially based. I think that's insulting to the Government and it's also insulting to many Australians who support the Government's policy.

Here, Howard responded directly to Jones by repeatedly using the term 'race' while arguing that the desire for protection against threats was a reasonable response based on legality, order and process. Australians remained open and generous in this conception, part of what Stefano Gulmanelli (2014, 582) identifies as Howard's advancement of 'ideas of inclusion and tolerance' as a key element of an attempted 'reshaping of Australia' and re-articulation of its shared values and history. Here, Australians were willing to be tolerant of those who entered the nation through the right channels with the right intentions but retain the power to control their borders, allowing or not allowing certain people to enter the national space and symbolic. This offered a sense of agency to those in the electorate who feel what Ghassan Hage (1998) has termed 'governmental belonging'. Two elements are central: first, the belief expressed by the party leaders in their own position as 'governors' of the nation (and their invitation to members of the national collective to see themselves in the same role); and second, the conception of others (whether immigrants, members of an 'ethnic minority' or even members of Australia's indigenous community) as 'people one can make decisions *about*' (Hage 1998, 16–17).

I Believe in the Values of the Old Australia

By 2007, the issues of 'illegal immigration' and border security that had dominated earlier campaigns had faded somewhat, and domestic policies were more prominent campaign features. Facing a challenge from an increasingly popular 'fresh thinking' opponent in Labor's new leader, Kevin Rudd, Howard sought to focus the campaign on his vision for the nation's future through his tried-and-true strategy: connecting his own plans and priorities to those of voters through an evocation of Liberal Party history and values.

Howard used his policy speech to provide voters with positive articulations of Australian identity and values. He delivered the hour-long address at Brisbane's Performing Arts Centre; his Labor opponent, Kevin Rudd, spoke from the same venue to deliver his own party's policy speech two days later. By 2007, newspaper coverage of these kinds of campaign events had responded to the increasingly fast-paced and competitive media market, shifting to providing opinion and analysis of campaign speeches (McNair 2000) rather than straight reporting of the speech itself.[6] Newspaper coverage focused less on the details of attendance numbers or audience response, as was common in reporting of early campaigns where broadcast or images of the speeches was unavailable. In addition, these details became less relevant as modern launches shifted to being invitation only events, meaning that a large and enthusiastic crowd is guaranteed. Rather, coverage in the era of the mediatized campaign illuminated for voters the strategies behind the leaders' announcements, and assessed their likely success. Howard's 2007 speech was reported as 'defensive' and 'lacking in inspiration' (Gordon 2007, 19); the *Age* (2007, 12) called it 'damage control to appease voters feeling the pinch'; while its big spending promises were dismissed as a 'naked, lover-like plea for another chance' (Overington 2007, 4). In contrast, coverage of Kevin Rudd's launch summarized the opposition leader's strategy as 'reassuring voters about Labor, and painting John Howard and the Coalition as politically desperate and reckless' (Grattan 2007, 1). The pageantry of the Labor launch was also a focus, in particular the unprecedented joint appearance in the audience of former prime ministers Whitlam, Hawke and Keating.

Both candidates, in 2007, provided positive definitions of Australian values in their policy launch speeches that echoed the broader identity discourses developed across their campaign language. In doing so, they battled over whose articulation would connect most effectively with voters. Howard (2007c) used his policy speech to construct his personal beliefs as in line with both the legacy of the Liberal Party and with the (current and traditional) values of the Australian people:

> I believe in the individual, I believe in the family as the cornerstone of our happiness and of our nation, I believe in free enterprise and reward for hard work, I believe in the values of the old Australia as well as sharing the excitement and the adventure of the new Australia, I believe very much in the vital role that small business plays in our economy, the two million small businesses that employ some 3.7 million Australians [...].

---

[6] Some newspapers, primarily the *Canberra Times*, continued to print full or edited transcripts until the early 1990s, but the focus of coverage shifted to summaries and costings, tactical and strategic analysis, opinion and metacoverage. By 2007, a political speech could be reproduced in full in video, audio or transcript form as an 'added extra' on newspaper websites, allowing these organizations to compete with broadcasters and other providers of political news.

This is a common discursive strategy in political language, which appeals to voters on the basis that a leader, their party and the people share the same values. It is a strategy that Howard perfected throughout his time in office. Here, voters were called on to align themselves with the so-called middle-class battlers and family values that Howard had moved to the centre of Australian politics since his 1996 defeat of the Keating Labor government. In his National Press Club address, later in the 2007 campaign, Howard referred explicitly to the bitterness and 'insecurity' felt by ordinary Australians that was a central theme of his in 1996. Responding to a question from the ABC political journalist Michael Brissenden about whether a similar 'mood for change' would lead to his own defeat, Howard (2007f) argued that in 1996 voters had been 'cranky' with 'lopsided cultural emphasis' and 'political correctness', and with a tendency in public and political debate towards 'condemning our past'. Howard (2007f), instead, presented his own approach as believing that 'we should preserve the best of the old Australia, the values of the old Australia' while at the same time 'being excited about the opportunities of new Australia'.

Howard emphasized these values and the family as the 'cornerstone of the nation'. He spoke in his policy launch and throughout the campaign about the central role of 'small business' and 'free enterprise', keywords that resonated beyond the political and religious right to appeal to those imagined as ordinary Australians. Johnson (2007, 197) has argued that Howard employed the language of values to 'endorse and influence particular forms of citizen identity', potentially marginalizing those who could not see their own identity reflected in Judeo-Christian or Anglo-Celtic family and political values. The dual emphasis on 'family' and 'free enterprise' was the foundation of Howard's campaign image of Australia as an 'opportunity society', where explicit markers of class, race, ethnicity, gender or religion were removed and national belonging was based on individual willingness to participate in the community and the economy (see Howard 2007c).

For Howard, in 2007, the 'opportunity society' was more than an expression of his own political beliefs and values; it was also a way to align his values, and those of the Australian people, with the Liberal tradition. In 2001, Howard (2001a) had claimed a role for his party in developing the Australian values of openness, generosity and social diversity with a long list of achievements he credited to Coalition governments: the end of the White Australia policy; overseeing the post–World War II immigration program; establishing support and settlement services for immigrants; and establishing the Special Broadcasting Service. During the 2007 election, Howard (2007c) aligned his party's vision of an 'opportunity society' both with the 'timeless hopes and dreams that transcend generations of Australians' and with the legacy of party founder, Robert Menzies. In his policy speech, this was a connection that specifically revolved around 'the desire […] for a place called home':

> The home being an almost sacred part of the Australian Liberal creed stretching back to Menzies' memorable evocation of homes material, homes human and homes spiritual in the forgotten peoples speech of 1942. And what unites our creed of optimism is the belief that the Australian people do not need governments instructing them about virtue. They are more than capable of charting their own course towards a good life for themselves and their families.

Howard linked the 'timeless hopes and dreams' of the Australian people to the Liberal tradition here, and located himself as the protector of those 'aspirational' values. In a doorstop interview the next day, Howard (2007d) reinforced that his leadership and policies were in continuity with his party's traditions, and explained he had deliberately drawn on Menzies' philosophy in his policy speech to emphasize this. This tactic, described in the *Sydney Morning Herald* (2007b, 12) as giving 'the white picket fence a me-too makeover', allowed the prime minister to claim these family and work-related values for his party and implicitly position his opponents outside the Australian cultural values of independence and entrepreneurship. In reassuring voters that they would be able to 'chart their own course' under his government, he evoked a discourse developed across decades of conservative political language in which Labor is imagined as extending state control over services and personal decisions.

Howard's attempt to claim Australian values for himself and for his party did not go unchallenged in 2007. When his opponent spoke at Labor's launch, reported as reminiscent of an 'evangelical tent show' (Wright 2007, 1), his language also privileged the positive values of the Australian identity, but connected these to the election of a 'new Prime Minister and a new government'

> who understand and respect the values upon which our nation has been built. Values of decency. Values of fairness. Values of respect. A new Prime Minister and a new government who believe that the great Australian value of a fair go for all has a future – and not just a past. Friends, Australians are a decent people. We don't ask for a whole lot. We want to have incentive to go out there and innovate, to build new businesses, to build our families and to build our lives. We're competitive, hard working and independent. (Rudd 2007c)

In a direct challenge to Howard's assumed ownership of the terrain of Australian values, Kevin Rudd linked traditional Labor values, such as the decency and mateship of the working class, to the middle-class family values that had been the domain of the Howard government since 1996 (Maddox 2005, 24). This was reinforced through his consistent campaign construction of the Australian 'working families' that had been forgotten by Howard, a discursive appeal to voters that evoked a collective vision of society and tapped into widespread disillusionment with the Howard government's controversial WorkChoices legislation. Drawing on both the Labor tradition of egalitarianism and assumed shared perceptions of the middle-class, Rudd asked voters to identify with what he presented as the values of ordinary Australians who were hard working, 'decent' and aspirational. This, ultimately, was a successful appeal, and on election day, both Howard's government and his own seat of Bennelong fell to Labor, ending more than a decade of Coalition rule.

A Common Endeavour, a Common Adventure

One of the most powerful mechanisms through which Australian values have been constructed in campaign discourse is through debates and discussions that evoke the national military myth, commonly evoked through what is referred to as the Anzac spirit. In these identity stories, the valour of Australian soldiers in historical or contemporary battles is mobilized in order to speak about the true nature of Australian values, and to reify a particular image of what it means to be Australian. Hawke and Howard stand out, in the post–World War II period, as two of the most effective leaders at harnessing military discourse to provide positive constructions of Australian values for voters.

To do so, both have relied on a discursive strategy that has been a powerful campaign tactic throughout Australian political history. Australia's lack of a revolutionary story or civil war to mirror the myths of North American nationhood (Watson 2001, 27) have influenced the common-sense feeling that it was Australia's involvement in international conflicts that signalled the nation's coming of age. Australia's contribution to these conflicts was often presented to voters as an alignment with the forces of good, and a necessary commitment to protect the global network of civilized spaces in which the Australian identity is secure. At the same time, these involvements stimulated a new image of Australian identity: the heroic digger. Emerging after World War I, this was a powerful construction that built on already existing images of colonial-settler identity in post–Federation Australia (White 1981, 125; see also Ross 1985; Day 1998b, 76). Over time the 'Digger at Anzac' was aligned with other familiar symbols of white-masculine identity: the Man from Snowy River, Clancy of the Overflow, the Wild Colonial Boy, Peter Lalor, Cazaly, Ned Kelly and Don Bradman (Ashbolt 1996, 374; see also Souter 2000, 285; Curran 2006, 347). In campaigns, mobilizing *the digger* was a discursive strategy through which party leaders could construct for voters an image of what their own identity could be at its best: egalitarian, principled and cool under pressure.

Campaigning leaders have evoked the values of the digger in explicit terms, referring to the 'democratic spirit' of the defence forces (Fisher 1913) or the 'intelligence and cool gallantry' of Australia's soldiers (Holt 1966). In doing so, they placed the image of the digger at the centre of the nation's emerging national identity, and political and popular culture references kept him there for more than a century as a guardian of traditional Australian identity. The ability to feel pride in, and connected to, the values of Australia's soldiers was reliant on a simultaneous presentation of Australia's role in international conflicts as noble and just. This discourse also allowed Australian voters to justify the sacrifice and loss experienced by the nation as a whole (Brett 2003, 75). In the 1940 election, for example, both Menzies (1940) and Curtin (1940) presented Australia's involvement in World War II as a battle to build a better world against an enemy who threatened the principles and institutions on which the nation was based. While Curtin emphasized the political-cultural values of freedom, justice and democracy as validating Australia's role in the war, Menzies combined this with an evocation of religious imagery. He mobilized the notion of a 'Holy War' for Christianity to explicitly ask voters to see themselves (and their allies) as fighting on God's side to protect 'all the things that our Faith stands for' from destruction.

In the political culture of the late twentieth and early twenty-first centuries, however, the Anzac legend no longer functioned as an unproblematically reassuring image of Australian identity. Seen by some as an outdated symbol of Australia's subservient place in the Empire, the story also does not speak to women, or to those whose ethnic heritage places them outside (or perhaps on the wrong side) of memories of Australians' wartime exploits.[7] Despite this, some contemporary leaders revived the Anzac and Gallipoli myths to fill in the blank spaces of the discourse of Australian values and offer identity security in the face of new challenges. The campaign language of Hawke and Howard stands out here, as both explicitly mobilized the Anzac legend to provide a reassuring construction of contemporary story of Australian values and identity.

Throughout his time in office, Bob Hawke aligned himself with both Labor tradition and Australian history more broadly. In the 1990 election, he emerged as a confident political performer whose victories in the previous three elections afforded him faith in his connection to the Australian

---

[7] For example, Labor prime minister Paul Keating has critiqued it as an event that was both a military failure and representative of Australia's subservient role in the Empire. Keating was still actively arguing this viewpoint in public statements as recently as October 2008, where he dismissed the view that Australian identity was born at Gallipoli as 'complete and utter nonsense' at a book launch, sparking a war of words in the media with then prime minister Kevin Rudd and Victorian premier John Brumby (Shanahan 2008).

electorate. In this campaign, held in the lead up to the 75th anniversary of the Gallipoli landing, Hawke evoked the nation's familiar history and identity stories to communicate his own political values and those of his party. Ten days before the election, the prime minister farewelled the crews of three Australian ships (the Sydney, Tobruk and Oxley) as they began a journey to Anzac Cove to mark the anniversary. This highly symbolic speech afforded Hawke (1990b) an opportunity to reflect on the 'true meaning of Anzac' and to recharge this symbol of unity in a time of economic and social change. Hawke (1990b) explored Gallipoli's 'power to grip the imagination and stir the spirit of the nation':

> In those terrible years, 1914–1918, Australians […] came together; and for the first time, shared a common endeavour, a common adventure, a common danger, a common sacrifice – not as Western Australians or South Australians, not as Queenslanders or Tasmanians – but as Australians. And bonding this splendid company of young Australians together, in an unbreakable mateship, was the very fact that they were all so far from home […] And for the first time, Australians, not just as individuals, but as a nation, came to realise how much they loved Australia, their home […] It is this that gives Gallipoli and all that followed its almost unbearable poignancy. It is this that gives it its true meaning, as a seed event in the growth of the Australian national consciousness […].

In this evocative passage, Hawke employs alliteration and repetition ('a common adventure, a common danger'), drawing on the potent language of mateship to explicitly position Gallipoli as a national founding myth. In doing so, and invoking a sense of an Australian (rather than Imperial) patriotism born at Gallipoli, he reappropriated what had traditionally been a symbol of British-Australian loyalty. Daniel Reynaud (2007, 244) has argued that the Anzac myth evolved from its Imperial beginnings to represent a sense of (at times anti-British) Australian nationalism in the 1980s. Hawke evoked and encouraged this in his construction of Gallipoli as the first time when members of the nation came together as Australians, using the upcoming anniversary to tap into these powerful shared notions of Australian identity and associate himself and his government with this military tradition. In the broader context of economic rationalization, social change and the increasingly visible local effects of globalization, this also functioned to reassure voters about the security of their collective identity by reminding them of the unity inspired by previous challenges.

John Howard, too, used the language and myth of the Anzacs to develop a particular image of Australian values and identity for voters. Judith Brett

(2005, 38) has highlighted Howard's deep identification with 'Australia's military past and present' and his role in turning 'Anzac Day into our de facto national day'. For Robert Manne (2004, 50), Howard's 'vision of Australia' became increasingly clear across his time in office, so that by his third term, it could be identified as

> centered on the Anzac tradition; mateship; military valour; mourning; remembrance; the martial defence of Western values; the most intimate association with Australia's two wartime great and powerful friends, the United Kingdom and the United States.

Historian Mark McKenna (2003, 169–70) has also argued that Howard, more so than any post-war prime minister except Billy Hughes, has 'sought to gain political advantage by wrapping himself in khaki' and sees the 'profound expression of Australian identity in military endeavour'. This strategy can be seen in its most explicit form in the 2007 election where Howard evoked Australia's involvement in previous conflicts to place himself and his party in line with this reassuring military tradition (a strategy challenged by his opponent, Kevin Rudd). Coming near the end of the campaign, the Prime Minister's Remembrance Day Address provided an opportune moment for Howard to reflect on war and sacrifice, part of what speechwriter Graham Freudenberg (2005, 282) has labelled the 'manipulation and politicization of the Anzac legend in the interests of the Liberal Party' that was the most 'disgraceful' aspect of his career. On October 17, Howard and Rudd had suspended campaigning to attend the funeral of two soldiers killed in Afghanistan. Their deaths, Howard (2007b) told voters on Remembrance Day almost a month later, were 'a vivid reminder of the ageless sacrifice on behalf of a free people' that Australia's soldiers had made. Howard's (2007b) address borrowed the symbolic power of Gallipoli to remind voters of Australians' willingness to stand up for their beliefs, and connected those fighting in current international conflicts to the mythologized sacrifice of previous wars:

> There is no hierarchy of sacrifice amongst Australia's war dead [...] All sacrifices represented an equal, selfless commitment to one's fellow man and to one's nation. And whether the deaths occurred in Gallipoli or the Somme, in the Western Desert, Kokoda or Milne Bay, in bomber command over Europe, in Long Tan or Uruzgan Province in Afghanistan, all Australians who've died in conflict – the more than 100,000 of them in all the wars in which our nation has participated – have died for a common ideal.

This passage, clearly written as the sound bite of the speech, was reprinted in the *Australian* (Stapleton and Maley 2007, 2) the next day. With these evocative words, Howard extended the symbol of Gallipoli to other conflicts and other times, using keywords that named specific battles such as Kokoda in World War II and Long Tan in the Vietnam War. In doing so, he reinforced his own close association with the digger tradition, speaking as a prime minister who had located the Anzac legend as central to Australians' sense of collective identity throughout his term in office. This strand was also picked up in media coverage of Howard's address, with the *Daily Telegraph* (2007, 6), *Courier-Mail* (Gartrell and Ja 2007, 30) and SBS Television's *World News* (2007) all noting the prime minister took the unusual step of mentioning the campaign in his address to link the sacrifice of Australia's soldiers to the process of democracy currently underway.

While lacking the ongoing association with Australian military values his opponent had established while in office, Kevin Rudd (2007a) took the opportunity in this campaign to challenge Howard for ownership of the khaki strand of Australian identity when questioned about proposals to mine copper along the Kokoda Track. 'The plan stinks', he told voters without hesitation during a press conference in Queensland, arguing that as someone who had walked the Track he felt it was 'part and parcel of the Australian soul […] it's the Australian continuing identity' (Rudd 2007a). Rudd embraced the relatively informal nature of the press conference to use colloquial, down-to-earth language ('It absolutely stinks'). However, his language here is richer than it may seem on first reading. Speaking of the 'sacrifice' of the Australian soldiers who 'pushed back the Japanese invasion' at Kokoda, he evoked deeply held racial fears. He also asked voters to remember his own personal connection, both with the Track and the image of Australianness it represents by reminding them that he had walked it himself, undergoing a gruelling physical journey with a symbolism second only to seeing Anzac Day dawn at Gallipoli.[8] This short comment allowed Rudd to dictate part of the day's media agenda, leading the coverage on ABC Radio News (2007), the *Sydney Morning Herald* (Pearlman 2007, 10), the *Canberra Times* (Peake 2007, 3), *Lateline* (2007) on ABC Television, the *West Australian* (Hatch 2007, 17), and Associated Press (2007).

These modern evocations of the Anzac myth in the language of Hawke and Howard demonstrate a clear shift away from the approach of their

---

[8] This reference also had problematic associations for Rudd. As shadow foreign affairs minister in 2006, he and Liberal MP Joe Hockey, regulars on Channel 7's morning program *Sunrise*, walked the Track and were criticized for wearing Channel 7 T-shirts while walking. A year later, a planned trip to Vietnam for the Anzac Day dawn service faced allegations, later disproven, that Rudd's office had asked Vietnamese authorities to delay the service in order to meet peak *Sunrise* viewing times (Shanahan 2007).

predecessors who asked Australians see involvement in conflicts as a defence of the institutions of the British race.[9] Hawke and Howard talked instead of the events that bought members of the national community together *as Australians*, recasting wartime involvement as forging a distinctive Australian national character whose values were worth protecting.

The Profound Expression of Australian Identity

The mobilization of Australian values, whether through explicit positive articulations, promises to return to a nostalgic shared past or evocations of a military history imagined as noble and heroic, is a key element of the discourse of identity security. If it is to be worth defending, Australian identity needs to be understood as *valuable*. Identity security requires this solid foundation, and one way to provide this is through positive articulations of national values that citizens feel connected to and can both understand and embrace. These discourses are complex, and any articulation of who and what *we* are will contain traces of what we are not. At times, these are explicit, and at others they lie well under the surface. This kind of political speech is reliant on a connection to the past and an understanding of the present, but in many ways must also speak to the future. When campaigning leaders reassure Australians that their way of life will be secure, they seek to account for the things that members of the imagined national community remember fondly about who we have been; the parts of who we are now that we value most; and our dreams about who we might be in the future. In these discourses, however, the security of Australian identity and values is always reliant on the voting choices of the electorate. In this context, it is a common campaign strategy to construct the election as a battle over which leader, and party, can best articulate and defend *true* Australian values. Here, the Australian way of life is always at stake in the campaign and voters are told that their decisions will significantly impact the security of their own values and community. Both Hawke and Howard were masters of this art: claiming for themselves (and by default, their parties) a unique understanding of the values of the Australian people and positioning themselves as the guardian of those values. This guardianship also requires drawing boundaries around the identity characterized by those values in order to defend it, and the next chapter will explore this element of the discourse of identity security.

---

[9] See Chapter 6 for a detailed discussion of this language and its evocation in the discourse of Australian security.

Chapter 5

COMMUNITY

The discursive construction of a distinctive Australian identity, whose values and characteristics are to be celebrated, will always be reliant on the placing of limits on that identity. Membership in the national collective cannot be an open proposition if it is to provide a sense of identity security. Jyoti Puri (2004, 2; 15), in her study of nationalism, argues that it is founded upon ideas of sameness and difference; that national identity is relational and the differences 'between insiders and outsiders are hardly fixed'. This identification of fluidity is vital, as constructions of national identity can and must change over time in response to broader changes in political, social and economic context. Setting and defending the shifting borders between those constructed as insiders and outsiders has been a consistent concern of campaigning political leaders, who have asked voters to consider the ideal size and composition of the Australian community.

These leaders have forged a connection to the electorate through identity stories that draw clear boundaries around the national community, working alongside political discourses that define Australian values and locate the nation in the global landscape as a mechanism to define and defend the national collective. This has played across a range of issues: in early campaign language, attempts to paint Australia as an idealized classless society both mobilized memories, and critiqued notions, of *home* in service of defining identity for the newly formed nation, offering a direct contrast to the stratified social and labour conditions left behind in Britain. In the campaigns of the twenty-first century, contentious and often highly emotional public debates over Australia's stance on asylum seekers and refugees have similarly offered political leaders the opportunity to evoke a national community both *welcoming* and *under threat*. This was perhaps clearest in 2001, an election that sits in popular memory as dominated by concerns about international terrorism and the perceived influx of asylum seekers (constructed in political language as 'boat people' or 'illegal immigrants'). Liberal prime minister John Howard's engagement with these issues sits alongside Gough Whitlam's *It's Time* campaign speeches as some of the most compelling and frequently analysed uses of political language in Australian political history.[1] As explored in Chapter 4,

---

[1] See, for example, Ward (2002); Solomon (2002); Simms and Warhurst (2002); Marr and Wilkinson (2003).

his 'devastatingly effective' (Glover 2007, 153) combination of national welcome and rejection allowed Howard (2001c) both to define the Australian community in positive terms as having a 'proud record of welcoming people' and also to reassert the community's right to control its borders: 'But we will decide who comes to this country and the circumstances in which they come'.[2]

Such evocative descriptions of the constitution and boundaries of the Australian community are rare. However, language that reflects the tension between mechanisms of welcome (which extend the boundaries of the national community) and control (which help to defend them) runs throughout Australian campaign history. One of the most consistent manifestations of this tension can be found in frequent, routine campaign discussions of immigration policy and population growth. Here, changes in demographics; social movements and identity politics; and the effects of globalization have influenced campaign language. These have informed the desire to define a racially, and later culturally, distinct Australian community as a means of finding identity security in the face of change. In some conceptions, Australian immigration policy has been positioned as a process of opening up to the world, moving from exclusive immigration control mechanisms to ensure a White Australia, through the post–World War II immigration waves, to the seeming embrace of diversity and multiculturalism in the late twentieth century. This familiar narrative of an expanding, diversifying Australian community has been both a source of pride and a contested domain,[3] whose key themes played out, for example, in controversial immigration debates in 1984 and 1988.[4] These debates about identity, race, culture and community cannot be separated from the role of class, an accompanying theme through which Australian social formations have been explored (Burgmann 2005, 2006; Connell 1997; Connell and Irving 1980). The link between the two was prominent in some reactions to the 1980s debates and in the rise of Pauline Hanson's One Nation party in the mid-1990s, a contest over belonging to the Australian community that can be seen as a response to the Hawke/Keating agenda of national reform. For Macintyre and Clark (2004, 109–11), however, it was symptomatic of the rise of neo-conservative politics in Australia, where those with the power to speak positioned themselves as representing 'the people' who were unmarked by 'gender, ethnicity, class, age, religion, or any of the other forms of social identity'. This was a battle over Australian collective identity: over who had the power to define the stories that would make up national memory and

---

[2] For a detailed analysis of Howard's discourse of border control in this campaign, see Brookes (2010).
[3] See, for example, Willard (1923); Palfreeman (1967); Collins (1988); Hage (1998); Jayasuria et al. (2003); Tavan (2005); Hammerton and Thompson (2005); Hodge and O'Carroll (2006); Jupp (2007).
[4] These immigration debates have been positioned by James Jupp (2007, 107) as signaling the end of bipartisan agreement on these issues.

culture (see Betts 1999; Davis 1999; Megalogenis 2003; West 2006). The neo-conservative perspective on Australian history challenged another that worked to explain (and contributed to) the rise of social movements in Australia in the 1960s and 1970s, in the context and aftermath of the Vietnam War. Central, here, were issues of sexuality, race and gender, such as women's history (Sawer 1990; Grimshaw et al. 1994; Dixson 1999; Bongiorno 2001; Summers 2002; Sawer et al. 2006) and the revival of indigenous histories (e.g. Rowley 1971, 1972; Reynolds 1996, 2001, 2005).

These shifts in narratives of the Australian community also have a broader international context. Robert Holton (1998, 198) has argued that Australian national identity is 'intimately bound up with processes of globalisation'. This is both because the development of national identity relies on a range of cross-national 'economic, political and cultural legacies' that are reworked in an Australian context; and because national identity creates and enables distance from the wider world providing 'resistance to perceived threats of globalisation'. Australian narratives of identity and community are therefore 'born of globalisation' and affected by it through issues such as immigration, multiculturalism and border security. It is in this context that broader Australian immigration debates are mobilized in campaign language. Campaign speech does not always match government programs and policies: leaders, and their parties and advisers, will choose to highlight or avoid issues depending on how these will play in the electorate. In doing so, their focus and language also responds to changing domestic and global conditions.

Campaigning leaders have consistently made complex appeals that invite voters to expand their ideas of who *counts* as Australian at the same time as reassuring them that they remain in control of an essentially unchanged national identity. This work of constructing the Australian community relies on a twin discourse of inclusion and exclusion. Positive articulations (who 'we' are, in leaders' spoken language) have been characterized by efforts to identify the markers of the national collective. Through this mechanism, campaigning leaders sketch the identifying features of the community through appeals to shared cultural histories and memories, and the summoning of common values and characteristics, as explored in the previous chapter. These narratives ask Australians to recognize themselves as members of the national community (a task easier for some groups than others) and are always accompanied by exclusionary mirror narratives. The overall trend in this discourse has shifted, since Federation, away from explicit discussion of race in favour of culture; however, the latter has not *replaced* the former. Rather, contemporary discourses of culture continue to be informed by earlier racial assumptions, and their legacy remains evident in contemporary campaign constructions of the Australian community.

It is vital that the practical and economic framing of these justifications, and their mobilization for both *inclusive* and *exclusive* purposes, is not overlooked. While explicitly race- and culture-based discourses of exclusion are relatively straightforward to recognize, the complex interconnection of these with economic and labour discourses (and the use of the latter to disguise or excuse the former) can be more difficult to identify. When campaigning politicians ask voters to extend their understanding of who might be included in the national community, they often do so in the context of skilled migration, labour and workforce policy. They are keenly aware of the security vulnerabilities of a small population conscious of its contingent and problematically-established 'ownership' of a large continent and of the population growth required for stability and prosperity. Rather than arguing for a change to the fundamental characteristics of the community, political leaders have tended to locate plans to restrict or expand immigration as economic proposals, which can be presented as routine, uncontroversial elements of establishing and protecting Australian prosperity. These rely on carefully constructed reassurances that only *useful* immigrants who can contribute to Australian prosperity without disrupting social stability will be chosen. Elsewhere, I have written about the complexities of balancing these priorities in political appeals, and the discursive construction of immigrants as either desirable or undesirable that has allowed campaigning leaders to offer voters a feeling of control over the nation's boundaries (Brookes 2010). Here, I develop this concept further, drawing together the economic security and racial/cultural justifications that are so often used in tandem in campaign constructions of the Australian community, and mapping their enduring influence in Australian identity stories.

This chapter begins with the leaders remembered as Australia's founding fathers, Edmund Barton and Alfred Deakin, whose campaign speech worked to construct the community upon which the new nation would be founded. It then moves to two leaders who have used discourses of economic and identity security to encourage Australians to expand their notion of who belongs while retaining the power to manage the community: Joseph 'Ben' Chifley and Malcolm Fraser. It engages with the language of their opponents, and maps the legacy of their narratives in campaign debates about skilled migration and border control mechanisms in the decades that followed. This illuminates the successful emotive connection afforded leaders who respond to voters' concerns about changing national demographics with empowering definitions of the Australian community.

Mapping the evolution of the frame of economic usefulness and the racial and cultural foundations on which it rests, this chapter asks: how have campaigning political leaders asked those who imagine themselves as Australian to welcome new entrants? What have been the reassuring mechanisms of identity and border security that have safeguarded the mainstream's power to manage the shape and size of the national collective? It engages with leaders' definitions and redefinitions of the boundaries of the Australian community and makes clear the importance of unpacking stories of inclusion and exclusion, and of collective identity and economic prosperity, together. These stories are based in and constructed through language and it is only through close attention to the spoken words of campaigning political leaders that their emotive power can be understood.

A Few Words about a Very Important Subject

In the first decade following Federation, public and political debate was driven by a desire to develop an Australian community that could maintain what was constructed as a white racial makeup in order to establish strong domestic industries and protect its links to the Imperial family. This was expressed, most clearly, in the introduction of the White Australia policy, famously the first piece of legislation passed by the newly formed Commonwealth Parliament.[5] While a wealth of literature across Australian social and political history has dealt with the workings of, and justifications for, this restrictive immigration policy[6], these often overlook the complex social and moral bases through which early leaders presented these policies to voters. Attention to the campaign language of Australia's first two prime ministers, who worked to sell the policy and the image of the Australian community it represented to voters in the decade following Federation, illuminates their careful balance between the necessary development of comforting identity stories to bind the new national collective and the decisions and policies that would lead to economic stability and prosperity.

The central issue of the 1901 election campaign was the economic policy that the newly federated Australian nation would adopt: the question of protection versus free trade that lent the newly formed parties their names. Discussions of other policies were held in the context of this overarching focus. Protectionist leader Edmund Barton was a familiar public figure from his central role in the Federation movement in New South Wales. Commissioned to take on the position of first prime minister by the governor general, Lord Hopetoun, he campaigned to be returned to the job in the 1901 election. He

---

[5] The White Australia policy remained in place until 1973 and was enforced through 'a complex set of legislative and administrative measures aimed at severely restricting non-European immigration' (Tavan 2005, 7) and maintaining the purity of Australia's white-British identity. For a detailed discussion of the introduction, operation and legacy of the White Australia policy see Tavan (2005).

[6] See, for example, Willard (1923); Palfreeman (1967); Birrell (1995); Jayasuria et al. (2003); Windschuttle (2004); Tavan (2005); Jupp (2007).

delivered what can be seen as Australia's first federal election policy launch speech in Sydney's Maitland Town Hall, and was repeatedly interrupted by cheers and applause (*Age* 1901, 5) as he delivered what the *Maitland Daily Mercury* (1901, 2) described as a 'lucid', 'well-considered' and 'concise' address.[7] The speech, written by both Barton and federal attorney-general Alfred Deakin (Simms 2001, 9; Murdoch 1999, 203) dealt with the White Australia policy in its prominent final section, following a discussion of universal suffrage. This featured in the headlines of both the *Age* (1901, 5) and *Sydney Morning Herald* (1901, 7) and was a key inclusion in reports sent by cable to other newspapers. Other reports listed the policies 'relating to the Federal Capital, to the alien immigration question, and to the uniform tariff' (*Maitland Daily Mercury* 1901, 2) as central features. The prime minister was greeted with 'loud and continued applause' (*Maitland Daily Mercury* 1901, 2) when he turned to saying 'a few words about a very important subject: that of a white Australia':

> Legislation against any influx of Asiatic labour we shall regard simply as a matter of course. As to Polynesians or kanaka labour, if we were at the beginning of it now we should have an equally strong objection to that, but we shall not be guilty of any oppression of those kanakas who are already in Australia, while we shall take to endeavour to restrict the importation of any more of them. (Barton 1901)

In this passage, Barton presented a potential 'influx of Asiatic labour' as the central justification for proposed immigration restrictions, invoking fears that predated Federation and were echoed by all parties contesting the election (Willard 1923, 120; Jaensch and Manning 2001, 100). In this way, from the outset he linked a desire for racial purity with labour issues, such as the protection of working conditions. These economic justifications, which persist in campaign language, must be understood in the context of long-running concerns about the presence of 'kanaka' (Pacific Islander) labourers in Australia's north. An editorial in response to Barton's speech in the *Maitland Daily Mercury* (1901, 2), which also published a full transcript of Barton's address, gives a clear insight into these broader debates. Here, 'alien races' are constructed as separate from an Australian community imagined as racially pure, a conception that ignores the significant racial diversity of the colonies, as well as the presence of the indigenous population (most commonly ignored altogether in leaders' early campaign language):

---

[7] Although ostensibly addressing the entire nation through newspaper reprints of the speech, it is important to note that the live speech was delivered to an all-male audience. Newspaper coverage at the time noted that 'the town was placarded with announcements that ladies would not be admitted to the hall' and 'consequently they were absent' (*Sydney Morning Herald* 1901, 7).

One of the happy circumstances attending the federation of Australia is the homogeneity of the people. We have no alien races to complicate the working of the machine of self-government. It rests with ourselves to maintain the purity and homogeneity of the people […]. (*Maitland Daily Mercury* 1901, 2)

Accompanying this racially based construction of the national community is a call for compromise to overcome the economic challenges of establishing sound local industry. The author/s argue that 'it is not yet proven that the sugar industry can be carried on by white labour', acknowledging the government cannot therefore 'consistently menace a native industry by denying it the labour that may be essential to its life and health'.[8]

A complex negotiation between competing desires is at work here, and it is in this context that political language both reassures voters and offers ownership of the national collective. This early tension between Australia's purist identity stories, and the contradictory need for workers to support development and encourage prosperity, resonates across Australian political history. It is accompanied in public debate, media coverage and campaign language by creatively conceived and presented solutions. The *Maitland Daily Mercury* editorial, for example, proposed the regulation of kanaka labour in such a way that 'the immigrants cannot, by becoming permanent elements of the population, menace homogeneity'. In offering a compromise in this way, the newspaper foregrounded a discourse of management and control that would be mobilized even more explicitly by Protectionist prime minister Alfred Deakin in later campaigns.

They Never Really Enter Australia

The reassuring discourse which presented border management as a mechanism that could protect the Australian community was developed further in the election that followed, the first held after the White Australia policy was introduced. Its clearest articulation was in the language of Protectionist prime minister Alfred Deakin, who had taken on the role when Barton retired. Deakin was no stranger to politics; he too had been one of the leaders of the Federation movement and as MP for Ballarat served as Attorney-General in Barton's government. MacCallum (2013, 17) describes his personal and political appeal: a 'suave and handsome' intellectual, a 'compelling orator' and 'visionary statesman' who was 'regarded with admiration and even awe,

---

[8] While explicit references to 'kanakas' do not appear after the first decade of the twentieth century, party leaders from both sides of politics continued to express their support for Australia's maintenance of a 'white' sugar industry well into the 1920s (see, e.g. Charlton 1925).

but not with affection' by voters. More deeply, Judith Brett (2012, 62) evokes a leader who was a 'puzzle to biographers' looking to reconcile the 'prodigious memory and verbal gifts' of an 'outwardly cheerful, successful man' with the 'detachment and loneliness' that emerges in his personal papers. His particular mix of talents meant he was well-suited to the times, applying his political skill to the negotiations required in the upheaval of the early post-Federation years, and his rhetorical skills to the vital task of drawing the newly conceived Australian community together (Hearn and Tregenza 2014, 177).

The campaign speech, delivered at a public meeting then reported in the next day's newspapers, was the dominant communication medium of the day. Deakin was a skilful public speaker, and coverage of his lengthy policy launch address for the 1903 campaign at Her Majesty's Hall Ballarat highlighted both his rapid pace and style of delivery. The *Sydney Morning Herald* (1903, 7) called it 'intensely interesting and seductive' while the *Argus* (1903, 4) credited his 'felicities of expression' and 'charms of delivery' for helping him achieve his 'eminent position':

> Never was his verbal witchery more freely manifested […] The audience was not roused to enthusiasm but it sat hour after hour with its senses pleasantly titillated and its critical faculties lulled, accepting vaguely the impression the orator wished to convey that the past of the federation had been all that could be wished and its future will be more than can at present be imagined or desired […] It was the triumph of the supreme word-spinner, and in this aspect it was entirely suited to the occasion.

These lengthy descriptions of speaker and speech, setting, and audience were often accompanied both by summaries of the key policy points and also a full transcript of the address itself. These transcripts provide a valuable record of the key concerns of early political speeches, giving insight into their themes, tone and style. Early policy launch speeches were lengthy and incredibly detailed. They allowed political leaders to present evidence-based arguments to support their achievements or proposals. Deakin took this approach when updating voters on the functioning of the newly introduced White Australia policy and claiming its success in offering those constructed as Australians control of the composition of the national community.

Deakin established a political discourse that would set the foundation for campaign language for more than a century. This discourse has, at its core, what anthropologist Ghassan Hage (2003, 47) calls the 'White paranoia' that has 'structured Australian nationalism from the time of its birth'. This is the paranoia of a colony distant from empire, manifesting as a 'fear of loss of Europeanness or Whiteness, and of the lifestyle and privileges' it affords

(Hage 2003, 49). The Australian community, here, is 'excessively fragile and constantly threatened' (Hage 2003, 49). In 1903, this 'white colonial paranoia' was evident in Deakin's policy speech report on the White Australia policy, in which he detailed the exact numbers, ethnic backgrounds, and working arrangements of those who had entered Australia since its introduction. Drawing a clear divide between 'Europeans' and 'coloured persons', Deakin (1903) reassured voters that mechanisms were in place to ensure that 'coloured aliens' who are brought to Australia on pearling vessels 'never really enter Australia', but instead 'simply fish for pearls in Australian waters':

> The arrangement we have made is that they land, sign their articles, and then they are taken away, and a guarantee is taken from those who bring them that they shall leave the country.

Deakin's (1903) development of this discourse of immigration management strikes a clear compromise between racial purity and economic prosperity: allowing a lucrative industry to continue while ensuring that 'undesirable aliens' are excluded from both the national space and community. Immigrant desirability is defined here in explicitly racial terms and is mobilized in aid of economic outcomes; Deakin goes on to develop this in a lengthy section of the speech addressing the true meaning of 'white Australia'. Here, the relationship between race, economics, and identity security in the construction of the Australian community becomes clear. He begins by arguing that the concept of a 'white Australia' does not simply refer to the 'complexion of the people of this country', locating it rather in the values and priorities of the national collective. A 'white Australia therefore depended both on populating a continent perceived as empty, in order to defend it, and ensuring that 'conditions of life fit for white men and white women' (Deakin 1903) existed within the national space. The threats to these conditions are expressed in the protectionist economic language that framed Deakin's policies. Here, a white Australia

> means protection against the underpaid labour of other lands. It means social justice as far as we can establish it, and the payment of fair wages (cheers). A white Australia means a civilisation whose foundations are built in healthy lives, lived in honest toil, in circumstances that do not imply degradation. A white Australia means protection (hear, hear). We protect ourselves from armed aggression; why not protect ourselves from aggression by commercial means? (Cheers.) We protect ourselves against undesirable coloured aliens. Why not protect ourselves against the products of undesirable alien labour? (Cheers.). (Deakin 1903)

In this passage the racially based exclusions necessary to create a white Australia are constructed as ensuring that those included in the core Australian identity can enjoy a prosperous, stable and just society. Civilization, honesty and 'fairness' are explicitly positioned as characteristics particular to a *white* community, which would come under threat if 'alien' labour or products were allowed to enter the country. Deakin combined the discourses of economic and identity security here, linking the values protected by a white Australia to those supported by the Protectionist movement. He defined the Australian community in reference to a particular set of values established and protected by the White Australia policy, founding a vision that is progressive in other ways (e.g. in its explicit inclusion of women) on an assumption about the existence of, and fundamental hierarchical differences between, whiteness and other races. He returns to these themes throughout the speech and at its conclusion, as a justification for his positions on other policy areas, such as population growth and immigration. When discussing his support for preferential trade with 'the mother country and our sister dominions', for example, Deakin (1903) portrayed the arrangement as vital to 'build up an Australia, white in race, under white men's social, political and rural conditions'; where the alternative was to 'abandon our birthrights to the alien'.

This discursive construction of an idealized white Australia operated both to close the borders of the national community to new entrants deemed undesirable and to exclude some groups already present from the national imaginary. Hage (2003, 53) has noted that the policy 'actually worked at making [Australia] even more homogeneous than it was at the time of Federation', using the expulsion of difference from narratives of identity, and from the national space, to reinforce the comforting sensation that Australians could recreate a white-British civilization in a new land. This expulsion of difference from the national imaginary applied to groups like the immigrants who came to Australia during the gold rushes of the 1850s and the Pacific Islander (or 'kanaka') labourers who worked in the sugarcane fields in Australia's north. It also applied to the indigenous population whose needs, stories, and very presence are strikingly absent from this early campaign language; a trend that continued in the century to follow (as discussed in Chapter 2). This, too, is an element of 'white colonial paranoia', a manifestation of the repressed, but always present, knowledge that 'Australia's "first world" wealth and democratic institutions' rest on 'the decimation of the continent's Indigenous population, and on the social, political and economic dispossession of those who remain' (Hage 2003, 48).

It is on this foundation of exclusion and dispossession that Deakin's nation-building rhetoric creates the safe and defensible space in which a community that privileges fairness and social justice can grow. Using his discussion of white Australia to serve both inclusive and exclusive purposes, Deakin lays the foundation for a political discourse designed to offer those voters who imagine themselves at the heart of the Australian community the power to control its borders. The tension it both draws on and helps to construct allowed party leaders, in the decades that followed, to explicitly paint some immigrants as *desirable* additions to the Australian community. The specific content of desirability is fluid, and has changed dramatically since early post–Federation campaigns. In the first three decades of the twentieth century, leaders argued that it was vital to attract white or British immigrants, offering voters both the right and ability to restrict entry according to this racially based criteria (see Deakin 1903; Fisher 1910; Bruce 1925). In these early elections, leaders debated development, settlement and defence with the assumption that the electorate largely supported the White Australia policy as a mechanism of connection to the British Empire.

The explicit emphasis on race as the primary criterion for constructing the Australian community, both in discussions of immigration policies and political discourse more broadly, declined in the wake of World War II. As a result, the emphasis shifted to skills and cultural compatibility as markers of the national collective. Historian Russel Ward (1988, 280; see also Stratton 1988, 72) has argued that this shift was a reaction to the policies of Nazi Germany, which demonstrated the extreme consequences of racially based extermination and prompted 'millions of whites around the world' to question their own assumptions. Alongside this was the realization that Britain might not be able to provide the numbers of migrants Australia needed. Therefore, in a global political and cultural environment where explicitly racial criteria were increasingly inappropriate, campaign language focused increasingly on immigrants' ability to contribute to national prosperity and fit in to the Australian way of life as a mechanism to keep out those classified as other. Welcoming those who would 'make a contribution' or whose presence would help strengthen national feelings of security, in this way, provided a morally and economically justifiable basis for excluding those who would not.

Embracing Desirable Immigrants

The struggle to extend the discursive boundaries of the Australian community while maintaining its essential character, in the post–World War II period, is clear in the campaign speeches of Labor prime minister Joseph 'Ben' Chifley and his opponent, Robert Menzies. Chifley's working class origins and 'humble, plain-spoken' style afforded him 'an affinity with ordinary men and women'; he is often talked of as Australia's 'best loved' prime minister (MacCallum 2013, 115). As treasurer and minister for post-war reconstruction during the war years, he was 'popular with a patriotic electorate' (MacCallum 2013, 118) and known within Labor ranks for his sharp political mind. He ascended to the prime ministership after his predecessor John Curtin's death in 1945, and took on the task of post-war reconstruction.

Chifley's government instituted the Department of Immigration in 1945 and implemented an immigration policy designed to provide the numbers needed to stimulate Australia's economy and complete large-scale development and infrastructure projects.[9] In his post-war campaign speeches, Chifley developed a discursive extension of the parameters of desirability that included non-British Europeans and other Commonwealth citizens. He presented the electorate with an immigration program that included 'other countries', without explicitly outlining *which* other countries it applied to:

> It is the Government's settled policy, by agreements with the British Government in the first place, and, by other means, embracing desirable immigrants from other countries, to build up a net gain of 70,000 a year in Australia's population. (Chifley 1946)

It is important to note that despite the extension of its boundaries, Chifley's language continued to be based on a hierarchy of racial difference: here, immigrants are sought first from Britain before looking elsewhere. His language echoed Deakin's narrative constructions of both the national collective and immigrants. While Australians are constructed as warm in their willingness to 'embrace' *desirable* immigrants in this passage, they also retain their ability to reject those who fall outside this definition.

Chifley's campaign descriptions of these immigration policies was neither impassioned nor particularly vibrant, and his ability to communicate both the benefits of this scheme and his government's broader achievements was hampered by his lack of comfort with broadcasting. The prime minister was known for his ability to feed off the energy and response of a live audience and he had difficulty translating his gravelly, off-the-cuff speaking style to the intimacy demanded by radio, which beamed leaders directly into voters' living rooms. Added to this were new time pressures for leaders whose speeches were being broadcast; running a few minutes long or short was now an issue, as radio stations allocated specific time within their schedules. Whether delivering a live speech or reading in a studio, campaigning politicians became aware of the perils of leaving 'dead air' or talking beyond their time slot. This rewarded those who were well prepared, and discouraged spontaneity. In

---

[9] Russel Ward (1988, 280) has highlighted the importance of Immigration Minister Arthur Calwell's intensive 'propaganda campaign' to support these new immigration policies by educating the public.

1949, for example, party leaders were allocated an hour of national broadcast, achieved through a hook-up of government and commercial stations, for their policy launch speeches. Both Chifley and his opponent Robert Menzies took this into consideration when planning and delivering their addresses. Menzies spoke at the Canterbury Soldiers' Memorial Hall in Melbourne, and realized as he neared the end of his address that he was going to run over his allocated hour. The *Sydney Morning Herald* (1949a, 4) reported that he was so anxious to 'have his peroration broadcast' that he omitted entirely the section on immigration and briefed the press later on his party's policies.

His opponent took a more radical approach, pre-recording his address in the 2BL Sydney studios a few days in advance for broadcast by ABC and commercial radio stations around Australia. In order to make it a truly national broadcast, a copy of the recording was flown to Perth to be played at 8pm local time. Media coverage reported it as 'one of the shortest government policy speeches ever made' at only 36 minutes, and the *Canberra Times* (1949, 1) noted that the prime minister had issued 'supplementary statements expanding on major areas of policy' that had been left out due to 'a limitation of time in broadcast speech'. Chifley's language reflected both the shortened nature of the speech and the lack of a live, reactive audience. His workmanlike presentation was in sharp contrast to his opponent's mastery (Crisp 1977, 226–28), and he was so uncomfortable that some in the ALP worried the whole campaign would prove as 'unreportable' as this policy address (Crisp 1977, 228). Newspaper coverage was particularly critical of the prime minister's decision not to broadcast the speech live from the studio. The *Sydney Morning Herald* (1949b, 1) noted that the prime minister didn't even listen to the broadcast and the *Age* (1949b, 1), with the headline 'Chifley Too Busy to Deliver Policy Speech', reported that Chifley spent the time in his office 'clearing up mail and other urgent matters' as he was due to leave on his election tour.

Chifley's pre-recorded policy speech signalled a shift from those of pre-radio days, which had included long, detailed reports on the government's previous term or the opposition's plans for the future. His address was framed as a report of Labor's service to the nation 'in war and in peace', and he spoke in broad brushstrokes about his party's values and achievements. He made a clear link between immigration and economic security, connecting these to Labor's key mission:

> To promote and maintain social and economic security for the people, higher living standards, and the progressive expansion of Australia as a nation in the world community of nations. (Chifley 1949)

It is in this context, after reporting that 'full employment has been maintained', that the prime minister pointed to the 'great headway' being made in implementing Australia's post-war migration program. The conditions of belonging to the Australian community were explicitly linked to the contribution that immigrants could make to the government's new infrastructure projects, located within the newly extended, but still relevant, boundaries of usefulness as a marker of 'whiteness'.

People of the Most Useful Sort

Chifley's opponent, Robert Menzies, also emphasized the economic value of those defined as desirable immigrants in post-war campaign speech. He presented the need for national development and defence as driving Australia's willingness to look beyond Britain for immigrants:

> We believe at this very moment there are in Great Britain, in Europe and in the United States of America, very many thousands of people of the most useful sort who could be encouraged and assisted to come and live in Australia. (Menzies 1946)

Menzies positioned Australia's racially and culturally appropriate allies as the ideal source of immigrants to strengthen economic and identity security. His language spoke implicitly of inclusion *and* exclusion; when highlighting the nations where people of 'the most useful sort' are found, he also constructed for voters a silent counter-image of those other nations whose people would not be 'encouraged and assisted' but rather actively barred from the nation.

Menzies' choice of the term *useful* highlights a further shift in the boundaries of collective identity, expanding desirability to include an emphasis on the expertise of potential immigrants. This interest in the skills potential new Australians would bring to the nation, and the contribution they could make to national prosperity, had been an element of leaders' campaign language since the first decade following Federation. In 1906, Prime Minister Alfred Deakin and Opposition Leader George Reid had agreed on the fundamental role of whiteness as an indicator of immigrant desirability, but presented voters with different images of the *skills* this white workforce would require. The prime minister used his Ballarat policy launch speech to emphasize that immigrants should be encouraged to settle and farm the 'millions of acres of land' which were 'well supplied with water in a healthy climate for a white population' (Deakin 1906). Free Trade leader Reid (1906) contested this, arguing that Australia needed factory workers instead: the labourer 'whose capital is in his brain and sinews'. These leaders debated what profession the ideal immigrant should have from a position that represented them only in terms of the contribution they could make to the nation's economic growth and stability. They relied on an unquestioned underlying commitment to the White Australia policy. Conservative political leaders have presented similar arguments to voters in elections over the century that followed. In 1972, for example, Coalition prime minister William McMahon and Labor opposition leader Gough Whitlam advocated different criteria for the selection of migrants. While in 1906, Deakin and Reid agreed that immigrants' skills were relevant in determining desirability, in 1972 the leaders debated the appropriateness of skills as the *sole* mechanism of choice. McMahon (1972) reinforced the importance of skills as a mechanism of immigration control, while Whitlam (1972) refocused the debate from skills onto the principle of family reunion in his now-famous *Its Time* policy launch speech, a theme that resonated in his later policy launch speeches (see Whitlam 1974, 1975, 1977).

A Policy of Assimilation and Absorption

As the requirements of immigrant desirability shifted and debates over skills and usefulness continued, concerns that those who could not, or would not, integrate into the mainstream would threaten the Australian way of life provided continuing justification for exclusion. This was a powerful and enduring theme in campaign language, an always-present mirror of the inclusive discourses outlined above. It worked by tapping into and evoking broader social and political concerns as Australia's international allegiances evolved over the course of the twentieth century. Familiar keywords of Australian immigration anxiety emerge here: for example, Andrew Fisher (1910) spoke of Australians' 'desire to welcome all races, except those who cannot assimilate', while Arthur Calwell (1966) argued for 'a policy of assimilation and absorption' as protection against 'any attempt to create a multi-racial society in our midst'. This language grants the positive agency to 'absorb' new entrants to the national mainstream, and only negative agency to the immigrants who 'cannot assimilate'. Threats to the Australian community have been constructed consistently in these terms by leaders from both sides of politics, who have asked voters to worry about the arrival of unassimilated groups of immigrants who would endanger the national way of life.

The lines of exclusion are therefore drawn to allow rejection of those immigrants who cannot, or will not, 'fit in' to Australian society, whether hampered by racial background or cultural incompatibility. Liberal prime minister William McMahon (1972) provides one of the clearest examples, arguing in the 1972 campaign that work was needed to maintain an integrated community in light of continued immigration:

> To ensure that we have one Australian society – a homogeneous and integrated community, not a community with enclaves of people who

cannot be integrated. We are committed to the policy of attracting new settlers from traditional sources and to control of the migrant intake by the Government. It will remain a selective policy, based on the skills of the migrants and their ability to integrate.

McMahon echoes the deeply held assumptions of his predecessors and taps into a rich legacy of immigration anxieties: Deakin's 1903 promises of control over immigration flows; Menzies's 1946 desire for immigrants from traditional sources; and Calwell's 1966 emphasis on assimilation to avoid the 'tragedy' of a multiracial society. These are concerns that flare up periodically at times of social contest, such as the rise of Pauline Hanson's One Nation Party in the late 1990s, the Cronulla riots in December 2005 and then-Immigration Minister Kevin Andrews's comments about the ability of Sudanese refugees to settle in Australia in October 2007. However leaders must speak to the concerns of the time in their campaign appeals, and Russel Ward (1988, 396) has positioned McMahon's 'old-fashioned attitude' to racial questions as one of his greatest problems in the campaign. He argues that the traditional Australian 'hatred and fear of foreigners' had weakened enormously by 1972, a change recognized and exploited by the Gough Whitlam and the ALP.

A New Deal for Migrants

In the 1970s and 1980s, alongside the declining cultural and political influence of the British Empire and rise of the American Alliance, Australian culture and society was influenced by the social movements that had gained prominence in many Western democracies in the 1960s (Lopez 2001, 32). Increasingly diverse immigration was changing the demographic composition of the Australian community. A new image of the national collective therefore developed in campaign language, both as a response to and guide for managing these changes. The term *multiculturalism* came to represent both the lived experience of change and a vision for the future; its use offered political leaders a discursive strategy for addressing population and immigration policy.[10] The discourse of multiculturalism, developed in its earliest political appearances by Malcolm Fraser, presented Australians' diversity and tolerance as defining positive images of the national collective. Fraser's role in this may seem to contradict political narratives which paint him as an arch-conservative whose actions led to the dismissal of the Whitlam government; however Jupp

---

[10] Gulmanelli (2014, 581) notes that the term 'experienced a bifurcation in its meaning' not long after its appearance in Australian social and political language in the 1970s. Here, multiculturalism came both to 'describe Australia's newly emerging demographic condition' while also 'acquir[ing] a strong ideological-normative' element.

(2007, 51) has argued Fraser's 'active endorsement of multiculturalism' was a significant departure from the 'assimilationist and Anglophile traditions' of his party. Mungo MacCallum (2013, 161), in his profile of Fraser, goes as far as to say that 'for older Australians there are two Malcolm Frasers': the 'capital-L Liberal ruthless right winger', and the 'small-l liberal caring humanitarian',[11] while Graham Little (1997a) provides an insightful analysis of the complex, contradictory politics of Fraserism.

The newly elected Whitlam Labor government had announced that race would no longer be a criterion for admission into Australia in 1972 (Ward 1988, 401), one of many small, quiet changes that had been made to the White Australia policy in the years preceding its official abandonment in 1973. At this time, moves were made towards adopting an official multicultural policy and the *language* of multiculturalism and diversity began to emerge in political discourse. In the 1970s and early 1980s, Prime Minister Malcolm Fraser's government 'vastly increased the immigration program', including a significant number of Vietnamese migrants and refugees; set up the Special Broadcasting Service to cater to the needs of minority groups; and founded the Institute of Multicultural Affairs (MacCallum 2013, 166) in response to a key recommendation of the Galbally Report (Koleth 2010, Part One). MacCallum (2013, 166) notes that Fraser 'would later claim the encouragement and recognition of a genuinely multicultural Australia as his finest achievement'. For all of its assumed cultural power, however, the *term* was used infrequently in campaign language and has all but disappeared in twenty-first century campaigns. This challenges the notion that multiculturalism was at the heart of an enduring reconceptualization of the Australian community. Close language analysis reveals that leaders either avoided using the term, or did so in a veiled, brief or tentative manner. Fraser's campaign discourses of community, for example, do not match the scope of his government's multicultural policy development and vision. Rather, his discussions of immigration, multiculturalism and identity were routine, featuring the managerial language of support services that placed the Australian mainstream in a privileged position. This bland, managerial language was an element of Fraser's speaking style; Little (1997a, 61) argues that his rhetoric worked to inspire fear and establish order, and that he 'seemed incapable of waxing lyrical about Australia [...] or about the nation's future'; he 'was no silky orator [...] his voice was grating, his speeches hectoring'.

---

[11] It is also illuminating, here, to note Fraser's frequent interventions into public debate following his time in office, through which he came to be seen as socially progressive in his criticisms of the Howard, Rudd/Gillard and Abbott governments' foreign policy positions and treatment of asylum seekers. Fraser was also involved in humanitarian work with organizations such as Care International and at the United Nations.

The 1975 election played out in the shadow of The Dismissal, remembered as one of the most dramatic events in Australian political history.[12] On 11 November the Whitlam-led Labor government was removed from office by Governor General John Kerr. Opposition Leader Malcolm Fraser was appointed as caretaker, and immediately moved to call a double dissolution election. In the month that followed, Fraser appealed to Australians to grant his party a mandate to govern in its own right. While the term multiculturalism would not appear in his campaign language until 1977, he spoke in his policy speech in this preceding election of the responsibility of the Australian community to care for 'the disadvantaged', a category that included 'handicapped, isolated, migrant and Aboriginal children'. This construction is also significant for its illumination of an approach to indigenous issues (identified in Chapter 2) which locates members of the indigenous community alongside other 'disadvantaged' groups for whom the mainstream is responsible, such as immigrants, and discusses policy commitments in tandem. In dealing with immigration, there is a shift here from previous campaigns. Rather than looking to restrict or expand immigration, or manage the Australian borders, Fraser asks Australians to extend support to those in need. He goes on to promise 'a new deal for migrants' already within the national borders:

> A Department of Immigration and Ethnic Affairs will be established. Adequate bilingual staff will be made available at government hospitals and public hospitals. The transmission and perpetuation of ethnic languages and culture in Australian and ethnic schools will be encouraged and supported. Measures will be taken to assist migrants to overcome the language barrier. (Fraser 1975)

From this passage he moves straight to indigenous issues, labelling Labor's approach to 'Aboriginal affairs' a 'disaster' and promising the maintenance of government support; a commitment to 'enable Aboriginals to be self-reliant'; and to 'introduce land rights legislation for the Northern Territory based on justice for all' (Fraser 1975). There is much to learn about Fraser's conception of the Australian community here. On the surface this can be read as an explicit attempt to include the challenges faced by, and concerns of, immigrant and indigenous Australians in political discourse and public debate. Both are visible and their needs acknowledged. In doing so, however, Fraser links the two groups, eliding their very different histories and experiences (much in the same way that the groups themselves are homogenized and vast differences

---

[12] For a more detailed account of The Dismissal, see Freudenberg (1977); Whitlam (1979); Kelly and Bramston (2015); Hocking (2016).

within indigenous and immigrant communities rendered invisible in this discourse). Here, both immigrant and indigenous Australians are located outside the symbolic space of Australian mainstream identity. They are positioned as having 'special needs' to be met and managed by the government on behalf of the Australian people through a discourse of *institutional caring*. In this way, Fraser's language constructs a nation whose fundamentally homogeneous core collective is called on to manage and be tolerant towards the groups of others who now cohabit (or who predate 'Western' presence in) the national space, echoing Deakin's positioning of those who worked on the pearling boats as 'never really' entering Australia.

The term multiculturalism appears for the first time in Australian campaign language in 1977, in Fraser's two most high-profile speeches of the campaign. In his National Press Club address and policy launch speech, the prime minister used the term to underscore his government's commitment to providing support for new immigrants. At the Liberal launch, he described Australia as 'a multicultural society' when introducing planned support services for 'our ethnic communities' (Fraser 1977a). Addressing the Press Club a few weeks later, Fraser (1977b) was even more explicit:

> Changes in the make-up of our population will bring challenges in adjusting our social security and other social policies to the changing needs of our community. We are a multicultural society. There is the constant challenge of encouraging the rich diversity that is in our midst.

Fraser issues a different kind of invitation to voters here, and with little fuss or fanfare develops a discourse of diversity that emphasizes both the potential richness of this diversity and also the challenges it would pose. While the use of the term *multiculturalism* is often seen to represent a radically new conception of Australian identity, what emerges most strongly in Fraser's language is the close continuity between this imagined multicultural identity and more traditional white-British identity. Although the markers of national inclusion at the boundaries had shifted, Fraser continued to place those imagined as the mainstream at the centre of society as generous providers of economic and social support for communities constructed as ethnic. Asking voters to align themselves with a government concerned to actively 'encourage' diversity, and through the simple use of the possessive pronoun when discussing *our* community and population he positions immigrant communities as needing to be managed by those who are unquestioningly part of the national collective. Even as he stretches the boundaries of inclusion, Fraser maintains the traditional hierarchy that places Australians who imagine themselves as white and Western at the core of the national identity. Multicultural diversity, in this conception, remains something that the mainstream owns and must manage. For some, this embrace of what Ghassan Hage (2003, 60) has called 'descriptive' rather than 'cultural' multiculturalism can be read as a response to the Whitlam years. In Hage's conception, descriptive multiculturalism is about 'welfare and cultural government' rather than national identity. He quotes Castles and colleagues (1988, 57) who note that the shift was 'a key strategy in a conservative restructuring of the welfare state whose main purpose was the demolition of Whitlam-style social democracy'.

A Classic Migrant Success Story

In these constructions of Australian migration and multiculturalism, the group constructed as the mainstream is rewarded both for its tolerance and its material support for immigrants by the contributions that those who are positioned this way make to national prosperity. The legacy of these discourses was clear in the 2007 election, where conservative prime minister John Howard drew on the themes of skills, cultural compatibility and integration when discussing immigration. Howard employed the discourse of *immigrant success*, one of few positive mainstream media discourses through which so-called ethnic minorities are constructed. In response to a talkback radio question about the recent death of high-profile businessman John Ilhan, Howard (2007a) outlined the economic contributions Ilhan had made to Australian society and praised his ability to fit into the Australian way of life. He tapped into key markers of desirability to represent Ilhan as a 'classic migrant success story':

> He came to Australia from Turkey at the age of three, had four children, he worked hard, he made a lot of money but he gave a lot back to the community. He was very philanthropic, the whole range of charities [...] And, on top of that, of course, he was very passionate about Australian Rules.

This language echoes more than a century of campaign constructions of usefulness and presents an image of the kind of immigrants of which Australians can be proud. Howard links these particular personal stories more broadly to the values of entrepreneurial hard work and community involvement that characterize the Australian Liberal tradition. This is a discursive strategy he used again, a month later, when launching the Coalition's 'Go For Growth' economic policy in Sydney. Howard (2007e) told the audience that he had visited the Vivo Café that morning, and described its owners, Angela and Con:

They started their businesses in 2003 and in that short period of time they have won numerous small business awards. They really are a wonderful metaphor for the modern Australia. Both of their parents emigrated to Australia in the 1950s from Greece, they both love Greece but they love Australia even more [...] they were very much the modern face of the optimistic, entrepreneurial successful small business Australia.

Howard placed John Ilhan and Angela and Con within a familiar narrative of Australianness and connected them to the values of the small business owners and so-called battlers at the core of his constituency. There is a strong economic aspect to this discourse, where the ability and willingness of immigrants to *contribute* to national prosperity eases anxiety about the cultural links they may retain. This construction also demonstrates the resonance of assumptions of essential difference between groups, and the preference for 'Western' (European or American) immigrants as more likely to become 'good Australians'. Howard's language both welcomes and rejects, outlining markers of successful inclusion that carry a trace of the immigrants who do not fit in as successfully as Angela and Con, and cannot be welcomed into the national community in the same way. He offered voters the power to define 'success', and to choose whether to include groups and individuals into the Australian community on that basis. His language demonstrates the interlinked discourses of identity (based on race and culture) and economic security developed in the earliest decades following Federation, and this echoed in the campaigns that followed. Issues of immigration and were recurrent, but not defining, themes in the 2010 and 2013 campaigns (Jupp 2015), both of which saw Liberal leader Tony Abbott contest the election against a newly minted Labor prime minister: Julia Gillard in 2010, and a reinstated Kevin Rudd in 2013.

Join Our Team

Alongside emotive debates about border control and so-called illegal immigration, the 2010 election saw Gillard and Abbott lock horns over population growth as part of an ongoing 'big Australia' debate. Discussions of population size have a long, 'fraught' history in Australian politics, and as Jacobs (2015, 804) argues they:

> often stand in for other more controversial points of contention within Australian society that are more difficult to articulate in the public sphere, such as immigration, social inequality and economic uncertainty.

Population debates will always, necessarily, incorporate 'questions [...] about race and the reproduction of the nation', either 'implicitly or explicitly' (Perera in Jacobs 2015, 803), and in 2010 also allowed for both leaders to position themselves strategically in relation to *identity security*. In October 2009, then prime minister Kevin Rudd was asked by ABC *7:30 Report* host Kerry O'Brien (2009) about 'startling new figures' for Australia's population growth that had been projected by Secretary of the Department of the Treasury Ken Henry. How would Rudd respond, he asked, to the 'whole spectrum of problems' thrown up by rising birth and immigration rates which Henry had predicted would lead to a 60 per cent increase in the Australian population in the coming four decades? Rudd (2009) had a positive answer for O'Brien that mobilized a discourse of security and sustainability:

> I actually believe in a big Australia [...] I think it's good for us, it's good for our national security long term, it's good in terms of what we can sustain as a nation.

In February 2010, the Department of the Treasury released its third *Intergenerational Report* (one is released once every five years), a document that projected a similar increase in population to that previewed by Henry. Rudd used the report to support his vision of a 'big Australia'. However, when he was replaced in June the new prime minister, Julia Gillard, distanced herself from his position. Gillard then repeated, in a number of 2010 election campaign interviews, speeches and events, that her vision was instead 'a sustainable Australia'. In the leaders' debate, she was challenged by her opponent to 'level with the Australian people' on this issue (Abbott 2010a). Her response used the same discourse of security her predecessor had mobilized in support of his own position to argue that a 'sustainable Australia' was about more than immigration policy:

> What I mean by a sustainable Australia is protecting our way of life. That's having a job, being able to aspire to own your own home, getting decent service, health and education, having access to wide open spaces. (Gillard 2010b)

The linking of *sustainability* with *protection* performed a powerful discursive and strategic role for Gillard. Jacobs (2015, 805) notes that her use of these terms allowed the prime minister to 'occlude any notion of risk or conflict' and offer 'symbolic reassurance to an anxious electorate that the future is assured under her watch'.

The 'big Australia' debate faded from prominence after the election. In the 2013 campaign Rudd and Abbott's constructions of the Australian community focused on two key policy areas: skilled migration and asylum seekers. A clear articulation was seen at the People's Forum held at the Brisbane Broncos League Club during the campaign. This 'televised town hall'[13] was moderated by Sky News' David Speers and saw the leaders appearing together to take questions from a crowd of undecided voters. One, a student named Josh, asked how they intended to 'maintain Australia's commitment to good international citizenship when it comes to asylum seekers?' The prime minister responded first, speaking about the 'regional resettlement arrangements' that the government had put in place, and then emphasizing that 'hard choices' were required when it came to the question of people smuggling:

> I think this is a very hard area of policy. It's one that doesn't lend itself to 3-word slogans. It's complex, it's difficult, it's hard. Getting the balance right between doing the right thing by the world and at the same time making sure that you're maintaining an orderly system of migration. (Rudd 2013f)

Rudd's emphasis on establishing an 'orderly system' mirrored his language from 2007, where the discourse of border management had dominated his responses on the issue. This reflected Labor's attempt to 'appeal to more conservative voters who might be contemplating a switch to the Coalition', while avoiding alienating those who might have been considering voting Green (McDougall 2013, 291). His opponent framed his own response in moral terms, reprising the '3 word slogan' that had become representative of his 2010 campaign. Abbott (2013g) argued that the 'most compassionate thing that we can do as a nation is to put in place policies that stop the boats'. The leaders then, after a question about environmental protection, were asked about skilled migration by Efra (who identified herself as a test analyst in the IT industry): 'What measures will your party take to ensure workers on 457 visas are not taking jobs that Australians could do?' Both candidates responded by speaking about the requirements for local labour market testing that were built into the system, and proposed ways of ensuring that this worked appropriately. In doing so, they both accepted the premise that there was a clear differentiation between local and overseas workers and supported the basic principle that it was vital to protect local jobs and industry, echoing more than a century of campaign debates. However, while the prime minister again spoke in managerial terms to reassure voters that 'we've now got the balance right', his opponent offered an impassioned defence of the 457 visa system:

---

[13] I have written elsewhere about the emergence of this genre in the 2010 election campaign; see Brookes (2011).

The last thing I want to do is anything that might end up demonising skilled migration to this country […] I don't think people who come to this country to work and pay taxes from day one are stealing our jobs. I think they're helping to build our country […] it is a good system and it's fully in accordance with the heroic tradition of this country to welcome people from the four corners of the earth […] who want to join our team and who want to be lifters not leaners. (Abbott 2013g)

Abbott's language demonstrates both the evolution of the discourse of community in Australian elections and the enduring legacy of early campaign narratives. Skilled immigrants are praised, here, for 'doing a good job in our economy'; being 'lifters not leaners'. However, their entry into the Australian community is dependent both on their desire to 'join our team' and our own 'heroic' (but always contingent) tradition of welcoming those who wish to contribute to national prosperity and economic security.

Dispensing their Wisdom and Announcing their Decisions

Abbott's broader discursive construction of the Australian community in this campaign should also be noted for the way in which it offers a rare exception to the traditional location of indigenous issues, and identity, on the fringes of Australian campaign conceptions of the national collective. Throughout the campaign, Abbott (2013d; 2013e) spoke consistently about issues specific to the indigenous community. He did this both in speeches and press conferences dedicated to the topic and, perhaps more significantly, as an element of his nationally focused policy launch speech (Abbott 2013j) and televised interviews (Abbott 2013f). While not a dominant issue in the campaign narrative overall, in these spaces Abbott worked to develop a discourse of inclusiveness. He spoke in explicit terms about how important it was that every member of the national community felt 'like a first-class Australian', while acknowledging that 'for too long Indigenous people have been second class citizens' (Abbott 2013f).

In a lengthy part of a campaign interview on Channel Nine's national morning show, Abbott (2013f) argued that more than 'full civic rights' was needed to achieve true equality. He listed education, life expectancy, job prospects and equality under the law as key elements required to 'turn this dream that every Australian cherishes into a reality for Aboriginal people'. This language was communicated both to a national audience through this interview, and to those in attendance at the Garma Festival, where Abbott (2013d) told the audience he would 'dispense with the prepared speech and talk to you from my heart' in the same way that Galarrwuy Yunupingu (who was present) had 'spoken from his heart to me'. From this constructed space of openness and spontaneity, Abbott (2013d) continued:

> Individually and as a nation, and as peoples, communities and families we are all on a journey. Where we want it to lead, is to a country where all of us can realise our dreams, where all of us can be ourselves, all of us can come closer to being our best selves. That's only going to happen if each one of us, as Australians, becomes better in the years to come than we have always been in the years that have been, at opening our hearts to one and another. It is very, very important that white fellas and blackfellas open their hearts to one and other.

Indigenous Australians are included in the discursive space of Australian identity here, implicated both in the work of realizing the shared hopes and dreams of the community and in the process of reconciliation and healing. Abbott's language is unusual but not entirely unprecedented in campaign history. It echoed that of previous leaders such as Bob Hawke, who dedicated a section of his 1983 policy launch speech to indigenous issues. He argued that as long as 'the first Australians' live under 'the worst conditions' in areas such as health, education, employment and education, as well as experiencing 'poverty and despair', 'we can never truly bring this country together' (Hawke 1983).[14]

Abbott's (2013d) emotive campaign appeals both constructed and mobilized his own personal history as he called for Australians to 'walk forward into the future as brothers and sisters'. In 2013, the Liberal leader put his years of 'involvement and engagement with the first Australians' to work in support of this vision, locating his own story as an example for all Australians: 'all of us need to engage better and more deeply with Aboriginal people if the soul of the country is to be made whole as it should be'. While not explicitly referring to the displacement and dispossession that had made this healing necessary, Abbott's pledge to move 'Indigenous policies and programmes' from being an 'afterthought' to 'the heart of a good Australian government' was a significant discursive shift. Again, here, elements of his language echoed previous leaders. In his 1977 policy launch speech, for example, Malcolm Fraser (1977a) pledged to 'end the paternalism of past policies' and 'encourage the self-management of Aboriginal programmes'. This resonated in Abbott's (2013d) promise at the Garma Festival to promote 'empowered communities' rather than continue

---

[14] While these issues were not prominent in Hawke's 1983 and 1984 campaign discourse, in the 1990 election he (Hawke 1990b) spent a portion of his 'National Agenda for Women' address speaking specifically about issues affecting Aboriginal and Torres Strait Islander women.

the history of 'white fellas turning up in black places and dispensing their wisdom and announcing their decisions'. It is important to note, however, that even here there is a problematic distinction between spaces imagined as black and white in Australia; Abbott's call for respect works against discourses that render indigenous Australians invisible, while at the same time reinforcing discourses of inclusion and exclusion by creating separate 'places' for separate communities.

Elements of this discourse echoed in the 2016 election, in the language of Labor opposition leader Bill Shorten. Shorten is the first campaigning leader to routinely include an 'acknowledgement of country' at the beginning of his formal campaign speeches. This is a short passage which allows non-indigenous Australians to pay respect to the land's traditional owners (Shorten 2016e):

> I acknowledge the traditional owners of the land upon which we meet,
> I pay my respects to their elders both past and present.

The inclusion of this acknowledgement is significant in that it routinely makes indigenous Australians visible in campaign discourse. More substantively, Shorten dedicated a trio of speeches to indigenous issues early in the campaign: an address in Darwin on National Sorry Day on 26 May (Shorten 2016a), and then to the Reconciliation Australia Dinner (Shorten 2016b) and Long Walk (Shorten 2016c) in the days that followed. This sustained attention to indigenous issues, over a number of days, in some ways echoed Abbott's approach in the previous campaign, particularly in its call for a search for 'common ground [… and] for the common good of our nation' (Shorten 2016b). However, while Abbott did not directly deal with the causes of ongoing inequality and injustice, Shorten sought to do so: acknowledging that 'this mighty continent is, was, always will be Aboriginal land'; referring to *terra nullius* as a 'disgraceful fiction' (2016b); and speaking of 'the generations of uncaring wrongs white Australia inflicted on people and cultures who have cared for this continent, their home' (2016a). This is a deliberate and explicit reconstitution of the national space, which relocates indigenous culture, identity and ownership in the present, acknowledges the contemporary existence of 'systematic racism' (2016b) and promises – as had Fraser and Abbott before him – to be 'guided by the wisdom of Aboriginal and Torres Strait Islander peoples' in addressing it (Shorten 2016a).

These kinds of constructions, in which the national space shrinks and expands in response to the political issues of the day and the particular campaign policies and values of the party and leader, endure in contemporary Australian political imaginings of identity. The next chapter explores the security aspect of these discourses of community more deeply, tracing how political leaders have worked with ideas of national values, community and belonging to reassure voters about perceived military and ideological threats.

Chapter 6

SECURITY

Concerns about the safety of the national way of life have consistently arisen in Australian election campaigns. These concerns have ranged from daily personal worries about family, finances and the future to larger scale threats to the nation's security. While the former are positioned in political and media discourse as domestic concerns, the latter tend to be perceived as foreign. As national citizens, we worry about military aggression or invasion; ideologies like socialism perceived as alien to the Australian identity; radical Islamic fundamentalism; and international terrorism. Political leaders have tapped into voters' fears of these real and perceived threats to develop a complex discourse of security. Addressing domestic and foreign threats has allowed them to demonstrate that they understand the anxieties of those constructed as ordinary Australians and can offer reassurance. Vote for me, they argue, because I understand why you're scared and I can help you solve the problem. This chapter explores the language of leaders who have mobilized voters' concerns about the security of the Australian way of life in the partisan battleground of campaign politics. Effectively presenting themselves, and their parties, as the custodians of national security offered a mechanism of connection with voters, and a means through which to position their political opponents as aligned with whichever threats were of key concern at the time. An exploration of these discourses of Australian security reveals the way that elections operate as a fundamentally partisan battle and illuminates how leaders have played into this battle, presenting themselves and their party as the natural choice to maintain identity security.

Campaign discourses that ask Australians to be concerned about domestic or foreign threats to identity security are complex. Political leaders use them to develop appeals to voters on a number of levels. First, leaders must construct the threat itself as real and vivid, with the most effective connecting contemporary concerns to long-held political, economic or cultural fears in the Australian imagination. Second, they present themselves and the party they represent as guardians of Australian security in the face of these threats, usually with reference to party history or tradition. And third, they must position their opponents either as a threat themselves, or as aligned with the enemy foremost in the public mind. Calling their opponents' allegiance into question, in this way, is designed to make it clear that under *their* stewardship of the nation risks would be heightened rather than mitigated.

Leaders on both sides of politics have contributed to the development of these sophisticated discourses, at times separating and at others drawing together domestic and foreign threat. The themes, keywords and touchstones of the discourse have varied depending on the political, cultural and economic contexts of specific campaigns and on the political alignment and personal inclination of the leaders. For example, a key element of the conservative discourse of security is leaders' alignment of their side of politics with Australia's foremost international allegiances, whether Imperial loyalty in the decades following Federation or the American Alliance after World War II. At the same time as presenting themselves as guardians of these strategic relationships, they developed a discourse in which their Labor opponents were a danger to Australian security because of their perceived foreign ties: to the union movement, socialism or communism. In a competing discourse, Labor leaders have both challenged this conservative construction and aligned themselves with what they have painted as a more sophisticated understanding of Australia's best interests. Here, campaigning Labor leaders have presented their opponents as subservient to those constructed as the nation's great and powerful friends and therefore unable to develop mature relationships and an independent Australian security.

This discursive strategy, which positions *us* as the guardians of secure Australian identity and *them* as putting that security at risk, allows a construction of threats as simultaneously external (aggressive armies beyond our shores, foreign ideologies that may disrupt domestic peace) and internal (the policies and values of the political opposition and their supporters). This chapter draws these elements together. It provides an analysis that locates discourses of military and ideological threat, in campaigns in the first half of the twentieth century, within a broader partisan contest to claim ownership of the security of the national collective. The chapter begins with the language of William 'Billy' Hughes, whose alignment with the project to protect the nation and her people from military threat during World War I earned him the title 'the Little Digger'. This persona allowed him to associate himself with the nation's troops and appeal to the hopes and fears of a country at war. Then, through a focus on the 1925 election, it explores the campaign battle between two leaders with strong competing visions of Australian identity and security: Stanley Bruce and Matthew Charlton. In this fiercely fought campaign, Bruce mounted a defence of British-Australian identity and security against the ideological threat of socialism. His opponent both rejected this characterization and aligned himself with a new vision of Australian identity marked by allegiance to the nation above the Empire. The chapter then moves to the campaigns of the twenty-first century, tracing the legacy of this language and mapping the domestic focus of the partisan battle for ownership of Australian security in two recent elections.

Imperial Loyalties, Foreign Ties

An understanding of Australia's involvement in, and response to, international military conflicts and ideological struggles provides vital context for analysing discourses of security in campaigns across political history. The nation's early colonial status and desire to prove its Imperial loyalty on the international stage has been given 'unusual significance' in the development of Australian definitions of nationhood and national identity (Alomes 1988, 59). As discussed in Chapter 2, the emergence of the digger or Anzac mythology in World War I was mobilized in political campaigns as a powerful positive construction of Australian values and identity. This national type was reinforced in World War II when advances in military and transportation technology meant that Australian sovereignty was felt to be directly threatened for the first time. The broader fear of military incursion coincided, here, with persistent anxiety about regional threats in the Australian imagination, highlighted by the February 1942 fall of Singapore (Curran 2006, 293). Labor prime minister John Curtin's speeches exemplify this complexity, valorizing the bravery of Australian soldiers in local theatres at Kokoda and throughout the Pacific while also looking to the United States for military assistance. Historian Russel Ward (1988, 248) has argued that it is impossible to 'overestimate the effects of these events' on the attitudes of a people who had assumed membership of the Imperial family guaranteed their protection against 'a "coloured" Asiatic invasion'. Australia's way of life and connection to its traditional cultural allies seemed under threat (Alomes 1988, 114–15; Macintyre and Clark 2004, 38), and this was compounded by later events that became powerful symbols in shared collective memory. The British withdrawal of its military presence east of Suez as the Empire declined in the decades following World War II, and its campaign to join the European Economic Community in the 1960s, seemed symbolic of the shifting global political landscape. This provided the context for the increasingly central place of the Alliance in security discourses in the campaigns that followed. These echoed decades later in Australia's membership of the US-led effort in the War in Afghanistan in 2001 and the Coalition of the Willing in Iraq in 2003. This demonstrated an eagerness both to align with those nations traditionally imagined as great and powerful friends and to safeguard the civilized, Western sphere of which they were a part and in which Australian identity was secure.

While the Anzac legend dominates popular memory of Australian wartime involvements, ideological threats have also been central in campaign discourses of threat. In the earliest decades following Federation, these concerns revolved around the foreign ideologies that were constructed as a potential disruption to an Australian social landscape imagined as a 'workingman's paradise' (White 1981, 34) free from the class conflicts left behind in Britain. They endured as a powerful element of the post–World War II climate, where Cold War fears of the communist threat (connected, for voters, to an Asian region already imagined as unstable and uncivilized) dominated Australian nationalism (Alomes 1988, 133). Robert Manne (1994, 113) notes that communism 'was an issue in every Australian election between 1949 and 1969', linking into long-held political and cultural discourses that presented socialism as both foreign and dangerous. The influence of Cold War ideological frameworks on Australian politics and society was evident both in the political language of the time, and in Liberal prime minister Robert Menzies' expressions of anti-communist sentiments, efforts to ban the Communist Party, and battles with Labor leader 'Doc' Evatt' (Cain and Farrell 1984; Burgmann 1984; Manne 1994, 126–68).

Campaign constructions of socialism and communism by (primarily) conservative leaders have represented both the ideologies themselves, and their supporters within and beyond the national borders, as either a *disease* or an *animal*. In 1903, Free Trade leader George Reid (1903) warned voters of the danger of the 'socialistic tiger' in his policy launch speech, telling them that the 'tiger cub of Australian socialism is [...] beginning to feel its claws and show its teeth'. In 1931, United Australia Party leader Joseph Lyons (1931) described communism as a 'serpent' and explicitly positioned it as anti-Australian *and* anti-British. Using a similar discursive technique, Robert Menzies told a crowd of more than 1,500 'cheering, stamping' (*Age* 1949a, 1) voters at a campaign meeting in suburban Melbourne, and those listening at home on the radio, that communism was an 'infection' and a 'growth'. Through this discourse of disease he constructed the political movement in Australia as a threat to its host and, reassuringly, provided hope that voting for him would provide the cure.

Australia's involvement in the Vietnam War has also become highly symbolic in the long-running battle against foreign ideology. Here, *our* efforts had the noble goal of halting the 'domino effect' of communism spreading from a North imagined in racial terms. This was a time of debate, contest and change in Australian society. Media coverage of the war (Payne, 2007) and deeply divided attitudes both to the war itself, and to the reintroduction of conscription (Grey and Doyle 1992; Langley 1992; Edwards 1997; Crowe 1999; Caulfield 2007), signalled the changing structures and priorities of Australian society. The notion that Australians needed to protect themselves from dangerous foreign ideologies, whether through domestic action or involvement in international conflicts, re-emerged after the terrorist attacks in the United States on 11 September 2001. The Coalition government's commitment of troops to US-led anti-terror efforts was met with a degree of public protest, demonstration and debate. In Howard's campaign language that year, the enemies of Australian security were clearly identified: al-Qaeda leader Osama bin Laden and his followers who hate both the United States (our ally), and the 'world system built on individual freedom, religious tolerance, democracy, and the international free flow of commerce' (Howard 2001b). This discourse had an ideological focus reliant on long-held assumptions of racial difference, evoking popular culture and media connections between Islam, Middle-Eastern or 'Arabic' cultural heritage and international terrorism to create a set of binaries. Douglas Kellner (2003, 63–64) has described this as an exercise in 'binary reductionism' where traits of 'aggression and wickedness' are projected onto the other 'in order to paint "ourselves" as good and pure'.

The Australian involvement in international conflicts spans from often-forgotten colonial and early post–Federation contributions to Imperial campaigns (such as Sudan in 1885 and the Boer War 1899–1902) to the ongoing commitment to the so-called War on Terror. It is World War I, however, that is memorialized as Australia's first significant contribution to an international conflict and that provided 'the Little Digger' an opportunity to develop a fiercely patriotic military discourse of Australian security that would resonate in campaigns for decades to come.

Sweep All Sectional Interests Aside

Australia was in the midst of its first double dissolution election when Britain declared war on Germany on 4 August 1914. This campaign would return Labor opposition leader Andrew Fisher for his third stint as prime minister, removing Joseph Cook who had taken office after an election held only a year earlier. Both leaders immediately pledged Australian support for the Imperial cause. Fisher had already promised Labor's support at a campaign meeting in Colac on 31 July, in anticipation of Britain's involvement. His words on the 'European situation' have become one of the best-remembered phrases of Australian politics: 'We will stand by our own and help the mother land to our last man and our last shilling' (Fisher in *Camperdown Herald* 1914, 2).

Fisher won the election, and when he resigned in October the following year William 'Billy' Hughes became leader of the Labor Party and prime minister. Hughes had represented Labor in the NSW Parliament before Federation, and in the new nation he served in the Federal Parliament from its first sitting in 1901 until his death in 1952. His biographer described him as 'one of the few genuine Australian wits', and one of Labor's 'most articulate advocates throughout the period of its rise and its first substantial tenure in Commonwealth politics' (Fitzhardinge 1954, 414). Hughes was a divisive figure throughout his career, despite consistent success in his own electorate. Fitzhardinge (1983) describes him as tall and thin, with a 'gnome-like appearance' that deepened with age. He was by turns 'abrasive and ruthless', 'charming and amusing' (Fitzhardinge 1983), and he used 'quickness of thought, caustic pungent wit, sardonic humour [and a] wicked sense of comedy' to great effect, having trained 'his voice and powers of expression so that they were formidable instruments of debate' (Cowper 1952, 7).

Hughes was prime minister for just over a year before his attempts to introduce conscription in support of the war effort caused a party rift. In November 1916 he was expelled, and established the short-lived National Labor Party with colleagues who had followed him before joining with Joseph Cook's Liberals to form the Nationalist Party of Australia. Hughes retained leadership of the new party and went on to win the next three elections, playing on a carefully constructed persona as 'a "win-the-war politician" who, unlike others in the [...] Parliament, was an effective wartime leader' (Andrews 2008, 240). A key element was his proud projection of himself as 'an imperialist and a race patriot' (Cotton 2015, 117) for whom 'nationalism' and 'imperial sentiment' were intertwined and interdependent. Eulogizing Hughes in *The Australian Quarterly* in December 1952, soon after his death, lawyer and United Australia Party politician Norman Cowper (1952, 6–7) wrote of his complex character, the 'impetuous fury' with which he dedicated himself to the war effort, and the 'surge of Australian nationalism' he inspired which 'insisted not on the severance, but on the strengthening of the Imperial connection'.

In this context, Hughes developed a myth of Australian identity that located pride in the wartime heroics of the diggers firmly within the scope of Imperial loyalty.[1] In associating himself, and his party, with both of these elements during elections, he shaped the contours of a partisan battle over Australian security that would echo in campaigns for decades to come. His campaign speeches during the war and in the post-war years demonstrate the power of political storytelling that mobilized military threat and heroic engagement in Australian security discourses. The specific content of this discourse changed as Hughes moved between parties in these politically unsettled years. After his split with Labor, he found a home in a coalition of conservative parties, and worked to paint his former colleagues as a significant threat to the nation's best interests.

---

[1] This myth would go on to be reworked and revitalized by prime ministers Hawke and Howard; see Chapter 4 for a discussion of their positive use of the Anzac myth to construct Australian values.

In order to mobilize Australia's wartime efforts into the partisan battle for political power, campaigning leaders during and after World War I constructed the nation's involvement as contributing to a noble cause. It was necessary for leaders hoping to align themselves with the diggers that Australian efforts were represented as a defining moment in the young nation's story. This is a common theme; for example, much scholarly literature positions war as 'a powerfully attractive means of asserting national identity' (Souter 2000, 261; see also Ross 1985; Robertson 1990, 191; Kelly 1994, iv–v). However, for leaders at the time, the identity born at Gallipoli was a mechanism for strengthening and taking pride in, rather than separating from, the nation's white-British identity. In 1917, media coverage highlighted the patriotic mood of crowds at Hughes' campaign meetings. At the Nationalist policy launch at Bendigo's Lyric Theatre, more than 3,000 people waited for him to appear by 'singing patriotic songs', waving flags and cheering 'the cause of Britain and the Allies' (*Age* 1917, 9). Once he began, the *Sydney Morning Herald* (1917, 11) reported his 'force as an orator' ensured that the crowd either listened 'in absolute silence' or was 'aroused to a pitch of wild enthusiasm' for two hours while he spoke.

Hughes painted the battles of World War I as an opportunity for Australians to prove themselves to be loyal defenders of the Empire. Australians, in his conception, were duty-bound *and* willing to fight 'on the battlefields of the old world':

> It is indeed imperative to do so for only by helping the Empire can we save Australia [...] there are many ways in which we can help the Empire, with men, with money, with our products. As to men, now that the people have decided against compulsion, the call of duty of patriotism of Australia, of Empire, must reach the ears of all our young men. Let them go forth and strike a blow for the land that has bred them. (Hughes 1917)

There is a strong element of self-interest in this language, which linked Imperial membership to Australian security when asking voters to support wartime policy proposals. Australians are called on to 'strike a blow for the land that has bred them' but this is positioned as a 'duty of patriotism' to both Australia *and* the Empire. The two are linked but not conflated, as Hughes argues that 'only by helping the Empire can we save Australia' and defend the source of our cultural and military security. This perspective re-emerged in campaign language during World War II, where Robert Menzies (1940) implored voters to exert 'every ounce of effort' for 'Australia's own safety, the freedom of the British Empire and the future of the world'. His opponent, John Curtin (1940), reaffirmed that Labor 'stands inflexible in support of the British cause'. In newspaper coverage at the time, the reaffirmation of Imperial loyalty was seen as the most important aspect of both leaders' speeches and these were reprinted as the key lines (*Melbourne Herald* 1940a, 8; *Sydney Morning Herald* 1940, 7; *Age* 1940, 8; *Canberra Times* 1940, 2).

With both threat and duty clearly established, Hughes worked in 1917 to align his newly formed Nationalist Party with Australian security, reassuring voters that it was precisely his party's commitment to the Empire that would protect national interests. Here, being 'for the Empire' meant that voters were 'true to Australia, to liberty, to ourselves' (Hughes 1917). This meant rising above partisanship, as in the context of such a significant threat all that mattered was whether voters (constructed here as male) were willing to 'put Australia first and sweep all sectional interests aside'. To shouts of 'hear, hear', Hughes (1917) continued with an attack on Labor, painting them as 'hostile to Britain' and beholden to 'other interests':

> The party, then, which opposed us is made up for the most part of men either hostile to or lukewarm on the war, indifferent to the Empire, or openly opposed to it; men clamouring for premature peace, men who forget that their first duty is to Australia, who put other interests before that of their country. And this party is absolutely controlled by men who are not seeking the suffrages of the people, by secret executives of persons not responsible to the electors.

Hughes implicitly evoked Labor's links to the trade union movement, and through them to international socialism in this passage. In the context of the fiercely patriotic battles over conscription and loyalty that were taking place in politics, public debate and the media during the war years, he asked voters to see Labor as a threat within the national space. Donald Horne (2000, 165) has described this as the development of 'the enemy within' in the conservative political repertoire, both before and during the Cold War. Hughes was a central figure in constructing 'the Labor Party's Bolshevism', which Horne (2000, 165) argues functioned as a rhetorical device to overcome the reality that the conservatives themselves did not have plans for the national defence, 'except in illusion, for party advantage, at election time'.

Hughes mobilized the discourse of Australian security as part of the campaign battle by placing his own party above any petty preoccupation with partisan differences. In doing so, he asked voters to understand that for his party *national* and *Imperial* loyalties would take precedence. However, this very assertion played into the partisan contest. By arguing that the Nationalists are willing to 'put Australia first' and 'sweep sectional interests aside', Hughes portrayed Labor as concerned with political power for its own sake rather than with Australia's success in the war. He told voters that 'the Caucus Party' had 'boasted' that they would prevent him representing Australia at the Imperial War Conference 'by the use of the majority in the Senate' (Hughes 1917). This action, in Hughes' emotive construction, would make Australia the only 'Dominion' whose voice was not heard at the Conference, betraying the legacy of the men who had fought in the war:

> The voice of Australia, this country whose sons have dyed the rocks and sand of Gallipoli and the great battlefields of France with the heart's blood, will be silent. What a humiliation to every loyal Australian this is. What will our soldiers, who have endured, fought, bled and sacrificed all things in order that the honour of Australia might be upheld – that victory might be achieved, say, when they learn that their country is not to share in these vitally important deliberations?

In this way, Labor was constructed as a direct threat to Australia's military security. Through this, Hughes positioned his political opposition as un-patriotic and even un-Australian. His explicit representation of his party as the protector of Australia's international relationships and interests was dominated by this lengthy and vibrant attack on his opponents, a campaign discourse which clearly linked positive self-descriptions to negative constructions of the opposition.

The conservative construction of Labor as a threat to Australia's military and cultural security endured in leaders' language across the campaigns that followed. In these, Labor was consistently painted by its opponents as having the *wrong* foreign allegiances, and as being unduly influenced or even controlled by these. Rather than loyalty to the Empire (and later the Alliance) Labor's true allegiance was constructed as being to the international union movement, to socialist ideology, and through these alignments to communist 'enemy' nations. The specific threat varied depending on the issues contemporary to each campaign. Across campaign history, voters were told that Labor's external ties would jeopardize the White Australia policy; Australia's British and Western relationships; the national way of life; and the institutions of freedom and democracy. However, the overall shape of the conservative critique of Labor's loyalties has been consistent. For example, in 1963, Australia's first 'major television election' and Prime Minister Robert Menzies' last as leader, he positioned Labor as compromised and untrustworthy. Menzies 'dispensed with the traditional public meeting' for his policy launch speech, instead presenting the first to be studio pre-recorded and nationally televised to an estimated audience of five million viewers (Whitington 1964, 68).[2] Broadcast directly into voters' living rooms, Menzies (1963) argued that his opponents could not be trusted because they were beholden to 'the thirty six "faceless men" whose qualifications are unknown, who have no elected responsibility to you'; a campaign theme that was 'devastating' for Labor (Freudenberg 1977, 89).[3] This image has become enduring political shorthand in critiques of Labor. In 2013, Opposition Leader Tony Abbott (2013a) used his opening press conference to remind voters that the 'caucus' and 'faceless men' had twice taken the choice of who would be prime minister away from ordinary voters since they had elected Kevin Rudd in 2007.

Safe, Sound and Solid

Campaign discussions of Australia's engagement in military conflicts, and valorization of the diggers as representative of the best elements of Australian identity, were mobilized in Billy Hughes' campaign language into the partisan battle for domestic political power. It is important to note, however, that the conservative construction of national and imperial loyalty exemplified by Hughes did not go unchallenged. Labor leaders developed their own counter-arguments in response. An exploration of these competing discourses of Australian security in 1925, a campaign dominated by concerns about political and ideological threats, illuminates the fraught nature of constructions of Australia's best interests. It also reveals the enduring nature of political attempts to lay claim to stewardship of those interests.

The construction of menacing ideological 'others' as enemies to be feared has been consistent across Australian campaign history, but flares up at times where these threats dominated the global political landscape. The discourse works on a number of levels. Initially, a clear distinction is drawn between *us* and *them*, allowing those identified as the enemy (whether socialists, communists or terrorists) to be separated from inclusion in the national identity. This allows leaders to then cast these ideological enemies (imagined as foreign) as heartless and brutal, highlighting the contrast with our noble, civilized selves. In this way, the threat posed by our enemies can be constructed as endangering the national way of life, and efforts to oppose this threat become noble attempts to protect the national identity.

---

[2] Goot and Scalmer (2013, 74) note that Menzies actually 'favoured studio broadcasts' because he 'found public meetings difficult', in part due to the 'vigorous heckling' he often faced.

[3] The '36 faceless men' reference asked voters to recall a famous image, taken by photographer Alan Reid, of Whitlam and Calwell waiting outside the Hotel Kingston in Canberra for the Labor Party Federal Executive to make a policy decision on the US plan to build a communications base at North West Cape in WA (NAA, undated).

This contest, within which party leaders have positioned themselves and their parties as custodians of secure national identity and their opponents as an ideological threat, has played out across the history of campaigns. One of the most prominent early campaign battles where ideologies constructed as external were positioned as a threat to the nation's security due to *domestic* political sympathies played out in 1925. A close analysis of the leaders' language in that campaign provides another perspective on the shape of the early partisan contest to define and protect Australian identity. Discussions of the parties' ideological sympathies were prominent and these discourses endured in the language of campaigning leaders in the decades that followed.

The 1925 election campaign was the first held after the introduction of compulsory voting in Australia; it was also the first of Australia's 'full-scale "Red scare" campaigns', an election issue that would be a central feature over the decades that followed (Edwards 1965, 114; also Brett 2003, 82). Debates over socialism and the perceived rising influence of so-called extremists in the trade union movement (exemplified by ongoing industrial tensions between the government and the Seaman's Union[4]) coloured discussion of other campaign issues, such as Australia's place in the Empire and fledgling independence in trade and foreign policy decisions. Two men with very different political personas vied for the prime ministership: Nationalist party leader and prime minister Stanley Bruce, and Labor opposition leader Matthew Charlton.

Stanley Bruce was born in Toorak, Melbourne but left Australia in 1902 to pursue his studies at Cambridge. He stayed in Britain after graduation, worked as a barrister and as Chairman of the Board of his family's firm Paterson, Laing and Bruce and served with a British regiment during the campaign at Gallipoli (Lee 2010, ix–x; Edwards 1965, 3–5). Judith Brett (2003, 78; see also Cumpston 1989, 267) has argued that he was 'able to pass as well as any Australian ever could as a member of the British governing classes'. A share in profits from the family firm had ensured he and his wife lived in 'affluence approaching luxury in the days before the First World War' (Edwards 1965, 3). He was initially an unwilling candidate for high political office after his return to Australia, but rose quickly once he entered public life. His public image as a formal, traditionalist 'toff' won him admiration rather than affection from the public and his speaking style did little to invoke voters' passions. His addresses were 'meticulously prepared and academic' rather than 'political harangues', 'worthy and heavy' rather than impassioned or inspiring (Cumpston 1989, 30).

---

[4] For a detailed account of these events, including Bruce's political battles with president of the Seaman's Union, Thomas Walsh, and his government's use of the *Navigation Act* 1925 and *Immigration Act* 1925 to counter union action, see Lee (2010, 48–58).

Matthew Charlton is all but forgotten in Australian political history. He is one of few party leaders who do not have a significant work of history or biography dedicated to them. This is perhaps because his challenges to Bruce in both the 1922 and 1925 election campaigns were unsuccessful and he never attained the office of prime minister. Charlton was the son of an English coal miner, born in Linton in country Victoria. He worked in the NSW coalmines himself and was active in the union movement until moving first into state, and then federal, politics. A sympathetic profile published in left-leaning Sydney tabloid the *Truth* (Burns 1925, 8) a month before the 1925 election describes him as a 'mild-mannered, gentle-spoken and medium-sized' man who 'impresses' with his 'sincerity and earnestness of purpose'. The article is headlined 'Matthew Charlton, MP: Safe, Sound and Solid', and is accompanied by a large illustration of Charlton, whose deep-set eyes gaze steadfastly out at the reader under heavy eyebrows. Even at the time, the writer acknowledged that Charlton's private life was little known but noted that 'his path [...] has not been strewn with rose petals', that he was 'no seeker of the spotlight' and 'no brilliant orator' (Burns 1925, 8).

The Chaos and Misery of Class War

When Stanley Bruce delivered his policy launch speech in 1925, it was to a crowd 'packed to the point of suffocation' into Dandenong Town Hall and filling the streets outside (*Age* 1925a, 11). The *Sydney Morning Herald* (1925, 9) reported that Bruce spoke 'in a clear and confident tone', and was interrupted at regular intervals 'by rousing cheers from an audience representative of all classes'. In office and during campaigns, the privileged 'British' identity that characterized his public persona gave the prime minister a unique speaking position from which to claim ownership of Australian security in the face of threat. With his 'Britishness' firmly established, Bruce (1925) called for Australia to have a voice in Imperial affairs, and a say in her own fate, without his dedication to Empire coming into question:

> The government stands whole-heartedly for the maintenance of the British Empire [...] One thing only do we ask – that in this assumption of responsibility we shall be treated as a partner and not as an appendage of Empire. Never again must we be involved in a war arising out of foreign policy in which we have had no voice [...] within the Empire we demand freedom, independence and the fullest consultation.

Bruce calls, here, for an Australian independence that would strengthen ties with the mother country. A true Australian, in this conception, should not need to choose between loyalty to nation or the Empire, as it is only when the two are combined that Australian security is guaranteed. In the introduction to his recent biography of Bruce, David Lee (2010, ix) argues against the traditional conception of Bruce as a 'man of two worlds'. Rather, he argues that Bruce 'sought to harmonize Australian nationalism, British imperialism, and internationalism'. It is from this position that the prime minister aligned himself and his party with the legacy of British-Australian nationalism, and could then position Labor as a threat to Australian security. In his address, Bruce (1925) painted his opposition (who were explicitly opponents both of Australia and of Empire in his speeches) as 'extremists' working to 'subvert democracy'. These extremists would threaten what Bruce (1925) presented as a time of 'prosperity' and 'opportunity'; they were:

> wreckers who would plunge us into the chaos and misery of class war [...] It is for you now to decide whether our free institutions of Government, our advanced civilisation, our enlightened industrial system and our prestige within the Empire and abroad are to be preserved, or whether they are to go down beneath the feet of men who care nothing for this country.

Here, Labor's ideological links were a direct existential threat to Australian security, as they would bring about 'class war'. Bruce returned to this theme in subsequent elections, although with different targets. In 1928, for example, the prime minister employed this discourse of Australian security to paint Labor's ideological position as endangering the White Australia policy, and through this Australia's white-British identity. In his policy launch speech, Bruce (1928) argued that the ACTU (the 'labour movement' which was connected to 'political labour') had been captured by 'un-Australian extremists' and was now linked to the Pan Pacific Trade Union Secretariat, whose aim was to fight exclusive immigration laws in the region. If they succeeded, he argued, this would sound 'the death knell' of the White Australia policy, which was supported by ordinary Labor voters:

> Yet so craven are the leaders of political labour that they dare not unequivocally denounce those extremists in their own ranks, who by insidious means are undermining Australia's great national ideal and substituting for it a policy framed in Asia. (Bruce 1928)

This reads, on paper, as a fiery denunciation of the leadership of the Labor Party. However, the speech was reported in the *Age* (1928, 9) as a 'monotonously measured' reading of the government's record, which, save for a group of interjectors, was 'appallingly dull' for the 1,500 attendees who sat through its full two hours. In this section, one of very few in which Bruce did not directly discuss industrial arbitration, the prime minister relied on a well-established conservative campaign strategy linking Labor to foreign interests. He made an important distinction between those who had supported and voted for Labor and the 'leaders of political Labor'. This allowed him to argue that Labor's leaders were so cowardly that they would not 'denounce' those among them aligned with the foreign organizations that threatened Australian identity security. This language worked on two levels: to avoid alienating those who had voted Labor in the past; and to appeal to the electorate on the basis of national rather than sectional identity. The notion that, if elected, Labor would replace what was framed as one of the central institutions of Australian identity security with a policy 'framed in Asia' evoked familiar Yellow Peril fears. This discourse relied, in part, on an assumption of voter awareness of other strands of the conservative critique of Labor. Elections take place in the context of previous campaigns, as well as the partisan battles that occur in parliament and the media in the intervening years. In this way, Bruce could evoke the passionate wartime debates over conscription, where Labor's Imperial loyalty was questioned, and the themes of the previous 1925 'red scare' election, to once again charge Labor with foreign allegiances.

Fake Fears and Frights

These charges did not go unchallenged. As opposition leader in two consecutive elections, Matthew Charlton both contested his opponents' positioning of Labor as a threat and reworked campaign discourses of Australian identity and security. In 1925, Charlton presented himself as working class and unpretentious, a representative of *true* Australianness in contrast to the 'toff from Toorak'. With this persona as a starting point, his speeches sought to reclaim the positive language of Australian security for Labor. Interviewed on 2 November, the afternoon before a campaign meeting at the Adelaide Town Hall, Charlton told *The News* (1925a, 1) that his speech would deal with 'the statements of Mr Bruce regarding the danger of extremists bringing about revolution', which the prime minister had attributed to 'their alleged domination of the Labor Party'. In response, Charlton said, he would convince voters that 'the policy of the Labor party is a better one in the interests of the future development of the Empire' (*The News* 1925a, 1).

This was Charlton's central task in 1925: to provide a vision of Australian security that aligned Labor's vision of the national interest with the security offered by Imperial membership, while rejecting allegations that the party was dominated by 'extremists'. That evening, at the Adelaide Town Hall, Charlton delivered a speech that *The News* (1925b, 7) described as devoid of 'fireworks, either rhetorical or political'. It was characterized instead by his 'earnest' speaking style: 'He is so obviously convinced he is right, and his every word carried the stamp of sincerity' (*The News* 1925b, 7). The Labor leader received an enthusiastic response from the crowd at two key moments of the speech. The first was when he expressed 'loyalty to the British Empire'; and the second came when he emphasized 'the moderate policy of his party' (*The News* 1925b, 7). Later that week, in a public address at Dean Square in Albury, Charlton developed the negative side of this discourse, accusing his opponents of 'insinuating' that Labor was working to undermine the Empire. The *Albury Banner and Express* (1925, 32) paraphrased this section of his speech before quoting Charlton directly:

> Labor's opponents were endeavouring to create an atmosphere in this country against Labor for the purpose of carrying this election in their favour. "There is no more loyal party", said Mr Charlton, "in the British Empire than the Australian Labor Party."

This was a key characteristic of Charlton's campaign narrative of Australian security. Here, he reclaimed ownership, and reworked the meaning, of the discourse of Imperial loyalty which had for two decades sat at the foundation of shared understandings of Australian identity and belonging. Charlton did not propose a disengagement from the safety afforded by membership in the Empire or a departure from common-sense understandings of Australian collective identity as white and British. In his speech at Albury, he reinforced that Labor's loyalty would continue to guarantee Australian security. However, he did call into question the *unthinking* Imperial loyalty he critiqued as characteristic of conservative approaches. This was a theme Charlton had introduced in his policy launch speech almost a month earlier, at the Sydney Town Hall. On 9 October, he had outlined the Labor policy in a 'very long' and 'completely prepared' address that was radio broadcast (*Age* 1925b, 17). A central element was his critique of the Bruce-Page Government's 'Men, Money, Markets' policy, through which Australia provided a market for British manufacturing in return for the supply of settlers and capital for rural development (Alomes 1988, 83). It was a policy that Charlton (1925) argued typified the government's misplaced loyalties, which should have been 'to provide work for its own people':

> Yet the Bruce-Page Government enters into a compact with the British Government that Australia will take British immigrants, put them onto the land, house them, train them, maintain them, and those it cannot put on the land it guarantees to provide with permanent suitable employment and 'after care'. The Labor party […] will regard it as a duty that guarantees of employment and 'after care' shall be furnished to Australians before being furnished to people from overseas.

Here, Charlton creates a distinction between Australians and 'people from overseas' that, significantly, locates British immigrants in the *latter* category. While not claiming a demographic shift for the Australian identity that will lead to a more racially or culturally diverse community, he does distinguish the national collective and the interests of its people from those of the mother country. Although white-British race identity remained the foundation of the national identity, Australianness was no longer directly synonymous with Britishness here. This was a challenging reimagining of the national identity, but was also a key element of Labor's attempt to reclaim the discourse of Australian security. The nation's true best interests, in Charlton's (1925) construction, would be served by the Labor Party who would put 'the development of our continent [and] the development of our race in body, in mind, and social status' above all else.

Charlton's critique of his opponents relied not only on questioning their ability to safeguard Australian security in light of their Imperial loyalties, but also on the mobilization of a deeper critique of their campaign methods. Not only did he challenge the alignment of conservatives with Australian security, he also accused them of conducting baseless 'scare campaigns' designed to inspire unfounded fear and insecurity in the electorate.[5] In a vibrant early passage of his policy speech, he painted the 'enemies of Labor' as reliant on a single method of preserving power: attempting to 'paralyse the mentality of the people with imaginary terrors' (Charlton 1925). To this end, he argued, they 'organise fake fears and frights, and conduct elections while the fright is on'. This tactic, for Charlton (1925), persists from campaign to campaign with the 'only variation [...] the name of the horror doing "scarecrow duty"' at any particular time. He outlines, and dismisses, the government's 'excuse', the assertion that:

> There are in Australia paid agents of foreign powers, working to subvert the government of this country, and that it has ample evidence of the men, their methods, their machines, and the sources of their tainted money. If that were true, it would be the duty of the Government to arrest treason and produce the evidence. It does not do so. (Charlton 1925)

Charlton predicted that the government's scare tactics would be unsuccessful in the campaign, as the strategy had failed them in recent state elections. Voters went to the polls on 14 November, compelled for the first time by compulsory voting laws, and more than 90 per cent of the eligible population cast

---

[5] This was an enduring charge; in the 2016 campaign, Labor opposition leader Bill Shorten accused his Liberal opponents of developing a scare campaign about 'illiterate' asylum seekers who would take Australian jobs (see Chapter 8 for a more detailed discussion).

their votes (Green 2011). Despite Charlton's confidence it was the so-called red scare strategy of the Nationalist incumbents that proved most effective. The government increased its majority in a decisive victory. However, Matthew Charlton's now mostly overlooked discourse of Australian identity security would provide the foundation for Labor leaders in campaigns for decades to follow.

The Australian Side of the Argument

Charlton did not allow conservative discourses of security to go unanswered. He challenged the very validity of the 'scares' he argued the conservatives were manufacturing. His Labor successors worked similarly in the campaigns that followed to contest the conservative claim to ownership of Australian military myth, Imperial and Alliance loyalty and national security. More deeply, however, Labor leaders not only attempted to reclaim these discourses, but also to rework their meaning. Australian studies scholar Nick Dryenfurth (2014, 164), in a detailed account of Labor's relationship to the Anzac legend, argues against histories that position 'both the Anzac legend and a hitherto progressive Australian nationalism' as '"hijacked" by conservatives for imperialist ends during the tumult of war'. Pointing to more nuanced revisionist histories, he argues that for much of the time between the first anniversary of Gallipoli and World War II, the Anzac legend 'was at once consensual and contested territory'; used by Labor to appeal to voters' patriotism but also mobilized to represent 'a vastly different set of political meanings' (Dryenfurth 2014, 188). These insights are useful when considering broader discourses of identity security, and the ways in which campaigning Labor leaders sought to align themselves and their party with these.

Alongside positive stories of Labor's loyalties and values, leaders developed critiques of the conservative side of politics. One prominent version of this critique painted Labor's opponents as more interested in maintaining Australia's safe junior position in the Empire (and later, the Alliance) than establishing an independent security position. This discourse, developed in one of its earliest forms by Matthew Charlton, has allowed Labor leaders to contest the notion that Australian safety is best secured through loyalty rather than independence. It echoes in more recent campaigns: for example, Labor leader Mark Latham (2004) framed his support for the American Alliance as secondary to his proud commitment to Australia's own interests, telling voters in 2004: 'if there's a difference of opinion […] between us and the United States, I'll always back the Australian side of the argument'. In the election that followed, new leader Kevin Rudd (2007b) emphasized that although he would maintain a 'a very close relationship with the United States', it was important for voters to remember that 'having an effective alliance with the United States' did not necessarily mean 'automatic compliance [...] on every element of foreign policy'.

On one level Labor leaders have positioned the conservatives' loyalty to those imagined as the nation's great and powerful friends as undermining Australia's interests and security. On a deeper level, they constructed such loyalty as outdated. This discursive strategy was developed by Gough Whitlam, who in 1972 argued that the policies of his opponents (who had been in power 23 years) would 'make Australia a backwater in our region and a back number in history'. More than three decades later Paul Keating (1996a) argued that his opponent, John Howard, 'has never been able to drag his feet from the sands of the past'. This construction was a feature of Keating's language as prime minister. In February 1992, he made a colourful attack on the Liberals' loyalties in parliament, and in later speeches 'pursued the claim that Labor had always championed the national interest while the conservatives still clung to an outmoded imperial past' (Macintyre and Clark 2004, 124). In 2007, Rudd drew on a similar discourse when arguing that the continued presence of the Howard government threatened Australia's competitive ability in the twenty-first century. Drawing on assumed voter knowledge of John Howard's age and time in parliament[6], and a broader *time for a change* mentality that often attaches to long-term governments, Rudd's (2007c) campaign focused on a 'new versus old' theme that painted his opponent as 'stuck in the past', out of touch with the challenges of the global era:

> Mr Howard [...] simply doesn't understand the new challenges that we face in the future. The challenges of climate change and water. The challenges of the digital economy. The challenge of the rise of China and India. The challenge to fix our hospitals, once and for all. And above all, the challenge to transform our education system.

Echoing Keating, Rudd's image of the prime minister was of someone fundamentally unable to address the new challenges the nation faced. He asked voters to see that voting for the Howard government would mean Australia was left behind, implicitly arguing that his (relatively) youthful 'fresh thinking' approach to problems meant he (and his team) would understand and be able to meet Australia's new challenges. While Rudd sought to redefine the discursive content of 'having Australia's best interests at heart' in domestic terms, he also contested the conservative claim to ownership of the domain of military security. In a speech at the Lavarck Barracks in Townsville, he told

---

[6] At the time of the 2007 election campaign, Howard was 68 years old, and Kevin Rudd 50.

voters Labor was 'fundamentally committed to the future of the US–Australia alliance', and claimed its provenance for Labor as it 'was formed during World War II under the prime ministership of John Curtin' (Rudd 2007b). This extended the traditional Labor critique of their opponents' unthinking loyalties, and operated alongside a broader discourse in which Labor would work in the interest of Australian security because of its closer connection to the values and ideals of those imagined as ordinary Australians.

The central battleground over Australian security had shifted by the 2007 campaign. In earlier campaigns the partisan battle to align oneself, and one's party, with these discourses played out in narratives that positioned foreign military or ideological forces as an existential threat to the Australian nation, its people and its way of life. While these elements did appear in 2007, the campaign was not dominated by concerns about military or ideological threats to the nation (despite ongoing Australian involvement in overseas wars, and the ever-present concern about international terrorism). Rather, the discourse of Australian security was domestically focused.

Are You More Secure? Is Our Nation More Secure?

This was a shift even more evident in 2013, where the battle over which party was best able to safeguard Australian security was fought on local turf. Ideological threat, in these contested discourses, would come from the historical and contemporary policy positions of the opposing party: from their values, alignments and past performances. In 2013, for both leaders, it was *our* party's job to safeguard Australians against *their* poor judgement and negativity. This is not to say that discourses of military and strategic threat played no part in the election. Both leaders spoke at Robertson Barracks in Darwin during the campaign, evoking Australia's proud military history and connecting it to the nation's contemporary involvement in the coalition of forces fighting in Afghanistan (Rudd 2013e; Abbott 2013h). While at these moments, and in ongoing debates about border security and the 'threat' of people smugglers and terrorism (Abbott 2013i), discussions of military and ideological threat did arise they were not the dominant location of the 2013 partisan battle over Australian security. Rather, both leaders located the most worrying current threat to Australian security in their opposition's ideological positions, current policies, past failures and internal dysfunctions.

Liberal leader Tony Abbott had brought his party within a seat of winning government in 2010. The election had gone down to the wire in the wake of Labor's replacement of Prime Minister Kevin Rudd with his deputy, Julia Gillard, leading to a hung parliament. In the weeks that followed, Labor successfully negotiated with Green and independent members of parliament to form a minority government. In 2013, Abbott was determined to win back power, and to do so in his own right. Across a range of policy areas he portrayed newly re-instated prime minister Rudd and his party as a threat to Australian security. In this context, his campaign communications were characterized by the development of a discursive link between *prosperity* and *security*.[7] This link was evident in the questions he posed to voters at Sky News People's Forum in Brisbane, almost a month into the campaign:

> Are we doing better now than we were six years ago? Are we more prosperous? Are we more confident? Are you more secure? Is our nation more secure? (Abbott 2013g)

Addressing the National Press Club, in one of the most high-profile events of the campaign, Abbott (2013k) once again laid out the fundamental contours of the battle for Australian security, which he pitched as between 'a strong and united Coalition team' and 'chaos and confusion under Labor'. The 'core issue' of the campaign, for Abbott (2013k), was 'economic management': not for its own sake but because 'everything else – national security, border security, the delivery of better schools and hospitals' was unsustainable without a strong economic foundation. These themes were developed throughout the campaign. They featured in interviews in which Labor was presented as untrustworthy because it had 'no ethical compass' or 'values-based core' (Abbott 2013b); and in press conferences and speeches where the political instability of the last two terms was characterized in terms of Labor's 'desperate' need to stay in power. Here, Abbott (2013c) challenged voters:

> What did we get from the Labor Party? In 2007 you voted for Kevin Rudd, you got Julia Gillard. In 2010 you voted for Julia Gillard, you got Kevin Rudd. In 2013 they want us to vote for Kevin Rudd and who knows who we might end up with? Maybe Peter Beattie, maybe Bill Shorten, you just don't know, nothing is certain under the Labor Party.

It is into this landscape that Abbott (2013b) inserted himself as saviour, able to provide the stability that would allow for a 'safe and secure' Australia founded on a 'strong and prosperous economy'. Labor's political desperation was the real threat here, and the negotiations that it had made to function in minority government meant that the Australian public had been subjected to 'betrayals […]

---

[7] Carol Johnson (2015, 36), in her analysis of the campaign, has noted that Abbott developed two key strategies to win the hearts of voters: encouraging 'voters to feel afraid and anxious' through a characterization of Labor as a 'threat to the economy […] and to border security', and an attempt to 'neutralise Labor fear campaigns against the Coalition'.

hopeless compromises [...] the abandonment of principle [and] the abandonment of commitments' (Abbott 2013b).

Abbott's development of an Australian security discourse mobilized one of the classic us/them distinctions of electoral politics, in which we are stable, united and principled while they are divided, unpredictable and lacking in moral courage. Johnson (2015, 37) has identified that this had a been a key feature of Abbott's term as opposition leader: a consistent 'encouraging of feelings of insecurity by suggesting that the minority Labor government was both dysfunctional and likely to fall at any time'. Engaging in this partisan battle, his opponent in 2013 also based his campaign communications on a familiar electoral trope where we are positive, policy-driven nation-builders while they are negative wreckers with no political values. Kevin Rudd developed these two strands across his campaign to paint his opposition as the true threat to Australian security and Labor as its guardians, locating the campaign battle in the domestic realm rather than inviting voters to worry about foreign military or ideological threat.

On 5 September, just two days before the election and three days after his opponent had stood in the same place, Kevin Rudd addressed the National Press Club in Canberra. Much like his opponent had only days before, he used this highly visible televised address to reiterate his central campaign message, painting 'the core mission of progressive politics, our Party and our Government' as being to do 'whatever we can to make life better' for Australians (Rudd 2013h). In this conception, Labor were committed to 'building an Australia of the future'; they were the ones who work to 'build the house up', while their opponents 'oppose, oppose, oppose and then tear the house down'. Rudd's key discursive strategy, here, mobilized a key theme he had developed throughout the campaign. Weeks earlier, Rudd was in Mackay, in Queensland, to launch Labor candidate Bronwyn Taha's campaign for the seat of Dawson. The prime minister used the opportunity to connect his government's positive plans for the Australian future to Labor history, and to position these nation-building enterprises as the true guarantee of Australian security:

> Who was it who went and commissioned the building of the Snowy Mountains Scheme? It was a Labor Government under Ben Chifley. When I look around the country and I see the big building projects of the past in the social domain like Medibank and then Medicare, it was only a Labor Government which delivered that for all Australians. When I look at all the major investments in our country's future, the reforms to our economy, the great investments in our future – they have come by-and-large through the initiatives of Labor Governments [...]. (Rudd 2013c)

Setting his opponents against this positive vision, Rudd (2013c) quoted former Labor prime minister Paul Keating as 'famously' saying that 'we make the history, they try and unmake the history', and positioned his opponents as advocating a return to 'some mythical point in the past' rather than embracing change. These themes also recurred when Rudd addressed the National Press Club, in a lengthy passage where he painted his opposition as both nostalgic and subservient. Rudd (2013h) critiqued Abbott's response to the allegations of human rights violations and atrocities in Syria. He claimed the Liberal leader was unwilling to be involved and thought Australia 'shouldn't be getting ideas above our station'. This, Rudd (2013h) argued, was 'symptomatic of a conservative view of Australia's future more generally':

> Conservatives often point to a mythical, almost mystical point in an elusive, imagined past. And the Conservative mission, sometimes explicitly stated as such, is to return us to that point in history when everything is imagined to have been just fine and dandy. In the case of Australia's conservatives, a cocktail of the 1950s, *Upstairs Downstairs* and *Downton Abbey* – where plainly everyone did know "their station".

Rudd (2013h) countered this with an attempt to align Labor with the 'true' Australian identity, and to position himself and his party as its guardians. This is a nation that takes risks, he argued, and having ideas above our station is one the things that 'defines us […] is carved in our hearts [and] is embedded in our identity'.

Across the campaigns analysed here, Australia's involvement in international conflicts provided fertile ground for political leaders who constructed these engagements as enduring symbols of a distinctive national character. Military threats were constructed as requiring, and inspiring, great acts of national unity and sacrifice to protect Australian identity. These representations operated in the context of partisan politics and both evoked and encouraged a broader national culture of commemoration (see, e.g. Damousi 1999; Reed 2004). These constructions of the nation's vulnerability were not limited to times of international conflict; in the face of internal and external threat (both real and perceived), voters were offered reassuring images of security which considered the protection of both the national space and identity. These combined positive and negative, inclusive and exclusive elements. The next chapter explores a discursive strategy that can, in many ways, be seen as the always-present mirror of campaign discussions of security and threat: the development and presentation of a positive vision for the Australian future.

Chapter 7

VISION

The presentation of a positive vision for Australian development and prosperity has been a central and enduring element of effective campaign communication. Party leaders vie for the prime ministership by asking voters to buy into a hopeful narrative of possibility; one that is always reliant on an explicit construction of, and implicit connection to, the shared cultural ideas of values, community, belonging and security explored in the previous chapters. Enduring political narratives of the Australian future combine these elements in their appeal to voters: *This is what your nation might look like, and who you might become, if you vote for us instead of them.* These appeals to possibility and hope are mechanisms of connection, through which a constituency can be constructed and maintained. In federal election campaigns this is the task of the party leader: to paint a picture for the nation's future that will personify the values central both to their party and to the Australian identity, and reflect both the electorate's frustrations with the present and dreams of the future.

Change of government elections offer the clearest window into the moments where a leader's vision connects with the electorate's priorities. Australians are notoriously loyal, and have voted an opposition in (or a government out) only six times in the elections held between the end of World War II and 2013: 1949, 1972, 1983, 1996, 2007 and 2013. These elections become part of political folklore, positioned as reflecting cultural and demographic shifts to herald a new era in Australian politics. In 1949, for example, Robert Menzies brought Labor's wartime government and post-war reconstruction to an end and gave voice to the 'forgotten people' he had been addressing in his radio broadcasts since the early 1940s (see Brett 1992). In 1983, a popular new leader restored Labor to power for the first time since the Whitlam government's 1975 dismissal (Haupt and Grattan 1983). In 1996, John Howard's vision of a 'relaxed and comfortable' nation brought Labor's record 13 years in government to an end (Williams 1997); and in 2013, a carefully controlled Tony Abbott came to power after a tumultuous period of Labor leadership changes and political uncertainty (MacCallum 2013). The specific social and economic issues that dominated these campaigns varied. Explanations for change ranged from the *it's time* factor (where the electorate tires of the incumbents and wants to give others a chance) to domestic debates around the economy, education or health care, and broader issues of national security or changes in the international environment.

Vision elections share three fundamental features which stand out in change of government campaigns: a leader who has developed an emotive connection with a constituency; a plan for the nation's future that connects the big picture with details that speak to voters' priorities; and an awareness of the mediatized nature of campaigns that embraces emerging media technology and opens up new ways to connect with the voting public. In these elections, leaders draw on popular understandings of the Australian identity and way of life to talk about the future, and also to paint an unsettling picture of what will happen if the government doesn't change. The political discourse of identity security functions on both these levels; to present an image of a future in which Australians are prosperous, secure and proud, and to sketch the darker alternative future that will unfold if nothing changes. Appeals to voters will always incorporate both aspects; and voting choices reflect the record of the incumbents at the same time as they indicate an opposition leader has communicated the party's plans in a way that connected with the values of the electorate and the requirements of the mediatized campaign.

This chapter explores two such campaigns: 1972, where Labor leader Gough Whitlam argued it was time for a change after 23 years of conservative rule; and 2007, which saw Kevin Rudd lead Labor to victory over John Howard's long-term Coalition government. These were moments in Australian history in which the opposition was able to develop a new constituency willing to embrace a positive new vision of Australian identity: whether in response to social changes brought about by the identity politics and progressive movements of the 1960s; or in the context of the global challenges of climate change, economic shifts, terror, conflict and displacement that characterized the first decade of the twenty-first century and seemed to call for reworked vision of the Australian future. What would Australian identity look like in the face of this change; and how might a positive story of the future help to reassure voters about the security of that identity?

These two campaigns, held more than 30 years apart, were strikingly similar in style and execution. Both saw a Labor opposition that had spent years in the electoral wilderness challenge an incumbent that seemed the natural party of government. Both saw unconventional Labor leaders overcome fractious relationships with colleagues and clashes with the party hierarchy through strong media performances and an ability to engage with voters. Both saw Labor capitalize on a perceived mood for change in the electorate, painting their leader as a visionary who could replace a stale and listless government with a passionate plan for the nation's future. And for both, Labor ran savvy media campaigns that demonstrated an awareness of the performative potential of political journalism and other forms of campaign communication. This allowed them to introduce their leaders and policies, communicate clear and consistent Australian identity stories and appeal to voters in a new way.

Personality Problems

Opposition leaders are like actors looking for their big break. They audition for the role of prime minister, eager to convince the crowd they are ready to play the lead. A vital element in winning the role is building a connection with the audience, gaining their trust well before election day. This was a key factor worrying Labor in the lead up to the 1972 election. They had been in opposition for more than two decades, unable to defeat Liberal Party founder Robert Menzies or his successors. Labor's electoral woes were a combination of internal conflict and broader context. Laurie Oakes and David Solomon (1973), in their insider account of the 1972 campaign, paint Labor in the 1960s as dealing with the legacy of the 1955 split which had left them ideologically divided. After more than a year of division between the party's national leadership and the Victorian-based Catholic Social Studies Movement, led by B. A. Santamaria, followers of 'the Movement' were expelled from Labor. They formed the Democratic Labor Party, which not only pulled voters away from Labor for the next two decades but also created an image of Labor as bitter and divided.

Gough Whitlam was a controversial figure in the party at that time. He had clashed with Labor leadership as he rose through the ranks, and spoken publicly about what he saw as an unrepresentative internal structure. His time as deputy under Arthur Calwell, from 1960 to 1967, was characterized by conflict. Calwell's biographer, Colm Kiernan (1978), attributes this to the two men representing different elements of Labor culture. Where Calwell emphasized the party's traditional style and trade union links, Whitlam represented a more intellectual approach, and an 'individual' leadership style. These issues came to a head after Labor's dramatic loss in the 1966 election. When Calwell stepped down the following year, Whitlam won the leadership and set himself a six-year timetable for gaining office. This was inspired, according to Oakes and Solomon (1973, 13), by Menzies's strategy when he took over leadership of the United Australia Party after their 1943 defeat.

Labor made significant gains in the 1969 election, reducing the lead of the Gorton government. When Gorton resigned the leadership, and prime ministership, after a tied party room vote in March 1971 William McMahon replaced him. There was a sense within Labor that the party stood a real chance against McMahon in 1972. While he was only eight years Whitlam's senior, he had come into parliament more than twenty years earlier when a reinvigorated Menzies won government in 1949. He was associated with the policies of the 1950s and the conservative era Labor was seeking to end. So, Labor's NSW branch asked their marketing team to develop a detailed media and advertising plan for the coming campaign.[1] In December 1971 the team delivered a 104-page document outlining a strategy that would become iconic. Two words shone off the plain cover: *It's Time*.

The proposal was quickly passed from state to national level. It offered some good news: 'a growing number of people are coming to believe that it is time for a change' (Shirley et al. 1971, 5). This may have owed more to the government's failings than the opposition's success. In her biography of Whitlam, Jenny Hocking (2008, 386–87) described how McMahon and his government were seen at the time as 'internally riven, ideologically uncertain and lacking a clear vision'. Ineffective in dealing with rising unemployment and inflation, they looked increasingly out of touch on issues such as Australia's relationship with China. Hocking recounts McMahon's condemnation of Whitlam for leading a Labor Party delegation to China and meeting with Premier Zhou En-Lai in July 1971. The prime minister described Whitlam as being 'captured' by the Chinese agenda, playing on common sense narratives that historically had linked Labor and communism. His attack was undermined, however, when US president Nixon announced he had accepted an invitation to meet with the Chinese premier himself the following year (and that Henry Kissinger had been in China at the same time as Whitlam to clinch the deal). McMahon was left looking out of step, and Whitlam seemed even more forward thinking in contrast. These distinctions gave Labor the chance to offer themselves as a real alternative.

But then there was the bad news. Labor had 'personality problems', and their 'lack of charisma' and 'pizzazz' was the biggest hurdle (Shirley et al. 1971, 15). Overcoming it would require a communication campaign that combined cutting-edge audience research techniques (such as focus groups) with a level of image management unprecedented in Australian elections. Whitlam was a major part of the problem. Edward Gough Whitlam had been Member for Werriwa for 20 years, 12 of those as deputy leader and the last five as opposition leader. Voters knew him, but they didn't like or trust him. They described him, in this research, as intellectual, evasive and beholden to Bob Hawke (then head of the ACTU). They used words like 'cold' and 'distant' (Shirley et al. 1971, 11). He talked too much, and his voice was 'oily'

---

[1] The team was composed of Mike Shirley and Paul Jones from Hansen-Rubensohn-McCann-Erikson, Wayne Young and Peter Shenstone from Spectrum International Market Services, and Tony Stevenson. For more detail on Labor's research and planning, see Oakes and Solomon (1973, 94–104).

and 'irritating'. This was a legacy of his battles within the party, his policy and personality clashes with Calwell and tendency to speak his mind in television and radio interviews. Whitlam wasn't seen as a team player. His party and its policies didn't fare much better. After 23 years in opposition, an internal split and conflicts over party structure and ideology, focus group participants saw Labor as 'communist-influenced' and internally divided: the losers' party (Shirley et al. 1971, 12). On the policy front, they were seen as no better equipped to deliver on education or to solve the issues faced by rural Australia than their opponents: unable to make good on their promises on pensions and with little idea how to manage Australia's security. Whitlam and Labor needed a political makeover if they were to connect more effectively with voters.

The 1971 ALP Federal Conference, held in Launceston in late June, saw the party address these issues and solidify the themes that would characterize their conversation with voters in the upcoming election year. Whitlam pledged to restore Labor's 'representative character', to listen to people's concerns, and communicate how the ALP's policies would address those concerns. 'The great changes we seek', he told the conference, 'concern the day to day life of our people here at home' (Whitlam 1971). To win the next election, Labor needed to connect their plans to renew Australian identity and secure the nation's future – plans that focused on social and urban renewal, commitment to equity in education and healthcare and repositioning of Australia's international relationships – to voter's priorities.

This was echoed in the Labor marketing document, where election victory was predicted to come from leadership based on listening to the people, and responding through the party's communications campaign. The plan to address Labor's personality problems combined pragmatism and idealism. With NSW as a test case, it proposed communications training for candidates in key electorates and set out media appearances week by week. Famously, it also outlined a multistage advertising plan that would begin by re-introducing Whitlam, projecting 'pure image' and then using this as a bridge to communicate 'logical policy information' (Shirley et al. 1971, 17). This would become *It's Time*, an advertising campaign whose central song remains Australia's best-known political jingle. Labor's marketing strategists commissioned it to have the characteristics of a Top 40 hit, hoping it would gain independent airplay and provide the ALP with free advertising. Sung by 21-year-old rock singer Alison MacCallum, the lyrics tapped into a feeling of unrest in the electorate without referring directly to Labor, Whitlam, or the upcoming election:

> It's time for freedom, It's time for moving, It's time to begin, Yes It's time
> It's time Australia, It's time for moving, It's time for proving, Yes It's time

Accompanying the television advertising, a new high profile role was also envisaged for Margaret Whitlam, showcasing her intelligence (as a contrast with Sonia McMahon who was 'not noted for her high IQ') (Shirley et al. 1971, 53). It was hoped that this, which included a series of electorate tea parties with Mrs Whitlam, would draw attention to the opposition leader's human side. This strategy was to be tested through a series of proposed focus groups in key NSW marginal electorates and adjusted accordingly as the election wore on.

Such detailed planning might seem at odds with the mythology of *It's Time* as a pure campaign of ideas. But the nostalgic longing for passionate off-the-cuff speeches delivered at packed public meetings distracts from the key question: is a leader speaking to voters' concerns and engaging them in a conversation about the nation's future? Does their vision of a secure Australian future resonate with voters' own deeply held, complex and multilayered notions of individual and collective identity? Labor's 1972 campaign was meticulously planned to address the frustrations some voters felt after more than two decades of conservative government, and drew on long-established themes. The language had a strong political pedigree: when Menzies' new Liberal Party swept into power in 1949, it was with the slogan *It's Time for a Change*.[2] In 1963 Whitlam's predecessor, Arthur Calwell (1963), told voters, 'It is time for a change. It is more than time for a change – it is time to give Australia a chance'. This reminds us that elections aren't waged in a vacuum. When voters listen to politicians make promises, watch their appearances on morning television, and read their campaign emails and tweets, they make judgements that take into account what they've been promised in previous years. They think about the conversations they've had with friends and family, and what they've seen, heard or experienced that has cultivated their trust or made them wary. Labor's task, as the 1972 election approached, was to give this ongoing conversation with voters a new sense of urgency. If there was an *opportunity* for change in 1969, in 1972 it was *time*.

Labor's planning showed a keen awareness of the potential power of political coverage that carried through to the campaign. This was evident in the carefully placed newspaper and television advertisements that accompanied the campaign, and exploited every time Whitlam stepped out onto the stage to deliver a speech with lights flashing and music playing. This was a campaign designed to appeal to the demands of television coverage and broadcast news, which understood that journalism's role was more complex than the straightforward transmission of messages to audiences. Australians are typically enthusiastic adopters of new technology. Television was introduced

---

[2] For more on this campaign, see Crawford (2004).

in 1956, and industry body *FreeTV* (2015) estimates that by 1960 70 per cent of homes in Melbourne and Sydney had a television set. That number had grown to 90 per cent of homes in established markets by the mid-1960s. While the 1972 campaign was the first to take full advantage of television as a medium of image, emotion and celebrity it was the Liberals' 1963 campaign that ushered in the era of televised politics. Prime Minister Menzies broke new ground by delivering his policy speech straight to camera, with no live audience. Although he claimed to be uncomfortable with the new medium he was, as noted in Chapter 5, a 'superb television performer' (Freudenberg 2005, 25; 209). The *Canberra Times* (1963, 1) estimated that his pre-recorded 40 minute speech reached five million people.

Labor's *It's Time* campaign built on the experiences of the previous decade and deliberately harnessed television's perceived ability to command viewers' attention and foster direct connection. McMahon also attempted to embrace the medium but was unable to match Labor's energy and enthusiasm. The Liberals filmed McMahon's policy launch speech from a mock-up of the prime minister's desk at the Channel Nine studios in North Sydney, and edited it with still images into a package broadcast the following evening (Oakes and Solomon 1973, 176–77). The *Sydney Morning Herald* (1972, 1) featured an awkward photograph of McMahon watching the broadcast from his home in Sydney's affluent Bellevue Hill. The prime minister looks elderly and patrician, sitting in his easy chair with his glamorous wife perched on the arm, with the headline 'McMahon aims for the young' running somewhat incongruously above (*Sydney Morning Herald* 1972, 1). Contrasting this domestic scene with Labor's celebrity-filled launch clarifies how important it is to understand the demands of, and be comfortable with, new media formats. Political journalist and author George Megalogenis (2010b) has argued that changes in media technology influence the way that prime ministers communicate with the electorate, and that 'really big changes' can help to make new governments dominant. Megalogenis is not arguing for a direct alignment of changes of government with media developments. Rather, his insight points to a dynamic that arises when a new opposition leader or prime minister embraces a new technology, often gaining unchallenged access to the audience it opens up. While the technology itself does not affect the ultimate goal of campaign communication (to connect with voters in order to secure their support) the ability to exploit new media formats and genres *can* influence effectiveness. As policy launches creep ever closer to election day, an innovative media campaign helps engage voters in a sustained conversation about a party's policy vision for the nation, or present an alternate narrative of the future of Australian identity.

    This longer-term commitment to a public conversation meant that *It's Time* was more than a catchy slogan. It stood in for a range of Labor's policies and plans for the future as well as the Whitlam candidacy, in the same way that *It's Time for a Change* did in 1949. Without this deeper dialogue, campaign promises can be hollow and fall flat. In 2010, for example, both the Labor government and Liberal opposition struggled to connect to a public still reeling from a year of dramatic political changes, and their slogans *Moving Forward* and *Real Action* reflected this. A successful vision campaign needs to combine big-picture ideas with a detailed, personal narrative, fitting policy proposals into each voter's central question: What will my life be like if I vote for you?

It's Time

Gough Whitlam was a political speaker who commanded attention. His undeniably Australian voice had a tone ideal for broadcast: crisp and clearly understood without sounding too rehearsed. This style was well suited to the televised policy launch, a big ticket speech that needed to inspire the live audience while also reaching out to those tuning in at home. Whitlam could boom to supporters crammed into the back of a public meeting, and also be intimate and engaging. Delivering Labor's 1972 policy speech, on 13 November, he used Curtin's preferred method of address both to appeal to voters through collective identity and to situate himself firmly within the Labor tradition:

> Men and women of Australia! The decision we will make for our country on 2 December is a choice between the past and the future, between the habits and fears of the past, and the demands and opportunities of the future. There are moments in history when the whole fate and future of nations can be decided by a single decision. For Australia, this is such a time. (Whitlam 1972)

Whitlam's language invited emotional, rather than purely rational, responses; with a sense of urgency, he called on voters to understand that the nation's future was at stake. If this was a vital time in Australian history then each and every voter had a role to play in deciding 'the whole fate and future' of the nation. Whitlam received a rapturous hearing from the 1,400 supporters crammed into the 1,100 capacity hall (Oakes and Solomon 1973, 162). Choice of venue is not incidental in policy launches, and speaking from the Blacktown Civic Centre (in Sydney's western suburbs) reinforced Whitlam's commitment to urban renewal, his understanding of the struggles and hopes of those Australians imagined (in positive terms) as *ordinary*. Here Whitlam (1972) drew on the rhythm and rhetoric of Labor's campaign advertising:

It's time for a new team, a new program, a new drive for equality of opportunities. It's time to create new opportunities for Australians, time for a new vision of what we can achieve in this generation for our nation and the region in which we live. It's time for a new government – a Labor government.

This is an explicit vision narrative of Australian identity that locates the security of that identity in bold, challenging ideas of change. Whitlam called on voters to see their own future happiness and the future of their collective values and priorities as reliant on their voting decision. To do so, he drew on a longer-term conversation built on detailed policy discussions and positions and connected both to shared cultural constructions of Australian identity. Whitlam's compelling opening was accompanied by 140 specific policy and reform proposals built around the key themes of domestic and international renewal. The *Age* (Barnes 1972, 1) described it as a 'cornucopia of promises', but noted that nearly a third of the 35-page long speech was edited out for the broadcast. Even in 1972 the ALP was aware that hours of policy detail, no matter how significant ('a Federal Labor Government will introduce a universal health insurance scheme'), would not play well for the television audience. Instead, Whitlam's speech, which he had worked on with Graham Freudenberg, was the centrepiece of a televised launch filled with colour. The audience was scattered with celebrities such as singers Little Pattie and Col Joye, writer Tom Keneally, and artist Clinton Pugh, as well as comedians and footballers. There were banners, flashing lights, and *It's Time* was playing on loop. The presentation and the content came together to promise that Whitlam's vision of a new and changing Australian future would remedy voters' feelings of lethargy in a way his opponents could not. This was an effective campaign strategy that Labor would seek to reprise more than three decades later.

My Vision is Very Simple

In 2007 the ALP conducted a vision campaign driven by an extended public and political discussion of their plans for Australia's future. In its style and execution, it recalled the innovative, passionate political battle waged by the party in the late sixties and early seventies. The *Kevin07* campaign saw Labor move into government after more than a decade in the political wilderness. It seemed, at the time, to reflect a fundamental shift in the country's social and cultural landscape; and it was the beginning of a period of political instability unprecedented in modern Australian political history.

In the years that followed *Kevin07*, Australians' relationship with Kevin Rudd evolved, impacted by a dramatic series of political scandals and events.

This was a time of upheaval mirrored only in the earliest years following Australian Federation. The Labor government changed leaders (and prime ministers) two years into Rudd's first term after a dramatic turnaround in the polls; won minority government in 2010 under their new prime minister, Julia Gillard; and reinstated her predecessor in June of 2013, only to see Rudd lose the prime ministership again in an election only months later. Media analyses, political judgements and insider accounts chronicled Rudd's fall from grace throughout this time: he appears as the unconventional Labor leader who lacked clear factional allegiances; the bureaucratic know-it-all who governed from the prime minister's desk. He was the prime minister unable to engage the electorate in an effective conversation about the government's agenda once in office; the advocate for climate change action who had abandoned the emissions trading scheme. He was the popularity-driven 'celebrity' politician (Wilson 2014) who embraced the art of the 'selfie' (Vanstone 2013; Leys 2013, 1). He was a leader whose personality flaws drove his colleagues to replace him when his poll numbers faltered[3]; the strategic 'saboteur' (Jensen 2013) who mounted a lengthy campaign to regain the prime ministership and then swiftly lost to Tony Abbott.

In the wake of the dramatic events that characterized Labor's two terms in office, it is easy to forget how effective a communicator Rudd was in 2007. It is easy to lose sight of the compelling story he told in his first campaign about the nation's future and his popularity with the voters he inspired to bring Labor out of the electoral wilderness. This popularity can be attributed, in no small part, to the way his campaign now-famously 'embraced social media platforms', demonstrating an understanding of their 'importance [...] in mobilising support among voters' (Burgess and Bruns 2012, 386). Rudd's media savvy approach to voter connection would reappear in brief flashes at unexpected moments, a powerful reminder of the resilience of the relationships that can be forged between a political leader's vision for the nation and citizens' hopes for the future.

One such moment was a press conference at Brisbane Airport, on 24 February 2012. Rudd had just flown in from Washington DC, where he'd resigned as Australia's foreign minister in a dramatic 1:20 am press conference. The former prime minister, and now former foreign minister, was in his

---

[3] Nicola Roxon spoke of a man who 'wasn't prepared to ask for advice' and treated staff poorly (Ireland 2012); Tony Burke told *7:30*'s Chris Uhlmann that Rudd was leading an 'undermining campaign', and that the stories 'of the chaos, of the temperament, of the inability to have decisions made' of the Rudd government were more than simply stories (in *7:30* 2012); while Wayne Swan released a statement expressing party room frustrations with Rudd: his 'dysfunctional decision making' and 'deeply demeaning attitude towards other people', his sabotage of the 2010 campaign and undermining of the Gillard government 'at every turn' (Swan 2012).

element as he faced a gaggle of journalists assembled at Brisbane Airport. His prepared statement was littered with references to the 2010 'midnight coup' when his deputy Julia Gillard had informed him she would challenge for the Labor leadership, and prime ministership, in the party room the next morning. Reacting skittishly to falling poll numbers, a majority of the Labor caucus pledged their support for Gillard. Without the numbers Rudd did not contest the challenge and Gillard was elected unopposed, ending Rudd's time as prime minister just over two years into his first term. In Brisbane, he told reporters that the 'shenanigans of the last few days' and attempts to discredit him reminded him of the 'shock and awe tactics' used in June 2010. When he called for questions he was instantly drowned out by the shouts of reporters all asking the same thing: will you challenge Julia Gillard for the leadership at Labor's caucus meeting? Rudd refused to answer. The consummate showman, he saved that announcement for a second press conference later in the day.

Months of media speculation had made this leadership spill seem inevitable. The *should Labor bring back Rudd?* question was a convenient way to talk about a prime minister who lacked conviction and legitimacy after her failure to win a majority in the 2010 election. The seeming effectiveness of Opposition Leader Tony Abbott's attacks on her minority government, and Labor's uninspiring poll numbers raised the inevitable question about whether replacing Rudd had been a mistake, and whether Labor's chances at the next election would be boosted by returning him to power. When he did challenge the prime minister a few days later, he lost the leadership ballot 71 votes to 31; he would need to wait until June to following year to mount a successful leadership bid. However, in the moments in Brisbane where Rudd spoke of something other than his betrayal by Labor's 'faceless men', there were flashes of the man who had won a historic victory in the 2007 election. Rudd (2012) called for 'some plain speaking about our country's future'. He emphasized that his actions in public life were driven by his enduring 'vision' for Australia:

> My vision is very simple. How do we prepare Australia for the huge challenges that we face in the future given the uncertain world in which we live, and how do we do so in a way which never ever throws the fair go, as I used to say, out the back door. (Rudd 2012)

This language recalled Rudd of 2007, who connected with the electorate when it mattered and made his vision of a 'fair go for all' relevant to the concerns and priorities of the people he dubbed Australia's 'working families' (Younane 2008).

You Make Your Own Luck

In April 2007, Kevin Rudd (in Ferguson 2015) had introduced himself to the ALP conference with a wave and a grin: 'My name's Kevin, I'm from Queensland and I'm here to help'. Here was a neat snapshot of the informal relationship he would seek to establish with voters. Every interview, speech and press conference Rudd gave between becoming leader in December 2006 and winning the November 2007 election was part of this 'getting to know you' process. His personal story was the platform from which he discussed his plans for the nation's future; his own ostensibly ordinary persona the mechanism through which he would lay claim to broader narratives of Australian identity.

Rudd had been building this public profile as he rose from diplomat to bureaucrat to member of parliament. 'Kevin from Queensland' was already a familiar figure for voters in early 2007, despite only having beaten Kim Beazley for the job of opposition leader a few months earlier. Elected in 1998 to the Brisbane seat of Griffith, he served as Labor's shadow foreign minister from 2001, and his growing national profile got a boost when he joined a weekly segment on Channel Seven's morning program *Sunrise*. In the brightly coloured studio, amongst breaking news bulletins and cheery celebrity guests, Rudd faced off against a Liberal opponent in the 'Big Guns of Politics' segment. Joe Hockey soon became his regular adversary, and hosts Mel and Kochie asked the big guns about everything from political scandals and government policies to sports news and celebrity gossip.

Sunrise served a vital purpose. It allowed Rudd to work outside of the scrutiny of the Press Gallery and develop a relationship with the people who would become his core constituency. Younger voters and working families were central to his election pitch: if talkback radio listeners were Howard's domain (Turner 2009, 422), then Rudd would make the FM radio and popular television audience his own. Polls in the lead up to the election showed Rudd had the support of more than 50 per cent of young voters; 40 per cent of voters aged 18 to 34 supported Labor on election day (Hollins 2011). As *Sunrise*'s ratings and popularity grew so did Rudd and Hockey's political profiles. Christine Jackman (2008, 30–31), in her insider account of the 2007 election, sees this as the time when Rudd 'learned to relax' in the public eye; for his staff, it was his chance to develop domestic policy credentials to bolster his foreign policy expertise. The segment continued until mid-April 2007 when new roles as opposition leader and workplace relations minister made continuing (in Rudd's words) 'too hard' (*Sydney Morning Herald* 2007a).[4]

---

[4] There was speculation that a minor controversy over the timing of a pre-dawn Anzac Day broadcast from Vietnam alerted both to PR issues with continuing (Grattan 2008, 41).

Kevin, Therese and the kids seemed refreshingly normal throughout 2007 when Australians read Rudd's 'award-winning' chocolate cake recipe in the *Women's Weekly* or watched the family relaxing at home on *Today Tonight* (Davis 2007). Voters were encouraged to think of this potential prime minister as 'Kevin'; this was what Mel, Kochie and his enthusiastic team of colleagues and recruits called him. 'Kevin' was a normal Aussie bloke with a compelling personal and political story to tell: things are changing, the Howard government is out of touch, and I have the 'fresh thinking' approach we need. Articulated with clarity, it was a reassuring message that made space for so-called ordinary Australians and the things that concerned them after more than a decade of Coalition government.

Rudd's attempt to bond with voters through the language of individual and collective identity was clearest on Australia Day 2007. The ALP (2007) released a slick 'getting to know you' television ad. It is a powerful 90 seconds of political communication, which previewed the themes and messages of Rudd's upcoming campaign. In the ad, the Labor leader wanders wistfully around his childhood hometown. This is the part of 'country Australia', Rudd tells the audience, where he was raised. The fair-skinned, bespectacled Labor leader looks only slightly awkward as he leans against a paddock fence post, his cream slacks impeccably pressed and his pale open-neck shirt clean and crisp. He gestures to the small schoolhouse where he got a good education 'by the standards of that time', establishing his rural roots (Rudd in ALP 2007). Faded family photos alternate with Rudd's to-camera monologue, underscoring that his political message comes from personal experience. This is a technique North American communications scholar Nicholas O'Shaugnessy (1990, 241) has identified as central to political marketing, allowing a candidate to 'connect with majority values'. While this doesn't mean that the candidate must literally have been 'born in a log cabin', they must demonstrate that they experience 'common emotion with uncommon intensity'; often playing on 'whatever suburban anxieties happen to be uppermost' while also communicating 'a fierce patriotism'. Once Rudd established his credentials in this way, the ad shifts gear and asks voters to think about the challenges their kids will face in the future. The lucky country's beaches and outback disappear when Rudd (in ALP 2007) tells the audience that he believes we 'make our own luck', and suddenly the images shift to classrooms and science labs while he talks about his plan for an education revolution. Australia is going to 'take on the world' by having the best-trained people, not by cutting wages and conditions.

This was a critique of the Liberals' unpopular WorkChoices industrial relations laws, which had been passed in 2005 when Howard's government commanded a majority in the Senate as well as the House of Representatives.

Labor had painted the laws as a betrayal of Howard's core so-called battler constituency, a fundamentally unfair attack on trade unions and ordinary Australians. Their narrative was reinforced by the *Your Rights at Work* advertising campaign, run by the Australian Council of Trade Unions and estimated to have cost $30 million (Muir 2008, 40). These ads featured Australians talking about how they had suffered under the laws, and ran throughout the 2007 election. WorkChoices framed the campaign narrative, and Rudd's opposition to the laws lent potency to his constant references to 'working families' and 'fairness'. The final seconds of the Australia Day ad crystallized the message that would take Rudd to election victory: 'The Australia I want for the future has a strong economy but one where we don't throw the fair go out the back door'. This opened up the themes that dominated Rudd's media appearances throughout 2007, a conversation from which to engage a constituency based on fairness, education and competitiveness. The ad was also slick piece of image management that defined Rudd's values and personality in the minds of voters. The key would be to turn the anti-WorkChoices rhetoric into a positive vision for the future that would last once the votes were counted and the new government was sworn in.

Fresh Thinking

Kevin Rudd drew on this year-long conversation with the Australian electorate when he stood at the lectern to deliver Labor's 2007 policy launch speech. The speech wove the strands of this dialogue together to paint the ALP as uniquely qualified to deal with the challenges of the future. His message echoed 1972 but his style reflected the changes that were an outcome of an ever-evolving media and political landscape (Young 2011, 259–78). Where Whitlam presented policy detail Rudd used broad brushstrokes. He began by re-asserting his own connection to the Australian community, his link to Queensland standing in for Australians' personal lived experiences of belonging. This anchored Rudd as he opened by welcoming those in the room, and the wider media audience, to his 'home state', his 'home town' and his 'local community'. He addressed his big picture narrative:

> It is great to be among people who are passionate about our country's future. On November 24, Australians will face a stark choice: a choice between the future and the past. Today the case I put before the Australian people is that if we are to secure the future for our families, for our communities and for our nation – the government of Australia must now change. (Rudd 2007c)

All of Rudd's central themes are in his first paragraph, ready to be lifted out and replayed in a short grab on the television news, or easily quoted in online news coverage. This is an important election, the choices we make will matter if we are to 'secure the future', and only a change of government that will achieve this. Rudd appealed to the electorate across levels of connection: family, local community and national identity. He argued that Prime Minister Howard 'simply doesn't understand the new challenges that we face in the future' (Rudd 2007c). Listing these, Rudd not only painted his opponent as backwards, but also fleshed out the priorities of his own vision: climate change and water; the 'digital economy'; the rise of China and India; fixing 'our hospitals'; and, above all, transforming 'our education system'. These priorities allowed Rudd to position himself within the Labor tradition as protector of Australian values and identity. If Rudd's Australia was to face these challenges, it needed to draw on long-held values which Rudd saw as distinctively *Labor*: taking advantage of opportunity while remembering that 'fairness is in our DNA'.

WorkChoices was the lens through which Rudd's assurances about fairness for those constructed as working families were to be viewed. John Howard had loomed as an unbeatable opponent over the precious decade, a wily operator whose connection to so-called everyday Australians meant Labor was exiled to the electoral wilderness. But the unpopularity of WorkChoices offered Labor a chance. In the style of contemporary big ticket speeches, Rudd fit already announced policies into his broader vision. These were the smaller scale personal concerns that helped voters to see the 'challenges of the future' as relevant to their own lives: help with family budgets; education and childcare tax rebates; dental care reform; a grocery price enquiry and Petrol Price Commissioner; healthcare reform; plans to deal with water shortages, to update infrastructure, to invest in broadband.

Rudd drew a clear contrast, here, between a Labor Party bursting with ideas to take the nation forward and a government that had 'run out of energy' and 'run out of time'. He painted Howard as a relic; someone who thought giving laptops to students was an 'exotic' idea. This played on Howard's halting forays into social media throughout the year. His awkward YouTube announcement of a new climate change policy on 16 July and relatively friendless Facebook page demonstrated a lack of comfort with social networking and other digital technologies.[5] Rudd, on the other hand, was much more comfortable on social digital platforms[6], and reached Facebook's 5,000 friend limit so quickly supporters were restricted to liking his page rather than 'friending' him personally (Walliker 2007). These strategies would also characterize Rudd's next

---

[5] See Flew (2008) for a more detailed discussion; also Burgess and Bruns (2012, 386).
[6] This would continue and would characterize his public profile in the tumultuous political time ahead – his time as foreign minister, on the backbench, and again as prime minister.

campaign as prime minister: in 2013, Labor 'used digital media in a more informal way to interact with its supporters', while the Liberals' 'emphasis was on provision of information' (Taylor 2013).

As opposition leader Rudd spoke the language of the future: a need to invest in 'twenty-first-century infrastructure'; a plan for an 'education revolution'. He asked voters to see his vision as a reflection of his life story, a coincidence between the values of his upbringing and his party that would also reflect their own personal experience:

> I would not be standing here before you today were it not for the encouragement, instruction and opportunity provided to me by the teachers who shaped my life. They made it possible for a kid like me from country Queensland to finish school, go to university, become a diplomat and stand here today seeking to lead our nation into the future. (Rudd 2007c)

An Australia that offered this education and these opportunities for a 'kid' like Kevin was an Australia that could face the challenges of the future. Rudd's Australia would be 'a leader in the global fight against poverty, disease and underdevelopment – starting right here in our own region, our own neighbourhood, our own backyard'. This was an Australian future that voters could be proud to be part of; and importantly, Rudd would deliver the 'new leadership' to make it happen.

Popularity Contest

The *Kevin07* campaign embraced commercial television and radio, social networking and digital technology to communicate Rudd's message to a new constituency. Australian political scientist Sally Young (2008, 71) notes that Rudd gave more than 40 FM radio interviews during the campaign, in stark contrast with the prime minister who gave only one in response to the hosts' 'running segment on their failed attempts to get Howard to appear'. In these appearances, Rudd spoke to breakfast and drive-time crews in brief interviews that were considerably lighter than traditional news or current affairs programs. He gave seven FM radio interviews on the final day of the campaign alone, and also made a much-publicized appearance on late night chat show *Rove*. His opponent stuck to his tried-and-true AM and talkback strategy, appealing to the constituency that had helped keep his party in power for just over a decade. Partly reflecting the personalities of the two leaders, this also reflected their positions as challenger and incumbent. Joe Trippi (2004), who is often credited with pioneering online grassroots campaigning for Howard Dean's tilt at the 2004 US Democratic nomination, argues while incumbents will usually use well-tested campaign strategies, it is the challenger who is able to push the boundaries. Rudd's strategy was praised for its groundbreaking use of social and digital media to engage young voters, but also critiqued as lowest common denominator politics devoid of serious policy discussion. Veteran ABC political journalist and host of the Sunday morning politics panel program *Insiders* Barrie Cassidy (Green 2007), perhaps stung by Rudd's refusals to appear on his own show, accused the opposition leader of deliberately avoiding 'detailed scrutiny as best he can'.

Kevin07's challenger strategy was built to match Rudd's message. It painted Rudd as the voice of a new generation while simultaneously making his opponent look out of touch. The website invited visitors to become 'part of the K07 community': 'Here at KEVIN07, we're doing things differently. We want to hear from you – your ideas, hopes and concerns. Have your say.' *Kevin07* combined new media technology with elements of more traditional grassroots campaigning to give Labor's campaign the feel of a community-led movement. These strategies have a legacy, both in Australia and elsewhere; in 1972 the ALP used a 'send us a dollar' advertising campaign to encourage voters to feel invested in the cause. *Kevin07*'s invitations for voters to make small donations, buy t-shirts and bumper stickers and share their ideas for the nation's future had a similar motivation. Despite its presidential focus on Rudd as leader, the *Kevin07* campaign made space for voters to feel involved; a strategy that would become immortalized in the following year in Democratic senator Barack Obama's 'hope and change', grassroots-focused campaign for the American presidency.

The creativity of this innovative strategy, which encouraged voters to feel ownership of the campaign and of the vision of the Australian future it projected, did not extend to the campaigns that followed. In 2010, Julia Gillard made a valiant if uninspiring effort to engage with social media, occasionally answering questions tweeted to her by supporters, while Tony Abbott tweeted less than ten times across the entire campaign. The 2013 election pitted a resurrected Kevin Rudd (restored to the prime ministership after three years out of the job) against Opposition Leader Tony Abbott in his second campaign in the role. But despite Rudd's use of selfies, and Abbott's engagement on Facebook, the campaign was flat in content and execution. In 2016, the parties made a more significant investment of energy and resources in their social media strategies, culminating in a Facebook Leaders' Debate which was hosted by the social networking site and News Corp Australia website news.com.au, and broadcast live on both – a significant development despite low viewer numbers.[7] This is an indication that the safe media strategies employed by both sides of politics in the campaigns immediately following *Kevin07* simply signal a lull in innovation in media strategy. More broadly, the lacklustre nature of these campaigns should not be read as the demise of the *vision* election. Rather, campaigns based on a vision for the nation's future require a coming together of the right leader, the right moment and the right message. Even those leaders that get it right, as the 'relaxed and comfortable' John Howard did in 1996, can lose this connection if the times and the electorate change.

An Iced VoVo and a Strong Cup of Tea

In 2007, Labor marked its historic victory with a party in the Members' Dining Room at Suncorp Stadium, home of local rugby league team the Brisbane Broncos. Rudd was beaming as he entered a room of cheering supporters, their cries competing with rock music being played over the sound system. He was perfectly groomed, and his photogenic family was in tow. The crowd was ecstatic. Labor had won the night and it was looking likely that their star recruit, former ABC journalist Maxine McKew, would knock Prime Minister John Howard off his perch in the Sydney seat of Bennelong.

This was a moment of triumph, and celebration was expected. Perhaps Rudd would reprise Paul Keating's 'true believers' rhetoric from 1993, reclaim the mantle of the 'light on the hill' or raise his fists in the air Rocky-style in recognition of his knockout blow. But as he stepped to the lectern, Rudd's first move was to call for calm; and the longer he spoke the damper the mood became. He delivered all the standard lines without poetry or passion. As he listed plans for government and thanked a seemingly endless list of supporters ('our party president, the national campaign team, my fantastic staff, a fantastic local team, my life partner Therese, my wonderful kids'), his managerial style evoked a CEO at a shareholder meeting rather than a political leader celebrating victory or re-articulating

---

[7] The 'Facebook debate' was the third leaders' debate of the 2016 campaign, and offered voters the opportunity to submit questions via social media as well as giving the small audience of undecided voters access to the two leaders. It was streamed on Facebook Live and news.com.au and had a live audience of approximately 120,000 (Gartrell 2016). Billed as Australia's first 'online leaders' debate', it followed two previous encournters between the leaders: the Sky News/*Daily Telegraph* People's Forum at the Windsor RSL, in western Sydney (featuring an audience of undecided voters asking questions, this is becoming a staple of Australian campaigns) and more traditional televised Leaders' Debate, held at the National Press Club (featuring a panel of journalists).

his vision. Labor, he pledged, would work hard to 'prosecute this agenda of work for the nation':

> We're ready for the long haul. You can have a strong cup of tea if you want in the meantime; even an Iced VoVo on the way through. The celebrations should stop there. We have a job of work to do. (Rudd 2007e)

Somewhere between the final votes being tallied and this passionless victory speech, *Kevin07* morphed into Kevin 24/7. Throughout 2008 and 2009 he developed a reputation for his workaholic tendencies. However, this was not what plagued Rudd, nor were rumours about his temper (tales in the news media that had him screaming at an RAAF flight attendant when he wasn't served a hot meal or throwing a tantrum on a trip to Afghanistan because he didn't have access to a hairdryer). Australians seemed willing to forgive their policy wonk prime minister so long as he remained a man of conviction. The early fulfilment of campaign promises to sign the Kyoto protocol and apologize to the Stolen Generations gave Rudd a Teflon-coating. At the end of March 2009, the *Brisbane Times* reported a *Herald*/Nielsen poll with the headline: 'The Rudd Supremacy' (Coorey 2009). With a 74 per cent approval rating he was the second-most popular prime minister since Bob Hawke, and had trounced Opposition Leader Malcolm Turnbull in the preferred prime minister stakes, 69 to 24 per cent (Coorey 2009).

This support began to waver as the year wore on, as Rudd and his team failed to prosecute the case for the things that really mattered to them and to the country. A vision for the nation, while often at its most vibrant during the campaign, needs to stretch beyond election night. To be effective, it must be a commitment between the leader and the electorate that animates policy decisions and drives the decisions of the government. After his 1972 election victory, Gough Whitlam continued to argue for the *It's Time* agenda even as the support of his colleagues and the public wavered. James Walter (1980, 171–75), in his political biography of Whitlam, dissects his personal characteristics in detail: the commitment to the pursuit of knowledge, professionalism and sense of the importance of language that saw him rise to the prime ministership; and the impatience, confrontational style and preoccupation with image that were a hindrance as well as a help. One stands out: Whitlam's commitment to stand by his vision for the nation. Walter (1980, 172) paints Whitlam as 'inflexible in his determination that the people had given him a mandate precisely for those decisions encapsulated in the 1972 policy speech'. Even after his government was dismissed and then failed to win re-election in 1975 Whitlam stayed on as opposition leader, fighting another unsuccessful campaign in 1977 before stepping aside. This was a leader who 'knew what he wanted for society [...] and refused to indulge in politicking about its essentials' (Walter 1980, 175).

His National Press Club speech during the 1977 campaign drew on the same vision of a just and equitable Australia that voters had heard since 1969. He argued that returning to Labor's policies was essential if Australia was to avoid losing 'its last chance of salvaging the hopes of a generation'. This was as much a comment on the values and priorities of Australian society as it was a critique of the government's failure on issues like joblessness. Whitlam (1977) appealed directly to voters' 'sense of obligation' to their fellow citizens who were 'being damaged so severely, so needlessly by present policies'.

Where Whitlam presented a consistent social and political vision for the nation over nearly a decade, Kevin Rudd's 'bond with the people began to fray' in December 2009 (Marr 2010, 2), after world leaders failed to deliver a comprehensive climate change treaty at the Copenhagen Conference of the Parties. That bond was torn apart four months later when his government announced the indefinite postponement of the Emissions Trading Scheme that had been a key feature of its first term policy agenda. David Marr's (2010, 86) Quarterly Essay, *Power Trip*, painted a vivid image of a deeply driven man, who had come through an emotionally challenging childhood with a 'rage at his core' that shaped his personality and defined his political values. Marr's eloquent examination of Rudd came at a time when the prime minister was visibly frustrated in his media appearances and unable to clearly articulate his government's agenda. The Rudd who had seemingly abandoned the 'greatest moral, economic and environmental challenge of our time' (van Onselen 2010) was a long way from *Sunrise* Kevin, and Marr (2010, 3) describes the savage reaction from the people and the polls:

> His leadership was in question. Rudd had sold himself to the Australian people as a new kind of leader: a man of intellect and values out to reshape the future. If he isn't that, people are asking, what is he? And who is he?'

Power Trip was published only three weeks before Rudd's replacement, but in documenting Kevin from Queensland's rise to power it also identified the very reason for his fall. Rudd's dominance in the Labor Party, for Marr (2010, 5), was 'first and foremost about the polls'. It was achieved by overcoming the qualms of some in his own party by 'appealing directly to the Australian people'. This was a strategy Rudd used again in his opening press conference of the 2013 election. Rudd (2013a) spoke of his own goal to bring 'the nation together behind a positive plan', contrasting his approach with his opponent's 'which tends instead to rip the country apart and polarise it'. Tapping into the common-sense narrative that Tony Abbott had embraced a negative style of politics as opposition leader, Rudd (2013a) worked to link his own positive approach to Australian values, arguing that this alignment would ensure the ongoing security and prosperity of that identity:

> Australians by their nature are a positive, practical people who believe in nation building and that approach is part and parcel of the values, ideas and policies we bring to bear for Australia's future.

Rudd's own personal vision and optimism mirrors Australians' hopes for the future here; a construction reliant on the establishment of a particular and unique connection between Rudd and his constituency. Rudd retained a deep faith in his own enduring popularity, in the relationship that had been built on familiarity, likeability and the promise to deliver Australia into a new future. This was based, in part, on the events of the past; Rudd (2013a) argued that Australians had 'seen me at my highest highs, and some of my lowest lows' and that 'as a result, you the Australian people, know me pretty well – warts and all'. At stake in 2013, he argued, was the same vision for the nation he had fought for in 2007, and that he and his government had relinquished in the second half of 2009; Australians needed to trust both in his vision, and his ability to deliver.

Chapter 8

HEARTS AND MINDS

> The essence of a speech is that it should reach the hearts and minds of our immediate audience. It must therefore be made *to* them, and not merely in their presence.
>
> Robert Menzies, *New York Times Magazine*,
> 28 November 1948

The words spoken by campaigning leaders throughout Australia's electoral history provide an invaluable, and often overlooked, window into contemporary national political, social and cultural life. Across elections, parties and politicians, the constructions of Australian identity analysed in this book provided *identity security* for voters. Campaigning leaders offered their constituents a chance to feel at home within, and in control of, the national space. Operating in cycles of anxiety and reassurance, these leaders reacted to the issues of the time while also evoking those of an imagined shared past. Speechwriter Graham Freudenberg (2005, 272) has argued that the issues that dominate Australia's contemporary political life are always about 'our history', and that 'the party political struggle increasingly involves a contest about who and by whom that history shall be interpreted'. This, then, is the key to understanding

> contemporary debate on the American alliance, the republic, our obligations under the United Nations charter, immigration, multiculturalism, Aboriginal rights, the stolen generations, reconciliation, Pauline Hanson's One Nation, industrial relations and the future of unionism. Even the great national celebrations, the Olympic Games, the Centenary of Federation, Australia Day and Anzac Day have been mobilised for service in Australia's history wars. In no other nation is that war carried on with deeper intensity. (Freudenberg 2005, 272)

This political 'struggle' is not just about the stories told about the past, and the flashpoints Freudenberg mentions could be updated to reflect those of any era. Rather, it reflects a much more immediate concern about who Australians are today. The enduring desire of campaigning political leaders to develop a meaningful discourse of Australian identity demonstrates the way in which constructions of the nation's collective past can offer a sense of belonging and ownership in its present and future. The battle for ownership of this discourse has played out in federal election campaigns since Federation.

Spoken language – the words political leaders speak to journalists, to each other and to their constituents – remains at the heart of mediatized election campaigns. This language is not in decline in Australia; nor is it dull or boring when compared to a fondly remembered 'golden age' of campaigning (Hudson 1978; Corcoran 1979; Watson 1995; Glover 2007). Of course, not every election is dynamic and engaging as those contested by the most effective speechmakers in our political history or at critical moments of change have been. However, leaders' campaign language has been, and continues to be, a powerful emotive mechanism of identification, even when it is mundane and banal – as Menzies's reference to 'hearts and minds', which was first introduced in Chapter 1 and which opens this chapter, evokes. It aims (and often succeeds) to speak to voters' lived experience, evoking a shared sense of Australian identity and reassuring them about their own belonging within that identity.

Campaigns themselves have changed dramatically since Federation, as has the media landscape in which they take place. The 'immediate audience' for political speech, as Menzies might have imagined it in 1948, has been dramatically extended and the volume of campaign speech has exploded. These trends have intensified in the last three decades alongside a diversification of other kinds of campaign communication and political coverage and are not limited to campaigns. As Dennis Grube (2013, 9) has noted in *Prime Ministers and Rhetorical Governance*, 'in many ways in the 21st century, to talk is to govern'. In 1901, candidates spoke at frequent political meetings and gave newspaper interviews where they defended their own plans and policies and attacked those of their opponents. On any given day during contemporary campaigns, however, leaders now communicate across different media and different states. For example, on 8 November 2007, Prime Minister John Howard gave a press conference with Treasurer Peter Costello in Melbourne, a radio interview on the ABC's national current affairs morning program, *AM*, and two doorstop interviews on interest rates. On the same day, Opposition Leader Kevin Rudd bookended his day with two national television interviews, on Channel Nine's *Today* show and the ABC's *Lateline*, gave a doorstop interview at a NSW hospital and was also interviewed for ABC Radio's *AM*. The ever increasing volume of words and messages help leaders shape campaign narratives in the era of the mediatized campaign, while also intensifying the competition for free media coverage. This competition plays out in the broader context of a 'high-choice' media environment in which, as Gibson and McAllister (2015, 339) identify, 'the rapid expansion of high-speed internet has had a major impact on the availability of political information'. Here, voters are able to 'access large quantities of political information on the web' through mobile and other media technologies which provide always-on and 'on demand' options (Gibson and McAllister 2015, 339). However, despite evolving demands and opportunities posed by new communication genres, the impact of broadcasting technologies and political professionalization on the length and format of political speech, the competition and opportunity posed by direct communication methods like social media and microblogging,[1] the words spoken by political leaders continue *matter*. They limit the parameters of debate and work to discursively define and defend Australian identity. Spoken campaign communications, whether a speech delivered before an audience of party faithful or a televised public forum, are at the centre of the election battle to connect voters' lived experiences to broader social debates and dialogues, and to secure their vote.

All the Spontaneity of a Priest Leading a Litany

However, to argue that political language remains a vital element of campaigns does not mean that this language has not changed. This change is less in the themes and issues addressed than in style and content. For example, policy launch speeches remain a key set-piece element of the contemporary campaign but their role, timing and style have shifted dramatically since Federation. The policy launch speeches of the first decade following Federation were held early in the campaign, quite literally launching the policy program that each party would take to the voters. They combined detailed, in-depth accounts of policies and plans with reflections on the specific achievements (or failures) of the previous government, attacks on political opponents and plans for the nation's future. The nation-building aspect of these speeches was, in many ways, a result of the historical context which allowed leaders to speak in lofty terms about the establishment of a High Court as 'a great Australian court for Australian matters' (Barton 1901) or the development of military resources for an 'Australian defence by land and sea' (Deakin 1910). This detail, at times, would have made for dull listening. Prime Minister Andrew Fisher (1913), for

---

[1] While not examples of direct political speech, these new digital media genres provide significant opportunities for campaigning leaders to communicate with citizens; see Chen (2014, 2) for a useful mapping of research in this area and insight into the way that 'the use of new media by major parties', organizations and candidates as individual campaigners has intensified' in the last few Australian election campaigns. Social media also opens space for change in political journalism and public debate; see Burgess and Bruns (2012) for a more detailed discussion.

example, used his 1913 policy launch speech to list and describe every bill passed by his government in their time in office, from the Australian Notes Act and Land Tax Amendment Act to the Sugar Excise Repeal Act and Judiciary Act.

This aspect has all but disappeared from the policy launches of the twenty-first century, which come later and later in the campaign; in 2016, Labor's was held two weeks before election day and the Liberals' only a week before. Contemporary launches combine repetitive, broad-brush constructions of Australian identity with carefully targeted policies. Rather than set a bold agenda or outline a detailed case against the opposition, as policy speeches of the early to mid-twentieth century tried to do, today's versions draw together the themes developed across weeks of campaigning and previous statements, press conferences, interviews, social media interactions, advertising and other campaign communications. The particular combination of detailed promises and expansive imagery characterizes policy launch speeches written for television, delivered live to air before an invite-only crowd of party faithful, and broadcast, streamed, live-blogged and live-tweeted across the news media. In 2013 for example, Prime Minister Kevin Rudd *listed* Labor's policy commitments – a small business tax boost; funding for TAFE and VET students; the continuation of previous policies such as *Better Schools*, the National Broadband Network and clean energy – and explained their relevance or benefits to voters rather than detailing them, relying for this on information provided in earlier announcements or supplementary press releases.

Another significant change is in the ability of political leaders to interact directly with voters as media technologies have developed. Early campaign meetings and speeches were characterized by protests and heckling, which were both included in published transcripts and noted in media coverage. Turnout was a measure of the health of a campaign, and a leaders' ability to deal with interruptions and hold the crowd's attention a mark of his or her political ability. In 1914, Joseph Cook silenced an interjector by promising to have a 'rough and tumble' with him another time (*Sydney Morning Herald* 1914, 9) while in 1961 Menzies ridiculed a crowd of students protesting the White Australia policy at his launch, imploring the crowd to take no notice of these 'yahoos' as they were 'just imposters posing as university students' who had 'never passed their matriculation' (*Sydney Morning Herald* 1961, 1). However, the increasing professionalization of campaigns and prevalence of campaign management has almost entirely removed this aspect of campaign language. The colourful and often humourous off-the-cuff remarks that leaders like Chifley, Evatt or Menzies were famous for directing at hecklers do not suit the broadcast campaign speech as they could be alienating and confusing for those at home. Even Menzies, in his radio broadcast policy launch speech in 1955, curbed his style to the demands of the medium:

> If it hadn't been for the broadcast, it could have been a lively meeting. That was because a small but noisy cell of active Communists came along [...] But the attempted demonstration was a fiasco against the resolution with which Mr Menzies, keeping his mind on the microphones and his watch, ignored tempting baits and stuck to his script. (Cox 1955, 4)

This awareness of broadcast changed the relationship between the speaker and the live audience, a shift further cemented by the rise of mediatized speech and interview genres in which those tuning in at home (and the journalists who report for them) were the key targets, rather than the live or studio audience. This not only influenced the length and style of leaders' campaign language, shortening both sentences and whole speeches, it also broadened the scope of that language. The *potential* audience of a speech, interview or debate now extends well beyond those who attend live or even those watching or streaming at home. The content must therefore have a broad appeal, and as a result the formal language of Australian campaigns is increasingly deliberate and careful, rarely deviating from prepared phrases and messages. This is a frequent cause of concern and critique; evident in journalists' analysis of the lacklustre 2016 televised leaders' debate in which both Prime Minister Malcolm Turnbull and Opposition Leader Bill Shorten said very little voters had not already heard (Gordon 2016; Shanahan 2016; Taylor 2016b).

At the same time, as language use becomes more deliberate, there has been a shift away from formal or set-piece speeches to interviews, press conferences, doorstops and, most recently, televised or streamed public forums. These genres characterize the modern mediatized campaign, and also influence the increasing intimacy of the language through which constructions of national identity are sold to voters. This is a theme identified by scholars of political language: the 'new eloquence' (Johnson-Cartee and Copeland 1997, 8) associated with the introduction of television. However, while the language of interviews, talkback radio, people's forums and other genres has taken on this conversational tone, some political speech retains echoes of the broad-based rhetoric thought to characterize an imagined golden era. These are the high-profile, predictable events of the contemporary campaign: the policy launch speech, National Press Club address and televised leaders' debates (which in 2016, were staged in three different formats as a people's forum, traditional leaders' debate and Facebook debate). In these, leaders aim to speak directly to the nation, whether through live broadcast or streaming, delayed coverage, edited highlights packages or the next day's coverage in traditional and emerging political journalism formats. Their words are addressed to the live audience *and* those watching at home, as well as the journalist mediator or panel at the debate and the assembled media listening and questioning at the Press Club. At these events, even more so than others, every word, gesture and stumble is reported, summarized and analysed. While the language can be colloquial or informal, it does not mirror the more intimate tone attempted in other genres.

Chapter 2, in its discussion of concerns about the decline of political language, introduced the perspective that in the era of constant media scrutiny and campaign professionalization political language has become 'banal, deadening chaff' overtaken by corporate language (Ramsey in Glover 2007, 148). This trajectory is apparent in the language analysed in this book, and the campaigns held between 2010 and 2016 seem particularly to have demonstrated the corporatization of language bemoaned by Ramsey and identified elsewhere by Don Watson (2003). The wit and inventive use of the Australian colloquial that characterized the earliest campaigns following Federation and re-emerged with more colourful leaders such as Menzies, Hawke, Keating and even Latham was entirely lacking in these humourless campaigns. Even their partisan attacks lacked the fire and substance of the battles between Bruce and Charlton in the 1920s, Hawke and his opponents throughout the 1980s, or Paul Keating's personal attacks on John Howard in the 1996 campaign. In contrast, Malcolm Turnbull's critique of Labor's economic policy in the 2016 National Press Club leaders' debate lacked passion. The only moment of real engagement came when Bill Shorten (2016e) attacked his opponent's lack of clear vision for the nation, quipping 'I genuinely lead my party, whereas your party genuinely leads you'.

The vast amount of material available from the election campaigns since 2001 (when parties began to make transcripts available on their websites) also reveals how repetitive the themes and phrases that dominate political language have become. Whether in a prepared doorstop announcement or in response to reporter on a current affairs program, leaders repeat arguments and ideas across the country, often with the same phrasing. This makes clear how truly rare it has become for politicians to speak spontaneously in the contemporary mediatized election campaign, and there is little sign that leaders make any attempt to avoid this repetition or are concerned by media market crossover. Rather, staying on message and having that message reported each day of the campaign is a communications victory. Despite this, coverage of campaigns has continued to judge political leaders according to their skill as speakers. In 1919, for example, the *Age* (1919, 7) bemoaned that Prime Minister Hughes 'kept religiously to his carefully prepared text in his policy speech, and therefore failed to arouse the interest of the audience'; while in 1925, it reported the audience's delight when Prime Minister Bruce 'flung down his notes and gave his audience a little more homely talk' (*Age* 1925a, 11) in his. The privileging of the off-the-cuff has endured, as discussed when considering the 2010 search for the 'real Julia' in Chapter 2. At times the role of speechwriters has also figured in this evaluation. Primarily this has been a concern about the fit, or lack of fit, between words and delivery. Coverage of Bob Hawke's formal speeches often focused on this aspect. In 1983, for example, Peter Bowers (1983, 1) noted in the *Sydney Morning Herald* that former Whitlam speechwriter Graham Freudenberg had been 'lent' to Hawke to 'give his election speeches a touch of class, but not too much'. In keeping with a persona constructed as ordinary, it felt that in the policy launch 'this Freudenberg speech was written for the plain man's plain orator', and was a good fit for Hawke. In contrast, in 1996 the *Australian*'s Jennifer Hewett (1996, 6) drew a distinction between the text of Keating's policy launch speech, which was 'well crafted by his speechwriter' Don Watson, and the prime minister's 'flat' delivery, which had 'all the spontaneity of a priest leading a litany'.

Another central marker of the effectiveness of campaign speeches is the suitability of the content, style and tone for its intended medium. Throughout Australian electoral history, leaders who have misunderstood or misjudged the demands of communication technologies have failed to connect with audiences. In these cases, media coverage has often picked up on this failure rather than the content. Ben Chifley's radio broadcast policy addresses in the 1940s, and McMahon's dense, fast paced live-to-camera policy speech in 1972 did not make use of the opportunities afforded by developing media technologies, and were critiqued accordingly. Those who excelled at meeting the demands of the medium are remembered as effective speakers: Menzies adapting to the clarity and intimacy required for radio speeches; Whitlam exploiting the colour and repetition needed for television; Howard's embrace of the direct connection offered by talkback radio. Paying attention to the medium earns leaders praise, such as Harold Holt's glowing reviews, in 1966, for 'skilfully measuring and tailoring the opening of his campaign to the special needs' of television, making it short and direct (Cox 1966, 7). In contrast, during John Howard's first stint as opposition leader he received scathing media reviews for his policy launch speech: for ignoring the image demands of television and taking 'a big leap into ordinariness' (Gawenda 1987, 1), and for his unvarying volume and pace, which made watching the launch 'a bit like spending the evening with a talking clock' (Pryor 1987, 1).

The importance of embracing the style and format of emerging communication media has shifted, in the last decade, to online communication. Australia is yet to see the level and professionalism of the direct speech developed for online streaming and on-demand viewing pioneered during the primaries for the 2008 US general election; in the eventual battle between Democrat Barack Obama and Republican John McCain; and in the election cycles that followed. In 2007, Prime Minister John Howard was ridiculed for using YouTube to record a brief speech launching a new climate change policy in the lead up to the campaign (for an analysis, see Flew 2008). The video featured an overly formal style and opened with the greeting 'good morning', demonstrating a clear misunderstanding of the tone and non-time-specific nature of the medium. In the campaign that followed, the more successful attempts of Labor's *Kevin07* campaign to harness video sharing and social networking technologies seemed to signal the possibility for political speech to also extend into this arena in future campaigns. This has not yet been the case; and the campaigns that followed have lacked innovation and creativity.

The most definitive aspect of effective political speech, however, has changed very little since Federation. Whether an address to a crowded public hall, a televised interview or a people's forum debate, the most effective political speech achieves a delicate balancing act. It is firmly of its time, and also transcends it. This election language works within the social, economic and political contexts of the campaign, speaking to voters about their immediate concerns and ideals. It offers a secure, comforting identity against contemporary challenges and connects these urgent debates to broader, ongoing narratives of Australia's history and identity. Although recognisably addressing the immediate context it connects to something more lasting to make sense of voters' daily experiences within the sweep of national change and continuity. Deakin's combination of visionary nation-building rhetoric and support for exclusive immigration policies; Bruce's promise to strengthen British ties and keep Australia safe from the 'reds'; and Howard's reassertion of mainstream agency over national borders all worked in the context of social and political upheaval. They spoke to voters' current concerns about the character of the fledgling nation and its problematic relationship to the land and its original inhabitants, the safety of their political-cultural ties and the strength of their borders in the face of terrorism and so-called illegal immigration through the reassuring discourse of *identity security*. In this way, the most successful political speech has excelled at the goal of *identification* (discussed in Chapter 2). It has been designed and presented with 'a complex understanding of the audience, their social norms, values, and fears' (Lilleker 2006, 183). Some of the most powerful examples came in change of government elections. At these times, opposition leaders were able to tap into, and help construct, a shifting national mood and exploit this opportunity to present a new vision of Australian identity or promise a return to an abandoned one. Hawke's call for a spirit of national reconciliation in 1983; Howard's promise to deliver an Australia that was 'for all of us' in 1996; and Rudd's 2007 promise of 'fresh thinking' to face

Australia's new challenges all exemplified this. They tapped into and were instrumental in constructing a mood of national change and renewal. Political language was not the only factor in determining the outcomes of these elections; however, these opposition leaders were able to have an impact on the campaign agenda through their speech, influencing the issues that would dominate the campaign and coverage.

Bounded and Particular

The framework of Australian identity has remained a central feature in achieving the goal of identification in Australian leaders' spoken campaign language since Federation. Specific words and issues have changed, but campaigning leaders have consistently asked the electorate to see a collective identity constructed as *national* as the foremost arena for shared experience; to think, act and vote in their role as members of this national community. This appeal was then inflected with the other levels of identity familiar from voters' daily lives, such as their roles as family members, workers or taxpayers. Federal elections play out on a national level, so while leaders do campaign in specific electorates and aim promises at targeted groups, it is the discursive arena of the *nation* that is the constant (spoken or unspoken) backdrop. If campaigns are to be seen as contests over Australian identity, and the security of that identity, then they also have a role to play in 'urgent theoretical and political issues' such as belonging (Gilroy 2004, 98). British sociologist Paul Gilroy (2004, 98) argues that the importance of belonging in the nation state is connected to the 'bounded and particular' nature of identity itself, which helps to 'reckon with the patterns of inclusion and exclusion that it cannot help creating'. This resonates with the notions of identity around which this book is formed: the language of identity appears whenever people determine the boundaries of belonging to a particular group and decide if, and how, these boundaries should be enforced. Political leaders from Barton and Deakin to Turnbull and Shorten appealed to Australians in their role as national community members, and in doing so drew spatial and symbolic boundaries around the national collective.

As times of potential shift and change, election campaigns are moments when normally stable connections to the national collective are threatened (Yuval-Davis 2004, 216), and when Australian identity and belonging are articulated. They call the boundaries of Australianness into question and invite contest over national values and identities. The notion of borders is therefore intrinsic to the idea of the Australian identity presented by political leaders. For the Australian nation to be successfully imagined, political leaders have needed to present voters not only with an image of who *we* are but also with an awareness of those who don't belong and spaces that are not part of the national space. It is here that the preoccupation with the limits of Australian identity emerges, linking into contemporary debates about immigration rates, asylum seekers, international terrorism, Australian values and indigenous reconciliation that have dominated debate in Australia and public discourse in the part of the world that imagines itself as Western and democratic in the years following 11 September 2001. If positive constructions of Australian identity are a marker of where we belong, then locating the borders is a precondition for securing the limits of that identity. It is a discursive act that allows members of what is imagined as the *national we* to differentiate between those who meet the conditions of belonging and those who do not. Control over the national borders was therefore an important mechanism through which political leaders evoked, and then neutralized, collective anxiety about the influence of those imagined as others on the nation. These threats were constructed both as external pressures on the borders of the nation state and as internal challenges to the boundaries of the national collective. They appeared in campaign language as the regional nations, imagined as uncivilized and unstable, that gave shape and contrast to ours; as the illegal immigrants who were seen as an invasion or cultural threat; the *internal* outsiders who were influenced by 'extremist ideologies'; the immigrants who could not contribute or assimilate; or the political opposition who challenged *our* values and traditions. The construction of these national boundaries relied on a rich and complex discourse, working both to 'proclaim identity' for insiders and to 'repel difference' (Wolin 1996, 31).

Australian identity itself, and the space in which it could be lived, was a dominant source of comfort presented to voters by campaigning leaders in the face of these threats. The construction of 'safe' borders offers to 'shield the national collectivity' from the unsettling changes associated with globalization and the fracturing loyalties of 'people's multi-layered citizenship' (Yuval-Davis 2004, 220). Appeals to Australian identity continue to be central in campaign language because of their power to:

> combine the abstract and the concrete in such a way that the individual who is subject to mass and impersonal forces, feels themselves to be situated within a meaningful cultural framework and way of life, and to have part of one's self as solid and immutable. (Rundle 2006, 12)

The same forces of change of global change that may seem, for post-nationalists, to be heralding the end of bounded nationalism have also contributed to its revival. What it means to be Australian, how that identity is defined and to whom membership is extended is therefore more potent in campaign language than ever. The construction of national borders marked out a place where members unquestionably belonged and the myth of homogeneity was sustained through the suppression and expulsion of difference. Significantly, it was when the limits of national belonging at the geo-political borders of the nation began to look vulnerable to infiltration (such as in the concern about illegal or undesirable immigrants) that the *internal* frontiers of belonging also become blurred. In times of threat, groups previously included in the Australian identity (even in low or precarious positions in the social hierarchy) come under renewed suspicion as the 'enemy within'. For example, in the 1996 election the economic challenges of globalization and Keating's big picture vision allowed his opponents to evoke discontent aimed at so-called special interests (recent immigrants, indigenous Australians and others); and in campaigns following 2001 political language tapped into broader social discourses in which undifferentiated clusters of Muslim and Arabic immigrants were cast as a threat to *our* safety. Aku Aksoy (2004, 225) has described the feeling in Britain, after 11 September, that some immigrants could 'no longer be trusted to share the same concerns and sensibilities as us'. At these times in Australia, this suspected 'enemy within' was watched out of the corner of our collective national eye, positioned as a potential threat to the Australian way of life or the jobs and values of those voters imagined as ordinary; echoing similar concerns about socialism and communism in the earlier language of Bruce, Chifley, Menzies and Evatt.

These broader social tensions and fears were reflected in election campaign language that betrayed the contingent and hierarchical nature of belonging to Australian identity, exposing formal citizenship as a limited guarantee open to challenge from those higher on the pecking order of national membership. The discourse of *identity security* plays a vital role in election campaigns in drawing people together to make decisions about the nation's future. In this way, elections not only offer citizens the feeling that they have a place in the national collective, but also that they are able to exercise some measure of control over it.

A Generous, Open-hearted People

It is in this context that we can begin to understand the long term and ongoing primacy of constructions of Australian identity as a framework for voter identification in election campaign discourse. Federal elections are revealed, in this research, as facilitating powerful discussions about Australian identity where leaders reinforce or extend national boundaries, and evoke and construct shared memories, collective values and national priorities in their language. We have seen in the previous chapters the powerful central place of the interlinked discourses of threat and security in this language, recurring as mechanisms that address (and engender) anxiety and offer reassurance and comfort. These nationalistic campaign appeals are commonly located as the particular domain of conservative politics. For Nira Yuval-Davis (2004, 216), it is often the political right that:

> exploits the love and hate, fears and hopes that are evoked in these situations in order to build higher walls around the boundaries and borders of the national collectivity and mobilise the people towards exclusionary politics.

This perspective was reflected in the tone of public debate, media discussion and scholarly analysis that characterized the 11-year term of the Howard Coalition government. Critique (commonly from the political left) focused on the government's apparent willingness to exploit exclusive race- and culture-based constructions of identity in order to get elected. This was noted as early as the 1996 election, when the Howard Liberal opposition's campaign pledge to govern *For All of Us* was seen by members of indigenous, ethnic and other communities positioned as minorities as a deliberate move away from the 'special interest' politics of the Hawke-Keating era to garner the support of the disaffected mainstream. This mainstream became known as the Howard battlers and were promised a return to a 'relaxed and comfortable' Australia. Similar critiques emerged in discussions of the history wars and culture wars, and in the 2001 campaign. Here, Howard's language in response to the 9/11 terror attacks, the *Tampa* and 'children overboard' affair was located as an appeal to the anxieties about the safety of Australian identity that are the foundation of national security discourse. It was in this campaign, as discussed in Chapter 4, that Howard (2001c) was able to offer voters a positive vision of themselves as a 'generous open-hearted people' that justified their desire to decide 'who comes to this country, and the circumstances in which they come'.

The previous chapters have engaged with these discourses; but they have also argued that identity security is not solely the domain of the conservative side of politics. While there are different traditions and touchstones in campaign language that emerge according to partisan alignments, leaders from both sides of politics have engaged in the battle to construct their opponents as a threat to the safety of the Australian identity and national space. The others, they argue, are weak on border security. Their policies on immigration are too harsh, or too lenient. They're dangerous because they are beholden to foreign ideologies, or because of their own internal divisions and instability. They have no regard for the positive values or day-to-day struggles of Australians imagined as ordinary, and they have no understanding or appreciation of the heroic moments of our national history.

The imagining of the Australian nation is ongoing and contested in these battles. In elections since Federation, leaders have taken part in this project by drawing on deeply held shared myths, assumptions, memories and experiences, mobilizing these into partisan campaign combat. Election campaigns *matter*, in this context, and mediatized political language is a powerful mechanism through which Australian identity is constructed for members of the national collective. Something deeper than strategic politics is at stake here, and the success of this project relies on a connection to a constituency that is not only about policy information or polling data. Voters must be invited to feel that they belong to something valuable, and that they have a stake in protecting it from internal and external threats. In the first half of the twentieth century, campaign images of a unified British-Australian identity helped to build a sense of common experience. As the security that came from familial notions of Imperial belonging declined, and reliance on racially based notions of identity became increasingly unsuitable, it was the imagery of shared common history or shared values that leaders increasingly relied on to provide reassuring identity security against threat. Over 115 years, Australian voters have been offered national identity and security in a number of forms: from the nation-building language of Deakin and the anti-communist imagery of Bruce; to the shifting alliances of Menzies and cosmopolitan diversity presented by Keating. They've been wooed by Charlton and his successors in their attempts to claim Australian security for Labor; asked to invest in Whitlam's self-conscious national modernization; and been drawn into the positive, comforting images of Australian identity developed by Hawke and Howard. They've also been offered stories of identity on a smaller scale: in the bland vision of a 'competitive' Australia presented by Rudd and the cautious, conservative discourses of nation that characterized the language of Gillard and Abbott.

We'll Put People First

It remains to be seen where the campaign conceptions of the leaders who follow will fit into the picture painted here. This concluding chapter was written in the final weeks of the 2016 election campaign, in which a new-to-the-job prime minister faced off against an only marginally less-new opposition leader. Both were conducting their first federal campaign, and at the outset it was unclear how well they would perform the task of affective connection. How effectively would Prime Minister Malcolm Turnbull link the Liberals' policies and plans to voters' lived experiences? How easily would Opposition Leader

Bill Shorten challenge this to create and appeal to a constituency aligned with Labor values? The campaign was long for the modern era, and felt particularly long for voters who had endured a period of unusual political upheaval since the election of the Rudd government in 2007. Australians have enjoyed a traditionally stable political landscape in the post–World War II period, concluding with 11 years with John Howard at the helm. In between the 2007 and 2016 elections the prime minister changed four times, and only one of these changes happened at the ballot box (Appendix 4). In the others, leaders were deposed through party room challenges, or forced to step down in the face of one.

In 2015, ongoing tensions within the government and leadership speculation in the media saw a spill enacted against Prime Minister Tony Abbott in February, which he defeated. Tension continued to build, however, and on 14 September Malcolm Turnbull, a former party leader and then communications minister, challenged the prime minister and won by 10 votes. Turnbull has held the blue-ribbon seat of Wentworth in Sydney since 2004. He was a high-profile figure before entering politics, known not only for his successes as a barrister and investment banker but also for his time as chairman of the Australian Republican Movement. A former Rhodes Scholar, Turnbull had a reputation before his ascension to the prime ministership as business-savvy political moderate, particularly on social issues such as the environment, marriage equality and the republic. This reputation faded somewhat in his first months in the job when progressive policies in these areas did not emerge. Instead, Turnbull's political persona combined an acknowledgement of his 'precocious brilliance' with 'questions about what [he] believes in'; a 'dilemma' that Andrew Clark (2016), writing in the *Australian Financial Review*, positioned as 'dogging' the prime minister as the 2016 election approached. This problem was exacerbated by Turnbull's stiff, uncomfortable manner in the early weeks of the campaign; he seemed ill at ease in many of his scheduled events, perhaps keen to get through the election and on to the real business of governing. In her profile of Turnbull, *Guardian Australia* journalist Lenore Taylor (2016a) argued that Turnbull 'seems to have stopped speaking in the way that for many years made him the country's most popular choice as leader'. This is a calculated risk: 'to win the chance to govern in his own voice', Taylor (2016a) muses, he seems to think that 'he has to temper himself, to stay on message, talk the talk of a more conventional candidate'. This 'risk-averse' strategy, which sidelines conviction and big picture politics, led to a campaign in which it was difficult to get a clear sense of Turnbull's vision of the Australian identity and the nation's future.

His opponent was also contesting his first federal election as party leader. Bill Shorten became Labor leader after Kevin Rudd's defeat in the 2013 election, winning the position with the support of party members as well as the caucus under the party's new voting system. He had been the Member for Maribyrnong, in Melbourne, since 2007 and before that had served a six-year stint as National Secretary of the Australian Workers Union. It was this role that first brought him into the national spotlight, when the Beaconsfield mine disaster saw him become the 'public face' of the rescue effort (Baird 2006) in a role that combined 'media spokesperson' and national 'counsellor'. Shorten has a reputation as the 'ultimate insider' (Murphy 2016). In his Quarterly Essay profile of Shorten, *Faction Man*, David Marr (2015, 2) argued that he 'built his career out of sight in the union movement' and has 'failed to emerge strongly as a leader'. While he 'still has a faint halo' from his involvement at Beaconsfield, he has since become known as 'the plotter who brought down two leaders to clear his own way to power' (Marr 2015, 2). Shorten was seen as likeable but not particularly charismatic in the lead up to the 2016 election; a solid negotiator who was interested in consultation but retained a 'hunger for public affection' (Marr 2015, 59) that was both a motivator and a weakness. This translated into photo opportunities in which Shorten seemed warm and relaxed on the campaign trail in an attempt to engage Australians with Labor values. It echoed in the branding of the ALP's campaign website: 'We'll put people first; Standing up for middle and working class people' but failed to translate into a clear story of Australian identity for Labor that resonated with voters.

Scare Campaigns and Pathetic Lies

The 2016 campaign saw the return of focused debate about an area that had been relatively muted in the previous few elections: refugees and border security. While these had been areas of passionate conversation and contest in between elections in public discourse more broadly, the basic level of agreement between the major parties on the viability (and desirability) of offshore processing had taken the urgency out of this as a campaign issue.[2] Since the 2013 campaign, however, the issue had escalated both in reality and the visibility afforded by the global refugee crisis. Public debate and political response seemed to flare up around particularly vivid and widely shared images: for example, of the death of a young Kurdish toddler in Turkey, in September 2015, or of those forced to seek shelter in the Calais 'jungle' while attempting to cross the Channel into England. In Australia, April and May of 2016 saw the issue return to the front page in two related

---

[2] There were some exceptions here with minor parties and independents. The Greens, for example, have been consistently vocal in their opposition to detention centres and offshore processing, with Senator Sarah Hanson-Young the party's most visible spokesperson on the issue.

developments.[3] On 25 April the Papua New Guinea Supreme Court ruled that the detention of asylum seekers on Manus Island, a key element of Australian offshore processing, was illegal (Tlozek and Anderson 2016). Then, in line with a longer history of protest, two asylum seekers set themselves alight at the detention centre on Nauru (Hasham 2016) in a matter of days in late April and early May. It was in this context that the issue of asylum seekers and border security re-emerged in the 2016 election campaign, with both leaders using language more emotive and vibrant in its constructions of Australian identity security than the bland, managerial language of the previous three campaigns.

A foreshadowing might have been found on 11 May, only three days into a campaign set to stretch for eight weeks. Peter Dutton, minister for immigration and border protection in the Turnbull government (a policy portfolio that itself signals the linkage of these two issues in policy and popular debates) was the keynote speaker at the National Security Annual Summit, *Safeguarding Australia 2016*. At this conference, which the organizers present as bringing together university, government and corporate experts in national security, he gave an address in which he attacked Labor for being 'on the wrong side of history' on 'people smugglers' and border security (Dutton 2016a). He linked national sovereignty, asylum seekers and regional instability to argue that 'as a liberal, tolerant and democratic society, Australia is a tempting target for international and home-grown terrorists' (Dutton 2016a). The address received almost no media attention but laid the groundwork for comments, a few days later, in which the minister sparked a passionate (if ultimately short-lived) national debate on asylum seekers and immigration. On 17 May, Dutton appeared on the panel program *Paul Murray Live* on Sky News, Australia's subscription-based 24-hour news channel. Conservative commentator and program host Paul Murray asked him about the Greens' proposal to increase Australia's humanitarian refugee intake: 'what does it mean if 50,000 people come here every single year?' When Dutton replied sedately that his concern was where to draw the line considering the large numbers of displaced people globally who might 'seek to come to a country like Australia', Murray followed up. What, he wondered, might be the impact on the Australian economy,

---

[3] The public, political and media debate about offshore processing and detention centres cannot be neatly separated from broader contemporary conversations about race and identity in Australia. For example, in the first half of 2016 these flared up around the increasing visibility and public interventions on the question of indigenous issues, race and the Australian 'dream' made by veteran journalist and broadcaster Stan Grant; the nomination of a number of non-white television personalities for the Gold Logie Award (Australia's less-glamorous answer to the Emmy Awards); and the appearances of British poet Kate Tempest during the Sydney Writers' Festival and on ABC Television's *Q&A* where she spoke about the 'deep and poisonous racism' at root in Australian society (Harmon 2016).

when you considered that 90 per cent of Afghan refugees in Australia were currently unemployed? Dutton (2016b) didn't hesitate in sharing his concerns in response:

> For many people, they won't be numerate or literate in their own language, and this is a difficulty because [...] these people would be taking Australian jobs, there's no question about that and for many of them that would be unemployed, they would languish in unemployment queues and on Medicare and the rest of it, so there would be huge costs.

In this ostensibly economically focused response, Dutton (2016b) raised the familiar historical spectre of the Yellow Peril, noting that there were people who 'would trek down through Malaysia and Indonesia' to reach Australia if border security measures were relaxed. In following this with the assertion that 'tough leadership' was needed for Australians to keep 'their families and our community safe' (Dutton 2016b), he implicitly constructed asylum seekers as a threat to the Australian identity, people and way of life. These comments sparked furious debate and almost blanket media coverage, with comments sought from other politicians and editorials published in support or criticism of Dutton's comments (e.g. *Age* 2016; *Australian* 2016).

Dutton's comments came to dominate the campaign narrative of the two leaders for a period of days, driven both by their own messaging and questioning from journalists. This can be a long time in deciding the central issues and momentum in an election, although in this instance there were still weeks left before election day. The day after Dutton's late night television comments Malcolm Turnbull was campaigning in Townsville and Bill Shorten in Sydney. Coincidentally, both made similar announcements at their press conferences: promising funding for freight rail infrastructure projects designed to increase productivity. In Townsville, the prime minister made his announcement and answered questions on local issues before being asked: 'Do you back the Immigration Minister's comments on refugees?' (in Turnbull 2016a). A lengthy answer followed, in which he first claimed that the fact that no 'unauthorised arrivals' had reached Australia by boat in 'more than 600 days' made Dutton 'an outstanding Immigration Minister' (Turnbull 2016a). Moving to the substance of Dutton's comments, the prime minister's language was an echo of the discourse perfected by John Howard, which as we have seen has a legacy stretching back to the campaigns of Alfred Deakin. He first claimed for Australians a unique generosity and compassion, reassuring voters that 'we are one of the most generous host countries for refugees' and spend more than $800 million a year in 'settlement services'. This spending was both to ensure that refugees are able to 'integrate' and to protect our position as 'the most successful multicultural nation in the world' (Turnbull 2016a). From this basis, where Australia's approach to asylum seekers was constructed as 'built on a pillar of compassion', Turnbull (2016a) then linked openness to control:

> We should never forget this – our success as a multicultural nation, our success depends on secure borders. Australians accept this high level of refugee intake, this large humanitarian program because they know that their government keeps their borders secure.

Turnbull's response demonstrates the complex interconnection between inclusion and exclusion that characterizes the Australian identity security discourses analysed throughout this book. At play, here, is a powerful positive construction of Australians themselves as generous, compassionate and multicultural but still in control: only willing to welcome those they can adequately support. Turnbull developed this further in an opinion piece published in the Fairfax papers on 20 May, in which his language mapped even more directly onto Howard's 2001 'we decide' speech. Here the prime minister argued that 'the reason Australians welcome high levels of immigration' is because 'we have confidence that our government is in control of our immigration and humanitarian program' (Turnbull 2016b). While this is a softer version of the discourse, in which the government is not only responsible for 'deciding who can come here' but also for 'ensuring that […] they receive the support they need', this support is aimed at *integration*. This, for Turnbull (2016a), is a 'nation-building' policy; an expression of a government 'concerned about ensuring that our extraordinarily successful multicultural society' is secure. The prime minister does not repeat, but also does not refute, Dutton's specific claims. Instead he shifts to a managerial discourse, but one reliant on an assumed shared Australian anxiety about being overwhelmed and displaced within the national space.

While the prime minister waited for a journalist to ask him about this issue during his Townsville press conference, his opponent took a different approach. After Shorten and the shadow minister for infrastructure outlined the rail upgrade they were proposing, the opposition leader spoke again. 'Before we take questions', he told the assembled media pack, 'I want to address the deeply divisive and offensive remarks made by the Liberal Party and Peter Dutton overnight' (Shorten 2016d). Shorten critiqued his opponents on three central issues: firstly, that there were more important issues that Australian voters wanted dealt with in the campaign; second, that Dutton's comments were part of a baseless fear campaign designed to scare people into voting for the government; and third, that the comments themselves were insulting to refugees and immigrants who had made a significant contribution to the nation.

Shorten (2016d) argued that Australians 'expect more from this electoral process' than 'scare campaigns and pathetic lies'. His critique extended to an explicit discussion of the Dutton's exploitation of his own position of social and political power: this was a 'vulnerable group being demonised by a man in a position of great authority'. Shorten (2016d) located this attack not as an individual strategy but a key element of how the Liberal Party historically operates in elections, linking to more than a century of Labor critiques of conservative 'scare campaigns'. 'What I know and what every member of the Labor Party […] know', he told voters, is 'you don't attack a whole group of people and demonise them to the Australian people'. The opposition leader claimed the moral high ground for himself and his party, aligning Labor with the compassion and decency he painted as characteristic of the Australian people. Significantly, however, his discourse displayed the same practical elements as the prime minister's, although along different lines. While Malcolm Turnbull took a managerial approach to ensuring that Australia's stable multicultural society would be secure, Shorten's defence of refugee communities located as its priority the *contributions* they had made and could make to mainstream Australian society. Dutton's comments, he argued, 'didn't just insult refugees' but also 'insulted the millions of migrants who've contributed to making this a truly great country':

> When we hear an attack on refugees, understand the contribution that some of them have made to this country. They're called Victor Chang, they're called Frank Lowy, they're called Richard Pratt, and there are hundreds of thousands of other people who are running small businesses, who are educating their kids, who are great neighbours, who are just building our communities and paying taxes. (Shorten 2016d)

Despite these detailed, at times emotive responses from the two leaders the discussion of scare campaigns, Australian generosity and border security did not remain dominant. It was fast overtaken by other issues in an era of information overload and ever-shortening news cycles. The issue faded from the headlines as the campaign wore on, although both leaders continued to refer to it in response to questions from journalists, voters, and their own big-ticket addresses. Both addressed it in response to a question from the political editor from the *West Australian*, Andrew Probyn, in the leaders' debate at the National Press Club on 29 May, while the prime minister also revisited the issue in his policy launch speech and appearance on ABC Television's *Q&A* program. Turnbull took up the issue again, although indirectly, when holding an iftar at Kirribilli House on 16 June. He was the first Australian prime minister in history to host the fast-breaking Ramadan feast – something he described as an 'honour' on his Twitter feed (SBS 2016) – and his address at the dinner briefly sparked renewed media coverage of his views on immigration and multiculturalism. In the speech, the prime minister implicitly countered Dutton's characterization of immigrants to Australia when describing the 'remarkable contribution that Muslims have made to Australian society', which he again referred to as 'the most successful multicultural society in the world' (Turnbull 2016c). Speaking to a multifaith audience that included young Muslim-Australian community leaders, he employed the discourse of familial belonging:

> I want […] to emphasise to each and every one of you that the Australian Muslim community is valued and respected – and is not confined to a narrow security prism – you are an integral part of an Australian family that rests on the essential foundation of mutual respect and understanding.

This is both an acknowledgement of existing, and call for further, 'understanding' which asks Australian citizens to be active participants in the 'extraordinary project of the nation'. In line with more than a century of political discourse on identity and belonging in Australia, it both presents an image of that nation that can be valorized ('This is a blessed country. This is a remarkable country') and also constructs perceived threat from a 'world of discord and disharmony […] in which there is so much hatred' that lies beyond our borders (Turnbull 2016c).

On 2 July, the vote was so close in key seats that neither party could claim victory. It took just over a week before the Coalition government secured a one-seat minority, with Shorten conceding and Turnbull claiming victory on 10 July. Despite the close result and the slipping of immigration and border control issues from the headlines in the last weeks of the campaigns, the re-emergence of this anxious discourse in the 2016 election tells us something about the enduring power of identity security, and reminds us of its cyclical nature. It illuminates the potential impact of political storytelling about Australian identity that crystallizes at moments of change and indecision, such as elections. In an increasingly globalized world, where the comfort of nationally bound identity continues to be vital, recurring cycles of anxiety and reassurance ensure that Australian political identity stories feature consistently in campaign language. It will be fascinating to see the discursive evolution and reformation of constructions of the national collective that future leaders will debate, contest and offer to voters to make sense of their collective experiences and to attract their votes.

APPENDIX 1

FEDERAL ELECTION DATES INCLUDED IN QUALITATIVE DISCOURSE ANALYSIS SAMPLE, 1901–2013

Election Year	Dates in Sample*
1901	17 January–30 March
1903	29 October–18 December
1906	17 October–12 December
1910	7 February–14 April
1913	31 March–2 June
1914	6 July–11 September
1917	26 March–6 May
1919	30 October–20 December
1922	24 October–5 February
1925	3 October–16 November
1928	4 October–18 November
1929	18 September–17 October
1931	28 November–20 December
1934	13 August–16 September
1937	20 September–24 October
1940	28 August–22 September
1943	16 July–22 August
1946	20 August–29 September
1949	31 October–11 December
1951	28 March–29 April
1954	23 April–31 May
1955	7 November–11 December
1958	15 October–23 November
1961	3 November–19 December
1963	1 November–1 December
1966	31 October–27 November
1969	29 September–26 October
1972	2 November–2 December
1974	20 April–29 May
1975	17 November–13 December
1977	10 November–10 December
1980	19 September–19 October

Election Year	Dates in Sample*
1983	4 February–6 March
1984	26 October–1 December
1987	5 June–11 July
1990	19 February–25 March
1993	8 February–14 March
1996	29 January–2 March
1998	31 August–3 October
2001	8 October–10 November
2004	31 August–9 October
2007	17 October–24 November
2010	19 July–21 August
2013	5 August–7 September

* Election dates included in the sample for the qualitative discourse analysis are counted from either the issuing of the writs or the policy launch speeches (whichever comes first, as in 1901–14, 1919–22, 1928–29, 1934–37, 1946, 1958 the policy launch speeches were given before the issuing of the writs) until the victory/concession speeches (or, in the case of very close results, the post-election speeches).

APPENDIX 2

AUSTRALIAN FEDERAL ELECTION DATES AND RESULTS, 1901–2016

Election	Polling Day	Campaign Length (days)	Result
1901	30 March	73	**Barton** (PM) PROT def. Reid (OL) FT
1903	16 December	49	**Deakin** (PM) PROT def. Reid (OL) FT
1906	12 December	57	**Deakin** (PM) PROT def. Reid (OL) FT
1910	13 April	66	**Fisher** (OL) ALP def. Deakin (PM) FUSION
1913	31 May	62	**Cook** (OL) LIB def. Fisher (PM) ALP
1914	5 September	61	**Fisher** (OL) ALP def. Cook (PM) LIB
1917	5 May	41	**Hughes** (PM) NAT def. Tudor (OL) ALP
1919	13 December	45	**Hughes** (PM) NAT def. Tudor (OL) ALP
1922	16 December	54	**Hughes** (PM) NAT def. Charlton (OL) ALP
1925	14 November	43	**Bruce** (PM) NAT def. Charlton (OL) ALP
1928	17 November	45	**Bruce** (PM) NAT def. Scullin (OL) ALP
1929	12 October	25	**Scullin** (OL) ALP def. Bruce (PM) NAT
1931	19 December	22	**Lyons** (OL) UAP def. Scullin (PM) ALP
1934	15 September	34	**Lyons** (PM) UAP def. Scullin (OL) ALP
1937	23 October	34	**Lyons** (PM) UAP def. Curtin (OL) ALP
1940	21 September	37	**Menzies** (PM) UAP def. Curtin (OL) ALP
1943	21 August	37	**Curtin** (PM) ALP def. Fadden (OL) CP
1946	28 September	33	**Chifley** (PM) ALP def. Menzies (OL) LP
1949	10 December	41	**Menzies** (OL) LP def. Chifley (OL) ALP
1951	28 April	32	**Menzies** (PM) LP def. Evatt (OL) ALP
1954	29 May	37	**Menzies** (PM) LP def. Evatt (OL) ALP
1955	10 December	34	**Menzies** (PM) LP def. Evatt (OL) ALP
1958	22 November	39	**Menzies** (PM) LP def. Evatt (OL) ALP
1961	9 December	37	**Menzies** (PM) LP def. Calwell (OL) ALP
1963	30 November	30	**Menzies** (PM) LP def. Calwell (OL) ALP
1966	26 November	27	**Holt** (PM) LP def. Calwell (OL) ALP
1969	25 October	27	**Gorton** (PM) LP def. Whitlam (OL) ALP
1972	2 December	31	**Whitlam** (OL) ALP def. McMahon (PM) LP
1974	18 May	29	**Whitlam** (PM) ALP def. Snedden (OL) LP
1975	13 December	27	**Fraser** (PM) LP def. Whitlam (OL) ALP
1977	10 December	31	**Fraser** (PM) LP def. Whitlam (OL) ALP
1980	18 October	30	**Fraser** (PM) LP def. Hayden (OL) ALP
1983	5 March	30	**Hawke** (OL) ALP def. Fraser (PM) LP

Election	Polling Day	Campaign Length (days)	Result
1984	1 December	47	**Hawke** (PM) ALP def. Peacock (OL) LP
1987	11 July	37	**Hawke** (PM) ALP def. Howard (OL) LP
1990	24 March	34	**Hawke** (PM) ALP def. Peacock (OL) LP
1993	13 March	34	**Keating** (PM) ALP def. Hewson (OL) LP
1996	2 March	34	**Howard** (OL) LP def. Keating (PM) ALP
1998	3 October	34	**Howard** (PM) LP def. Beazley (OL) ALP
2001	10 November	34	**Howard** (PM) LP def. Beazley (OL) ALP
2004	9 October	40	**Howard** (PM) LP def. Latham (OL) ALP
2007	24 November	39	**Rudd** (OL) ALP def. Howard (PM) LP
2010	21 August	34	**Gillard** (PM) ALP def. Abbott (OL) LP
2013	7 September	34	**Abbott** (OL) LP def. Rudd (PM) ALP
2016*	2 July	55	**Turnbull** (PM) LP def. Shorten (OL) ALP

Note: Data compiled by the author from the sample and AEC (2007; 2008; 2016). Campaign dates are measured from the policy launch speeches or issuing of the writs (whichever comes first) until polling day. * The 2016 election, held at the time of writing, was not formally included in the sample for the detailed qualitative analysis, but is drawn into the discussion where relevant in this book.

APPENDIX 3

MAJOR AUSTRALIAN POLITICAL PARTIES, 1901–2016

Party	Year Formed	Details
Australian Labor Party (ALP)*	1891	Has contested every federal election 1901–2016; changed name from 'Labour' to 'Labor' in 1912; underwent major schisms in 1916, 1931 and 1955, leading to formation of NAT, UAP and DLP
Protectionist (PROT)	1889	Led by Edmund Barton and Alfred Deakin (Australia's first two prime ministers); needed early support of ALP to govern
Free Trade (FT)	1889	Focused on tariff abolition and later anti-socialism; predominantly active in NSW; led in federal elections by George Reid
Commonwealth Liberal Party (LIB)	1909	Formed as a 'Fusion' between FT and PROT; initially led by Alfred Deakin
Nationalist Party (NAT)	1917	Formed a merger between the LIB Party and Billy Hughes' National Labor Party, which had split from the ALP in 1916
United Australia Party (UAP)	1931	Replaced the NAT Party, formed through an alliance with Labor defectors Joseph Lyons and others
Country Party (CP)*	1920	Has been the minor party in Coalition with the UAP/LP since the 1940s; since renamed The National Party of Australia, then The Nationals
Liberal Party of Australia (LP)*	1944	Founded by Robert Menzies; replaced the UAP after its 1943 election loss

* Remains active in Australian federal politics.
Source: Compiled from Jaensch (1994); Brett (2003); AEC Online (2008). Major parties are included according to their ability to win government at an election or hold the prime ministership through coalition.

APPENDIX 4

CHANGES OF GOVERNMENT, PRIME MINISTER AND LEADER, 1901–2015

Date	Change	Details
1903 September	Change of prime minister	Barton (PM) PROT retired; succeeded by Deakin PROT
1904 April	Change of government	Deakin PROT resigned; succeeded by Watson ALP
August	Change of government	Watson ALP resigned; succeeded by Reid FT
1905 July	Change of government	Reid FT voted out by ALP and PROT members; succeeded by Deakin PROT
1907	Change of leader	Watson ALP resigned; succeeded by Fisher ALP
1908	Change of government	Deakin PROT forced from office after losing support of ALP; succeeded by Fisher ALP
1909 May	Change of government	Formation of LIB Party changed numbers in parliament and forced Fisher ALP from office; succeeded by Deakin PM
1910	Change of government	Fisher (OL) ALP def. Deakin (PM) LIB Fusion; Deakin resigned, succeeded by Cook LIB
1913	Change of government	Cook (OL) LIB def. Fisher (PM) ALP
1914	Change of government	Fisher (OL) ALP def. Cook (PM) LIB
1915 October	Change of prime minister	Fisher ALP resigned; succeeded by Hughes ALP
1916	Change of leader	Hughes ALP left party and formed NAT party; Tudor became new ALP leader
1923 February	Change of prime minister	Hughes NAT resigned; succeeded by Bruce NAT
1929	Change of government	Scullin (OL) ALP def. Bruce (PM) NAT
1931	Change of government	Lyons (OL) UAP def. Scullin (PM) ALP
1939 April	Change of prime minister	Lyons UAP died in office; caretaker PM is Page CP; succeeded by Menzies UAP

Date	Change	Details
1941 August	Change of prime minister	Menzies UAP resigned; succeeded by Fadden CP
October	Change of government	Fadden CP resigned; succeeded by Curtin ALP with support of two independent MPs
1945 July	Change of prime minister	Curtin ALP died in office; caretaker PM is Forde ALP; succeeded by Chifley ALP
1949	Change of government	Menzies (OL) LP def. Chifley (PM) ALP
1951	Change of leader	Chifley ALP died; succeeded by Evatt ALP
1960	Change of leader	Evatt ALP retired; succeeded by Calwell ALP
1966	Change of prime minister	Menzies LP resigned; succeeded by Holt LP
1967 February	Change of leader	Calwell ALP resigned; succeeded by Whitlam ALP
December	Change of prime minister	Holt LP died in office; caretaker PM McEwen CP; succeeded by Gorton LP
1971 March	Change of prime minister	Gorton LP def. as leader in tied party room vote; succeeded by McMahon LP
1972 December	Change of government	Whitlam (OL) ALP def. McMahon (PM) LP; McMahon resigned and was succeeded by Snedden LP
1975 March	Change of leader	Snedden LP defeated in second leadership challenge from Fraser LP after winning vote after the 1974 election loss
November	Change of government	Whitlam government is dismissed by Governor-General Kerr; replaced with Fraser LP who goes on to win the December 13 election.
1977 December	Change of leader	Whitlam ALP resigned leadership after election loss; succeeded by Hayden ALP
1983 February	Change of leader	Hayden ALP resigned under pressure from colleagues; succeeded by Hawke ALP
March	Change of government	Hawke (OL) ALP def. Fraser (PM) LP; Fraser resigned and was succeeded by Peacock LP
1985 September	Change of leader	Peacock LP resigned leadership; succeeded by Howard LP
1989 May	Change of leader	Howard LP is defeated in surprise leadership challenge by Peacock LP
1990 April	Change of leader	Peacock LP resigned after 1990 election loss; succeeded by Hewson LP
1991 December	Change of prime minister	Hawke ALP defeated by Keating ALP in second leadership challenge, after unsuccessfully challenging in June

CHANGES OF GOVERNMENT, PRIME MINISTER AND LEADER

Date	Change	Details
1994 May	Change of leader	Hewson LP is defeated in leadership ballot by Downer LP
1995 January	Change of leader	Downer LP resigned; succeeded by Howard LP
1996 March	Change of government	Howard (OL) def. Keating (PM) ALP; Keating is succeeded by Beazley ALP
2001	Change of leader	Beazley steps down as leader after 2001 election; succeeded by Crean ALP
2003 November	Change of leader	Crean ALP resigned after losing party support; succeeded by Latham ALP
2005 January	Change of leader	Latham ALP resigned as party leader; succeeded by Beazley ALP
2006 December	Change of leader	Beazley ALP is challenged for leadership and def. by Rudd ALP
2007 November	Change of government	Rudd (OL) ALP def. Howard (PM) LP; Howard loses his seat, steps down as leader after 2007 election; succeeded by Nelson LP
2008 September	Change of leader	Nelson LP is defeated in leadership ballot by Turnbull LP following spill motion
2009 December	Change of leader	Turnbull LP is defeated in leadership ballot by Abbott LP
2010 June	Change of leader	Rudd ALP resigned from prime ministership after losing party support; succeeded by Gillard ALP
2013 June	Change of leader	Gillard ALP is defeated in leadership ballot by Rudd ALP
September	Change of government	Abbott (OL) LP def. Rudd (PM) ALP
2015 September	Change of leader	Abbott LP is defeated in leadership ballot by Turnbull LP

Notes: Compiled by the author from the sample and Australian Electoral Commission political history data, *AEC Online*, http://aec.gov.au/Elections/Australian_Electoral_History/. Only changes of leader relevant to election campaigns are included.

REFERENCES

Printed Sources

AAP [Australian Associated Press]. 2007. 'Rudd Says Plan to Mine Kokoda Track "Stinks"'. *AAP General News*, 1 November. Factiva Source Document AAP0000020071101e3b1001me.

———. 2009. 'PM's Slang "A Throwback to Bazza McKenzie": Abbott'. *Sydney Morning Herald*, 10 June. http://www.smh.com.au/national/pms-slang-a-throwback-to-bazza-mckenzie-abbott-20090610-c36k.html.

AEC [Australian Electoral Commission]. 2007. 'Federal Election Timetable: Issue of Writs'. *AEC Online*, accessed 30 September 2008. http://www.aec.gov.au/Elections/australian_electoral_system/Electoral_Procedures/Feder al_Election_Timetable.htm#Issue_of_writs.

———. 2008. 'Australian Electoral History: Prime Ministers and Opposition Leaders'. *AEC Online*, accessed 24 September 2008. http://www.aec.gov.au/Elections/Australian_Electoral_History/pm.htm.

———. 2016. 'Election Dates (1901–Present) House of Representatives'. *AEC Online*, accessed 29 June 2016. http://www.aec.gov.au/Elections/australian_electoral_history/hor_dates.htm.

Aksoy, A. 2004. 'Some "Muslims" Within: Watching Television in Britain After September 11'. In *Media, War and Terrorism: Responses from the Middle East and Asia*, edited by P. van Deer and S. Munshi, 224–50. London: Routledge.

Albury Banner and Express. 1925. 'Federal Elections: Mr Charlton in Albury'. *Albury Banner and Express*, 13 November: 32.

ALP [Australian Labor Party]. 2007. 'Kevin Rudd – Australia Day Advertisement'. Transcript from the *Australian Labor Party Website*, accessed 26 November 2008. http://www.alp.org.au/features/alptv/kraustraliaday.php.

Age. 1901. 'Mr Barton's Speech: Policy of the Federal Cabinet'. *Age*, 18 January: 4–5.

———. 1917. 'Fusion Government's Policy: Prime Minister at Bendigo'. *Age*, 28 March: 9.

———. 1925a. 'Issues of the Elections; War on All Extremists'. *Age*, 6 October: 11.

———. 1925b. 'Labor's Policy: Mr Charlton's Opening Speech'. *Age*, 10 October: 17.

———. 1928. 'Federal Elections: Mr Bruce's Policy Speech'. *Age*, 9 October: 9.

———. 1940. 'Every Ounce Behind War Effort: Government's Policy'. *Age*, 3 September: 8.

———. 1949a. 'Joint Opposition Policy Defined'. *Age*, 11 November: 1.

———. 1949b. 'Mr Chifley Did Not Listen'. *Age*, 15 November: 1.

———. 2007. 'If John Howard Wants to be PM Again, He'll Have to Do Better'. *Age*, 13 November: 12

———. 2016. 'Australia's Disgraceful Inhumanity to People Seeking Asylum'. *Age*, 18 May. http://www.theage.com.au/comment/the-age-editorial/australias-disgraceful-inhumanity-to-people-seeking-asulym-20160518-goy8cu.html.

Airne, D. and W. L. Benoit. 2005. '2004 Illinois US Senate Debates: Keyes Versus Obama'. *American Behavioural Scientist* 49(2): 343–52.

Alomes, S. 1988. *A Nation At Last? The Changing Character of Australian Nationalism 1880–1988*. North Ryde, NSW: Angus and Robertson.

Alomes, S. and C. Jones. 1991. *Australian Nationalism: A Documentary History*. North Ryde, NSW: Angus and Roberston.

Althusser, L. (1970 [1995]) 'Ideology and Ideological State Apparatuses (Notes Towards an Investigation)'. In *Mapping Ideology*, edited by S. Zizek, 100–40. London: Verso.

Anderson, B. 1983. *Imagined Communities: Reflections on the Origin and Spread of Nationalism*. London: Verso.

Andrews, E. M. 2008. '"For Australia's Wartime Interests": W.M. Hughes and the Push Against Asquith, Britain March–July 1916'. *Australian Journal of Politics and History* 41(2): 239–52.

Ashbolt, A. 1966. 'Godzone 3: Myth and Reality'. *Meanjin Quarterly* 25(4): 373–88.

Archer, J. 1997. 'Situating National Identity in Theory and Practice'. In *The Politics of Identity in Australia*, edited by G. Stokes, 23–36. Melbourne, VIC: Cambridge University Press.

Archer, R. 1988. 'The Australian Accord'. *International Review of Applied Economics* 2(2): 213–32.

Argus, The. 1903. 'Friday, October 30, 1903'. *The Argus*, 30 October: 4.

Atkins, D. 2008. 'Kevin Rudd's Big Year in Canberra'. *Courier-Mail*, 26 December. http://www.news.com.au/couriermail/story/0,23739,24843958-27197,00.html.

Australian. 2009. 'Bush Awards "Good Friend" John Howard with Presidential Medal of Freedom'. *Australian*, 14 January. http://www.theaustralian.news.com.au/story/0,25197,24911062-2703,00.html.

———. 2016. 'Shrill Reaction On Refugees Exposes Labor's Weakness'. *Australian*, 19 May. http://www.theaustralian.com.au/opinion/editorials/shrill-reaction-on-refugees-exposes-labors-weakness/news-story/db0ff82a7fafe15ace28fe5702ee7fff.

Australian Broadcasting Corporation [ABC]. 2013. *Keating: Episode Four*. ABC Television, 3 December. http://www.abc.net.au/tv/programs/keating/.

———. 2010. 'Abbott Quizzed on Mixed Messages'. *The 7:30 Report*, ABC Television, 17 May. *The 7:30 Report* program archive. http://www.abc.net.au/7.30/content/2010/s2901996.htm.

ABC Radio National. 2007. 'Unforgettable Speeches'. *ABC Radio National Online*, Features. http://www.abc.net.au/rn/features/speeches/.

———. 2008. 'Official Farewell for Former Australian PM'. *ABC Radio National Online*, 8 May. http://www.radioaustralia.net.au/news/stories/200805/s2238442.htm?tab=latest.

ABC Lateline. 2007. 'Alarm Grows Over Kokoda Re-Route Plan'. *Lateline*, ABC Television, *Lateline* Program Archive. http://www.abc.net.au/lateline/content/2007/s2079453.htm.

Baird, J. 2006. 'Bill Shorten: The Voice of the Beaconsfield Mine Rescue'. *Sunday Profile*, ABC Radio National, 14 May. http://www.abc.net.au/sundayprofile/stories/s1637536.htm.

Banwart, M. C. and M. S. McKinney. 2005. 'A Gendered Influence in Campaign Debates? Analysis of Mixed-Gender United States Senate and Gubernatorial Debates'. *Communication Studies* 56(4): 353–73.

Barnes, A. 1972. 'Star-Bright Audience Cheers Him'. *Age*, 14 November: 1.

Benhabib, S. 2002. *The Claims of Culture: Equality and Diversity in the Global Era*. Princeton, NJ: Princeton University Press.

REFERENCES

Bennett, S. 1996. *Winning and Losing: Australian National Elections*. Carlton VIC: Melbourne University Press.

Benoit, W. L. 2003. 'Topics of Presidential Campaign Discourse and Election Outcome'. *Western Journal of Communication* 67(1): 97–112.

Berger, A. 2000. *Media and Communications Research Methods: An Introduction to Qualitative and Quantitative Research Methods*. London: Sage.

Berkovic, N. 2010. 'Abbott Says Gillard Controlled by Labor Party Machine'. *Australian*, 2 August. http://www.theaustralian.com.au/national-affairs/abbott-says-gillard-controlled-by-labor-party-machine/story-fn59niix-1225900017216.

Bertrand, I. and P. Hughes. 2005. *Media Research Methods: Audiences, Institutions, Texts*. New York: Palgrave Macmillan.

Betts, K. 1999. *The Great Divide: Immigration Politics in Australia*. Potts Point, NSW: Duffy and Snellgrove.

Billig, M. 1995. *Banal Nationalism*. London: Sage.

Birrell, R. 1995. *A Nation of Our Own: Citizenship and Nation-Building in Federation Australia*. Melbourne, VIC: Longman Australia.

Blainey, G. 1967. 'Godzone 7: The New Australia – A Legend of the Lake'. *Meanjin Quarterly* 26(4): 365–80.

Blumenthal, S. 1980. *The Permanent Campaign: Inside the World of Elite Political Operatives*. Boston, MA: Beacon Press.

Bodey, M. 2010. 'MasterChef Tops 3.9 but Debate Not Far Behind'. *Australian*, 26 July. http://www.theaustralian.com.au/business/media/masterchef-tops-39m-but-debate-not-far-behind/story-e6frg996-1225896908998.

Bongiorno, F. 2001. '"Every Woman a Mother": Radical Intellectuals, Sex Reform and the "Woman Question" in Australia, 1980–1918'. *Hecate* 27(1): 44–65.

Bowers, P. 1983. 'Hawke Winds Up As Fraser Winds Down'. *Sydney Morning Herald*, 17 February: 1–2.

Brady, H. E. and R. Johnston (Eds). 2006. *Capturing Campaign Effects*. Ann Arbor, MI: University of Michigan Press.

Brett, J. 1992. *Robert Menzies' Forgotten People*. Chippendale, NSW: Macmillan Australia.

———. 1994. 'Words Fail Us – Political Language in the 1990s'. In *The Abundant Culture: Meaning and Significance in Everyday Australia*, edited by D. Headon, J. Hooton and D. Horne, 150–55. St Leonards, NSW: Allen and Unwin.

———. 2003. *Australian Liberals and the Moral Middle Class: From Alfred Deakin to John Howard*. Port Melbourne, VIC: Cambridge University Press.

———. 2004. 'The New Liberalism'. In *The Howard Years*, edited by R. Manne, 76–93. Melbourne, VIC: Black Inc.

———. 2005. 'Relaxed and Comfortable: The Liberal Party's Australia'. *Quarterly Essay* 19. Melbourne, VIC: Black Inc.

———. 2012. 'Alfred Deakin's Childhood: Books, a Boy, and his Mother'. *Australian Historical Studies* 43(1): 61–77.

Brookes, S. 2010. 'Exclusion and National Identity: The Language of Immigration and Border Control in Australian Federal Election Campaigns'. Refereed paper presented to the *Australasian Political Science Association Conference*, University of Melbourne, 27–29 September.

———. 2011. '"Unscripted and Unpredictable": Communication and Connection in Televised Town Halls, Australian Federal Election 2010'. *Communication, Politics and Culture* 44(2): 57–75.

———. 2012. '"Secure in Our Identity": Regional Threat and Opportunity in Australian Election Discourse, 1993 and 1996'. *Australian Journal of Politics and History* 58(4): 542–56.

Burgess, J. and A. Bruns. 2012. '(Not) The Twitter Election: The Dynamics of the #ausvotes Conversation in Relation to the Australian Media Ecology'. *Journalism Practice* 6(3): 384–402.

Burgmann, M. 1984. 'Hot and Cold: Dr Evatt and the Russians, 1945–1949'. In *Australia's First Cold War, 1945–1953: Vol. 1 Society, Communism and Culture*, edited by A. Curthoys and J. Merritt, 80–108. North Sydney, NSW: George Allen and Unwin.

Burgmann, V. 2005. 'Language and the Labor Tradition'. In *A Passion for Politics: Essays in Honour of Graham Maddox*, edited by T. Battin, 15–26. Sydney, NSW: Pearson Education.

———. 2006. 'Contesting the Injuries of Class'. *Journal of Australian Studies* 89: 91–104.

Burke, A. 2008. *Fear of Security: Australia's Invasion Anxiety*. Cambridge: Cambridge University Press.

———. 2010. 'Questions of Community: Australian Identity and Asian Change'. *Australian Journal of Political Science* 45(1): 75–93.

Burke, T. 2012. Interview with Chris Uhlmann in 'Burke Gives Frank Assessment of Developments'. *7:30*, ABC Television, 22 February. http://www.abc.net.au/7.30/content/2012/s3437238.htm.

Burns, R. N. 1925. 'Matthew Charlton: Safe, Sound and Solid'. *The Truth*, October 11: 8.

Button, J. 2012. *Speechless: A Year in My Father's Business*. Carlton, VIC: Melbourne University Press.

Cain, F. and F. Farrell. 1984. 'Menzies' War on the Communist Party, 1949–1951'. In *Australia's First Cold War, 1945–1953, Vol. 1: Society, Communism and Culture*, edited by A. Curthoys and J. Merritt, 109–28. North Sydney, NSW: George Allen and Unwin.

Caldas-Coulthard, C. R. and M. Coulthard (Eds). 1996. *Texts and Practices: Readings in Critical Discourse Analysis*. London: Routledge.

Calhoun, C. 2004. 'Is it Time to Be Postnational?' In *Ethnicity, Nationalism and Minority Rights*, edited by S. May, T. Modood and J. Squires, 231–56. New York, NY: Cambridge University Press.

Camperdown Herald. 1914. 'Mr Fisher at Colac'. *Camperdown Herald*, 8 August: 2.

Canberra Times. 1940. 'Mr Menzies Outlines Policy For Elections'. *Canberra Times*, 3 September: 2.

———. 1949. 'Chifley Government to Stand on Record'. *Canberra Times*, 15 November: 1.

———. 1958. 'Political Leaders Differ Sharply on Major Issues'. *Canberra Times*, 17 November: 1.

———. 1963. 'ALP Promise of a New Economic Era'. *Canberra Times*, 7 November: 1.

Cashman, R. 2002. *Sport in the National Imagination: Australian Sport in the Federation Decades*. Sydney, NSW: Walla Walla Press.

Castles, S., W. Foster, R. Iredale, and C. Withers. 1988. *Immigration and Australia: Myths and Realities*. Sydney, NSW: Allen and Unwin.

Cathcart, M. and K. Darian-Smith. 2004. *Stirring Australian Speeches: The Definitive Collection from Botany to Bali*. Carlton, VIC: Melbourne University Publishing.

Caulfield, M. 2007. *The Vietnam Years: From the Jungle to the Australian Suburbs*. Sydney, NSW: Hachette Livre Australia.

Charlton, P. 2002. 'Tampa: The Triumph of Politics'. In *Howard's Race: Winning the Unwinnable Election*, edited by D. Solomon, 79–107. Pymble, NSW: Harper Collins.

Chen, P. J. 2014. 'New Media Electioneering in the 2013 Australian Federal Election'. *Global Media Journal: Australian Edition* 10(1): 1–17.

Clark, A. 2016. 'The Still Unknown Malcolm Turnbull Goes to Voters'. *Australian Financial Review*, 28 April. http://www.afr.com/news/politics/national/the-still-unknown-malcolm-turnbull-goes-to-voters-20160428-gohep4.

Clark, T. 2013. 'Keating's Redfern Speech is Still Worth Fighting Over'. *The Conversation*, 9 December. https://theconversation.com/keatings-redfern-speech-is-still-worth-fighting-over-21118.

Cole-Adams, P. 1995. 'Mr Reasonable Has His Day'. *Canberra Times*, 31 January: 1.

Coleman, S. 2015. 'Elections as Storytelling Contests'. *Contemporary Theatre Review* 25(2): 166–76.

Collins, J. 1988. *Migrant Hands in Distant Lands: Australia's Post-war Immigration*. Sydney, NSW: Pluto Press.

Coorey, P. 2009. 'The Rudd Supremacy'. *Sydney Morning Herald*, 30 March. http://www.smh.com.au/national/the-rudd-supremacy-20090329-9flo.html.

Connell, R. W. 1977. *Ruling Class, Ruling Culture: Studies of Conflict, Power and Hegemony in Australian Life*. Middle Park, VIC: Cambridge University Press.

Connell, R.W. and T. H. Irving. 1980. *Class Structure in Australian History: Poverty and Progress*, 2nd Edn. Melbourne, VIC: Longman Cheshire.

Cope, B. and M. Kalantzis. 2000. *A Place in the Sun: Re-creating the Australian Way of Life*. Sydney, NSW: Harper Collins.

Corcoran, P. 1979. *Political Language and Rhetoric*. St Lucia, QLD: University of Queensland Press.

Cottle, S. 2004. *The Racist Murder of Stephen Lawrence: Media Performance and Public Transformation*. London: Praeger.

———. 2006. *Mediatised Conflict: Developments in Media and Conflict Studies*. Berkshire, England: Open University Press.

Cotton, J. 2015. 'William Morris Hughes, Empire and Nationalism: The Legacy of the First World War'. *Australian Historical Studies* 46(1): 100–18.

Cowper, N. 1952. 'W.M. Hughes'. *The Australian Quarterly* 24(4): 5–7.

Cox, E. H. 1955. 'Mr Menzies' Policy Speech'. *The Melbourne Herald*, 16 November: 4.

———.1958. 'Labor States Poll Policy: Family-Aid Key in Evatt's Power Bid'. *The Melbourne Herald*, 16 October: 7.

———. 1966. 'Thanks for the Delivery'. *The Melbourne Herald*, 9 November: 7.

Crawford, R. 2004. 'Modernising Menzies, Whitlam, and Australian Elections'. *The Drawing Board: An Australian Review of Public Affairs* 4(3): 137–61.

Crisp, L. F. 1977. *Ben Chifley: A Political Biography*. London: Angus and Robertson.

Crowe, A. 1999. *The Battle After the War: The Story of Australia's Vietnam Veterans*. St Leonards, NSW: Allen and Unwin.

Cumpston, I. M. 1989. *Lord Bruce of Melbourne*. Melbourne, VIC: Longman Cheshire.

Curran, J. 2006. *The Power of Speech: Australian Prime Ministers Defining the National Image*. Carlton, VIC: Melbourne University Press.

Curran, J. and S. Ward. 2010. *The Unknown Nation: Australia After Empire*. Carlton, VIC: Melbourne University Publishing.

Daily Telegraph. 2007. '2007 Election: Battle for NSW: Soldiers' Sacrifice A Reminder To All'. *Daily Telegraph*, 12 November: 6.

Daly, F. 1984. *From Curtin to Hawke*. South Melbourne, VIC: Sun Books.

Damousi, J. 1999. *The Labour of Loss: Mourning, Memory and Wartime Bereavement in Australia*. Melbourne, VIC: Cambridge University Press.

Davis, M. 2007. 'Share Success Puts Icing on their Family Cake'. *Sydney Morning Herald*, 15 February. http://www.smh.com.au/news/national/share-success-puts-icing-on-their-family-cake/2007/02/14/1171405299811.html.

Davis, M. 1999. *Gangland: Cultural Elites and the New Generationalism*. St Leonards, NSW: Allen and Unwin.

Day, D. (Ed.). 1998a. *Australian Identities*. Melbourne, VIC: Melbourne Scholarly Publishing.

———. 1998b. 'The Demise of the Digger: Australian Identity in a Post-colonial World'. In *Australian Identities*, edited by D. Day, 73–95. Melbourne, VIC: Melbourne Scholarly Publishing.

———. 2001. *Chifley*. Pymble, NSW: Harper Collins.

Deane, J. 2015. *Catch and Kill: The Politics of Power*. St Lucia, QLD: University of Queensland Press.

Diaz, J. 2010. 'One Year: Storyteller-in-chief'. *The New Yorker News Desk*, 20 January. http://www.newyorker.com/news/news-desk/one-year-storyteller-in-chief.

Dickerson, J. 2009. 'The Storyteller'. *Slate Politics Blog*, January. http://www.slate.com/articles/news_and_politics/politics/2009/01/the_storyteller.html.

Dixson, M. 1999 [1976]. *The Real Matilda: Woman and Identity in Australia, 1788 to the Present*. Sydney, NSW: University of New South Wales Press.

Dryenfurth, N. 2014. 'Labor and the Anzac Legend, 1915–45'. *Labour History* 106 (May): 163–88.

Dutton, P. 2016a. 'The Border and Beyond: Australia's 21st Century Border Security System'. Speech at the *Safeguarding Australia 2016* Conference, Canberra, 11–12 May.

———. 2016b. Election Interview with Paul Murray. *Paul Murray Live*, Sky News Televsion. Transcribed from video on *Sydney Morning Herald Online*, 'Dutton: These People Will Take Australian Jobs', 17 May. http://www.smh.com.au/video/video-news/video-national-news/dutton-these-people-will-take-australian-jobs-20160517-4f5ph.html.

Edwards, C. 1965. *Bruce of Melbourne: Man of Two Worlds*. London: Heinemann.

Edwards, P. G. 1997. *A Nation At War: Australian Politics, Society and Diplomacy During the Vietnam War, 1965–1975*. St Leonards, NSW: Allen and Unwin.

Elder, C. 2007. *Being Australian: Narratives of National Identity*. Crows Nest, NSW: Allen and Unwin.

Ellis, B. 1983. *The Things We Did Last Summer: An Election Journal*, Sydney, NSW: William Collins.

Ewart, H. 2010. 'The "Real" Julia Gillard'. *The 7:30 Report*, ABC Television, 2 August. http://www.abc.net.au/7.30/content/2010/s2971415.htm.

Fairclough, N. 1995. *Media Discourse*. New York, NY: St Martin's Press.

Ferguson, S. 2015. 'Rudd Fronts the ALP Party Conference'. *The Killing Season*, Episode 1, ABC Television. Online footage, 5 June. http://www.abc.net.au/news/2015-06-05/2007-alp-party-conference/6524280.

Firth, M. 1996 'Leader Gets High on Scent of the Political Prize'. *Age*, 29 February: 11.

Fitzhardinge, L. F. 1954. 'W.M. Hughes and "The Case for Labor"'. *Meanjin* 13(3): 414–23.

———. 1983. 'Hughes, William Morris (Billy) (1862–1952)'. *Australian Dictionary of Biography*, National Centre of Biography, Australian National University. Published first in hardcopy 1983, accessed online 24 March 2016. http://adb.anu.edu.au/biography/hughes-william-morris-billy-6761/text11689.

Flew, T. 2008. 'Not Yet the Internet Election: Online Media, Political Commentary and the 2007 Australian Federal Election'. *Media International Australia Incorporating Culture and Policy* 126: 5–13.

Fulilove, M. (Ed.). 2014. *Men and Women of Australia! Our Greatest Modern Speeches*, Revised Second Edition. Melbourne, VIC: Viking.

Franklin, B. 2004. *Packaging Politics: Political Communications in Britain's Media Democracy*. London: Arnold.

FreeTV Australia. 2015. 'History of Australian Television – Inside the Industry'. *FreeTV Australia*, accessed 24 June 2016. http://www.freetv.com.au/content_common/pg-inside-the-industry.seo

Freudenberg, G. 1977. *A Certain Grandeur: Gough Whitlam in Politics*. South Melbourne, VIC: Macmillan.

———. 2005. *A Figure of Speech: A Political Memoir*. Milton, QLD: John Wiley and Sons.

Garrett, P. and A. Bell. 1998. 'Media and Discourse: A Critical Overview'. In *Approaches to Media Discourse*, edited by A. Bell and P. Garrett, 1–20. Oxford: Blackwell.

Gartrell, A. 2016. 'Federal Election 2016: The Third Election Debate Was the Best of the Bunch'. *Age*, 17 June. http://www.smh.com.au/federal-politics/federal-election-2016-opinion/federal-election-2016-the-third-election-debate-was-the-best-of-the-bunch-20160617-gpm2wk.html.

Gartrell, A. and L. Ja. 2007. 'Remembering the Brave'. *Courier-Mail*, 12 November: 30.

Gawenda, M. 1987. 'After All The Glitter, A Big Leap Into Ordinariness'. *Age*, 26 June: 1.

———. 1996. 'Notebook: Big Picture Man A Cardboard Cutout'. *Age*, 15 February: 1.

Georgakopolou, A. and D. Goutsos. 2004. *Discourse Analysis: An Introduction*, Second Edition. Edinburgh: Edinburgh University Press.

Gibson, R. and I. McAllister. 2015. 'New Media, Elections and the Political Knowledge Gap in Australia'. *Journal of Sociology* 5(2): 337–53.

Gilroy, P. 2004. *Between Camps: Nations, Cultures and the Allure of Race*. London: Routledge.

Gleeson, K. 2014. *Australia's 'War on Terror' Discourse*. Surrey, England: Ashgate.

Glover, D. 2007. 'Speechwriters and Political Speech: Pitting the Good Angels Against the Bleak'. In *Government Communication in Australia*, edited by S. Young, 147–57. Melbourne, VIC: Cambridge University Press.

———. 2010. 'Redfern Speech Flatters Writer as Well as Orator'. *Australian*, 27 August. http://www.theaustralian.com.au/national-affairs/opinion/redfern-speech-flatters-writer-as-well-as-orator/story-e6frgd0x-1225910609841.

Goldsworthy, D. 2002. *Losing the Blanket: Australia and the End of Britain's Empire*. Melbourne, VIC: Melbourne University Press.

Goot, M. and S. Scalmer. 2013. 'Party Leaders, the Media, and Political Persuasion: The Campaigns of Evatt and Menzies on the Referendum to Protect Australia from Communism'. *Australian Historical Studies* 44(1): 71–88.

Gordon, M. 2007. 'Rudd Puts The Lid On'. *Age*, 15 November: 19.

———. 2016. 'Leaders' Debate: Malcolm Turnbull on Message, Bill Shorten Goes the Biff, and the Voters Lose'. *Age*, 30 May. http://www.theage.com.au/federal-politics/federal-election-2016-opinion/leaders-debate-malcolm-turnbull-on-message-bill-shorten-goes-the-biff-and-the-voters-lose-20160529-gp6r58.html.

Grattan, M. 2007. 'Rudd Assails "Reckless" PM'. *Age*, 15 November: 1.

———. 2008. 'Eyes on the Prize; *The Age*, 23 April, 2007'. In *The Best Australian Political Writing 2008*, edited by T. Jones, 38–42. Carlton, VIC: Melbourne University Press.

———. 2010. 'PM Gets the Job Done at Low-key Launch'. *Sydney Morning Herald*, 17 August. http://www.smh.com.au/federal-politics/political-opinion/pm-gets-the-job-done-at-lowkey-launch-20100817-127js.html.

Gray, G. and C. Winter (Eds). 1997. *The Resurgence of Racism: Howard, Hanson and the Race Debate*. Melbourne, VIC: Monash University.

Grey, J. and J. Doyle (Eds). 1992. *Vietnam – War, Myth and Memory: Contemporary Perspectives on Australia's War in Vietnam*. St Leonards, NSW: Allen and Unwin.

Green, J. 2007. 'Who Would You Turn Gay For? Not Barrie Cassidy'. *Crikey*, 15 November. http://www.crikey.com.au/2007/11/15/who-would-you-turn-gay-for-not-barrie-cassidy/.

Green, A. 2011. 'Turnout at Australian Elections 1901–1925'. *Antony Green's Election Blog*, ABC Elections, 15 April. http://blogs.abc.net.au/antonygreen/2011/04/turnout-at-australian-elections-1901-1925.html.

Griffen-Foley, B. 2007. 'Talkback Radio and Australian Politics Since the Summer of 1967'. *Media International Australia Incorporating Culture and Policy* 122: 96–107.

Griffiths, M. and M. Wesley. 2010. 'Taking Asia Seriously'. *Australian Journal of Political Science* 45(1): 13–28.

Grimshaw, P., M. Lake, A. McGrath and M. Quartly. 1994. *Creating a Nation*. Ringwood, VIC: McPhee Gribble.

Grube, D. 2013. *Prime Ministers and Rhetorical Governance*. Basingstoke, UK: Palgrave Macmillan.

Gulmanelli, S. 2014. 'John Howard and the "Anglospherist" Reshaping of Australia'. *Australian Journal of Political Science* 49(4): 581–95.

Gupta-Carlson, H. 2016. 'Re-imagining the Nation: Storytelling and Social Media in the Obama Campaigns'. *PS: Political Science & Politics* 49(1): 71–75.

Gurr, M. 2006. *Days Like These*. Carlton, VIC: Melbourne University Press.

Hage, G. 1998. *White Nation: Fantasies of White Supremacy in a Multicultural Society*. Melbourne, VIC: Pluto Press.

———. 2003. *Against Paranoid Nationalism: Searching for Hope in a Shrinking Society*. Annandale, VIC: Pluto Press.

Hall, S. 1983. 'The Problem of Ideology – Marxism Without Guarantees'. In *Marx 100 Years On*, edited by B. Matthews, 57–84. London: Lawrence and Wishart.

Hammerton, A. J. and A. Thomson. 2005. *Ten Pound Poms: Australia's Invisible Migrants*. New York, NY: Manchester University Press.

Hanska, J. 2012. *Reagan's Mythical America: Storytelling as Political Leadership*. New York, NY: Palgrave MacMillan.

Harmon, S. 2016. 'Kate Tempest: "There is a Damaging and Poisonous Racism at Root in Australia"'. *The Guardian*, 19 May. https://www.theguardian.com/stage/2016/may/19/kate-tempest-sydney-writers-festival-poisonous-racism-australia.

Hart, R. P. 1994. *Seducing America: How Television Charms the Modern Voter*. New York, NY: Oxford University Press.

Hart, R. P. and J. P. Childers. 2005. 'The Evolution of Candidate Bush: A Rhetorical Analysis'. *American Behavioural Scientist* 49(2): 180–97.

Hart, R. P. and S. E. Jarvis. 1997. 'Political Debate: Forms, Styles and Media'. *American Behavioural Scientist* 40(8): 1095–122.

Hart, R. P., S. E. Jarvis, W. P. Jennings and D. Smith-Howell. 2005. *Political Keywords: Using Language That Uses Us*. New York, NY: Oxford University Press.

Hart, R. P. and M. C. Johnson. 1999. 'Constructing the Electorate During Presidential Campaigns'. *Presidential Studies Quarterly* 29(4): 830–50.

Hasham, N. 2016. 'Second Refugee Sets Herself on Fire'. *Sydney Morning Herald*, 3 May. http://www.smh.com.au/federal-politics/political-news/reports-of-second-refugee-setting-themselves-on-fire-at-nauru-20160502-gokg9y.html.

Hatch, D. 2007. 'New Battle Flares Over the Kokoda'. *West Australian*, 2 November: 17.

Haupt, R. and M. Grattan. 1983. *31 Days to Power: Hawke's Victory*. Sydney, NSW: George Allen and Unwin.

Hay, J. 2011. '"Popular Culture" in a Critique of the New Political Reason'. *Cultural Studies* 25(4–5): 659–84.

Hearn, M. and I. Tregenza. 2014. '"The Maximum of Good Citizenship": Citizenship and Nation-building in Alfred Deakin's Post-Federation Speeches'. In *Studies in Australian Political Rhetoric*, edited by J. Uhr and R. Walter, 177–94. Canberra, ACT: ANU Press.

Hewett, J. 1996. 'Ascent of Homespun Howard'. *Australian Financial Review*, 19 February: 6.

———. 2010. 'A Confused Nation Asks, Will the Real Julia Gillard Stand Up?'. *Australian*, 31 July.

Himmelfarb, G. 2002. 'The Illusions of Cosmopolitanism'. In *For Love of Country? The Limits of Patriotism*, edited by M. C. Nussbaum, 72–77. Boston, MA: Beacon Press.

Hocking, J. 2008. *Gough Whitlam: A Moment in History: The Biography*. Carlton, VIC: Melbourne University Publishing.

———. 2016. *The Dismissal Dossier: Everything You Were Never Meant to Know About November 1975*. Carlton, VIC: Melbourne University Publishing.

Hodge, B. and J. O'Carroll. 2006. *Borderwork in Multicultural Australia*. Crows Nest, NSW: Allen and Unwin.

Hogan, M. 2006. 'Reid, George (later Sir George) Houstoun'. In *The Premiers of NSW, Volume 1: 1856–1901*, edited by D. Clune and K. Turner, 191–208. Annandale, NSW: Federation Press.

Holbrook, T. 1996. *Do Campaigns Matter?* Thousand Oaks, CA: Sage Publications.

Hollins, K. 2011. 'Youth Voters Seek Refuge in the Australian Greens'. *Online Opinion*, 21 July. http://www.onlineopinion.com.au/view.asp?article=12337.

Holton, R. 1998. 'Globalisation and Australian Identities'. In *Australian Identities*, edited by D. Day, 98–211. Melbourne, VIC: Melbourne Scholarly Publishing.

Horne, D. 1964. *The Lucky Country*. Ringwood, VIC: Penguin.

———. 2000. *Billy Hughes*. Melbourne, VIC: Bookman Press.

Howard, J. 2010. *Lazarus Rising: A Personal and Political Autobiography*. Sydney, NSW: Harper Collins.

Hudson, K. 1978. *The Language of Modern Politics*. London: Macmillan Press.

Hudson, P. 2010. 'Julia Gillard Vows to Take Control of Her Election Campaign'. *Herald Sun*, 2 August. http://www.heraldsun.com.au/news/special-features/julia-gillard-vows-to-take-control-of-her-election-campaign/story-fn5ko0pw-1225899749875.

Hudson, W. and G. Bolton (Eds). 1997. *Creating Australia: Changing Australian History*. St Leonards, NSW: Allen and Unwin.

Ireland, J. 2012. 'Roxon Says She Won't Work with PM Rudd Again'. *Sydney Morning Herald*, 24 February. http://www.smh.com.au/federal-politics/political-news/roxon-says-she-wont-work-with-pm-rudd-again-20120223-1trqn.html.

Jackman, C. 2008. *Inside Kevin07: The People, The Plan, The Prize*. Carlton, VIC: Melbourne University Press.

Jacobs, K. 2015. '"Hurtling Down the Track": The Significance of Australian Population Debates in an Era of Anxiety'. *Journal of Sociology* 51(4): 799–811.

Jaensch, D. 1994. *Power Politics: Australia's Party System, 3rd Edition*. St Leonards, NSW: Allen and Unwin.

Jaensch, D. and H. Manning. 2001. '"We Want a White Man's Continent": The Free Trade and Protection Campaigns'. In *1901: The Forgotten Election*, edited by M. Simms, 95–116. St. Lucia, QLD: University of Queensland Press.

Jayasuria, L., D. Walker and J. Gothard (Eds). 2003. *Legacies of White Australia: Race, Culture and Nation*. Crawley, WA: University of Western Australia Press.

Jean, P. 2008. 'Bob Hawke Tells Kevin Rudd to Find a Speechwriter'. *Herald Sun Online*, 20 November. http://www.news.com.au/heraldsun/story/0,21985,24677949-662,00.html.

Jensen, E. 2013. 'The Saboteur: Kevin Rudd's Unrelenting Campaign to Regain Power'. *The Monthly*, May. https://www.themonthly.com.au/issue/2013/may/1367364737/erik-jensen/kevin-rudd-s-unrelenting-campaign-regain-power.

Johnson, C. 1998. 'Pauline Hanson and One Nation'. In *The New Politics of the Right: Neo-Populist Parties and Movements in Established Democracies*, edited by H. G. Betz and S. Immerfall, 211–18. New York, NY: St Martins Press.

———. 2000. *Governing Change: From Keating to Howard*. St. Lucia, QLD: University of Queensland Press.

———. 2002. 'Australian Political Science and the Study of Discourse'. Refereed paper presented at the *Australasian Political Studies Jubilee Conference*. Australian National University, Canberra, 1–4 October.

———. 2005. 'Narratives of Identity: Denying Empathy in Conservative Discourses on Race, Class and Sexuality'. *Theory and Society* 34: 37–61.

———. 2006. 'John Howard's UnAustralia'. Paper presented to *UnAustralia: The Cultural Studies Association of Australasia Annual Conference*. University of Canberra, 6–8 December.

———. 2007. 'John Howard's "Values" and Australian Identity'. *Australian Journal of Political Science* 42(2): 195–211.

———. 2009. 'The Hawke Government and Consensus'. In *The Hawke Legacy*, edited by G. Bloustien, B. Comber and A. Mackinnon, 3–14. Kent Town, SA: Wakefield Press.

———. 2015. 'The Battle for Hearts and Minds'. In *Abbott's Gambit: The 2013 Australian Federal Election*, edited by C. Johnson and J. Wanna, 35–48. Canberra, ACT: ANU Press.

Johnson, C., P. Ahluwalia and G. McCarthy. 2010. 'Australia's Ambivalent Re-imagining of Asia'. *Australian Journal of Political Science* 45(1): 59–74.

Johnstone, A. 1991. 'Political Broadcasts: An Analysis of Form, Content, and Style in Presidential Communication'. In *Mediated Politics in Two Cultures: Presidential Campaigning in the United States and France*, edited by L.L. Kaid, J. Gerstle and K. R. Sanders, 59–72. New York, NY: Praeger.

Jupp, J. 2007. *From White Australia to Woomera: The Story of Australian Immigration, Second Edition*. Port Melbourne, VIC: Cambridge University Press.

———. 2015. 'Ethnic Voting and Asylum Issues'. In *Abbott's Gambit: The 2013 Australian Federal Election*, edited by C. Johnson and J. Wanna, 332–40. Canberra, ACT: ANU Press.

Kabanoff, B., W. Murphy, S. Brown and D. Conroy. 2001. 'The DICTION of Howard and Beazley: What Can Computerised Content Analysis Tell Us About the Language of Our Political Leaders'. *Australian Journal of Communication* 28(3): 85–101.

Kane, J. 2014. 'Introduction'. In *Studies in Australian Political Rhetoric*, edited by J. Uhr and R. Walter, 3–16. Canberra, ACT: ANU Press.

Katz, E. and Y. Warshel. 2001. 'Introduction'. In *Election Studies: What's Their Use?*, edited by E. Katz and Y. Warshel, 1–14. Boulder, CO: Westview Press.

Kavanagh, D. 1995. *Election Campaigning: The New Marketing of Politics*. Oxford: Blackwell.

Keane, B. 2009. 'Fair Shake of That Sautéed Tomato Preserve in a Bottle'. *Crikey*, 12 June. http://www.crikey.com.au/2009/06/12/fair-shake-of-that-sauteed-tomato-preserve-in-a-bottle/.

———. 2010. 'Jubilation, Expectation, and a Whole Lotta' Nuthin – The Liberal Launch'. *Crikey*, 9 August. http://www.crikey.com.au/2010/08/09/jubilation-expectation-and-a-whole-lotta-nuthin-the-liberal-launch/?wpmp_switcher=mobile.

Keating, P. 2010. 'On That Historic Day in Redfern, the Words I Spoke Were Mine'. *Sydney Morning Herald*, 26 August. http://www.smh.com.au/federal-politics/political-opinion/on-that-historic-day-in-redfern-the-words-i-spoke-were-mine-20100825-13s5w.html.

Kavanagh, D. 1995. *Election Campaigning: The New Marketing of Politics*. Oxford: Blackwell.

———. 2003. *From 9/11 To Terror War: The Dangers of the Bush Legacy*. Lanham, MD: Rowman and Littlefield.

Kelly, P. 1994. 'Foreword'. In *The Battles That Shaped Australia: The Australian's Anniversary Essays*, edited by D. Horner, v–vi. St Leonards, NSW: Allen and Unwin.

Kelly, P. and T. Bramston. 2015. *The Dismissal: In the Queen's Name*. Melbourne, VIC: Penguin.

Kemp, R. and M. Stanton (Eds). 2004. *Speaking for Australia: Parliamentary Speeches that Shaped the Nation*. Crows Nest, NSW: Allen and Unwin.

Kenny, M. 2009. 'PM Discovers A New Language – Strine'. *Courier Mail*, 10 June. http://www.couriermail.com.au/news/kevin-rudd-discovers-a-new-language-strine/story-e6freon6-1225731846527.

Kiernan, C. 1978. *Calwell: A Personal and Political Biography*. West Melbourne, VIC: Thomas Nelson.

Kingston, M. 1999. *Off the Rails: The Pauline Hanson Trip*. St Leonards, NSW: Allen and Unwin.

Koleth, E. 2010. 'Multiculturalism: A Review of Australian Policy Statements and Recent Debates in Australia and Overseas'. *Australian Parliamentary Library Research Paper No. 6, 2010–11*. http://www.aph.gov.au/About_Parliament/Parliamentary_Departments/Parliamentary_Library/pubs/rp/rp1011/11rp06#_Toc275248119.

Krippendorf, K. 2004. *Content Analysis: An Introduction to Its Methodology, Second Edition*. London: Sage.

Laing, M. and B. McCaffrie. 2013. 'The Politics Prime Ministers Make: Political Time and Executive Leadership in Westminster Systems'. In *Understanding Prime Ministerial Performance: Comparative Perspectives*, edited by P. Strangio, P. T'Hart and J. Walter, 79–101. Oxford: Oxford University Press.

Langley, G. 1992. *A Decade of Dissent: Vietnam and the Conflict on the Australian Homefront*. North Sydney, NSW: Allen and Unwin.

Lee, D. 2010. *Stanley Melbourne Bruce: Australian Internationalist*. London: Continuum Books.

Lewis, S. (Ed.). 2014. *Stand and Deliver: Celebrating 50 Years of the National Press Club of Australia*. Melbourne, VIC: Black Inc.

Leys, N. 2013. 'Selfie-Obsessed PM Misses the Mark'. *Australian*, 10 August: 1.

Lilleker, D. G. 2006. *Key Concepts in Political Communication*. Thousand Oaks, CA: Sage.

Lion, P. 2012. 'Former Prime Minister Bob Hawke Thrills SCG Cricket Crowd Skolling a Beer'. *Daily Telegraph*, 6 January. http://www.dailytelegraph.com.au/former-prime-minister-bob-hawke-thrills-scg-cricket-crowd-skolling-a-beer/story-e6freuy9-1226238455269.

Little, G. 1997a. 'Malcolm Fraser: A Strong Leader Revisited'. In *Political Lives*, edited by J. Brett, 52–70. St Leonards, NSW: Allen and Unwin.

———. 1997b. 'The Two Narcissisms: Comparing Hawke and Keating'. In *Political Lives*, edited by J. Brett, 16–27. St Leonards, NSW: Allen and Unwin.

Lopez. M. 2001. 'The Origins of Multiculturalism in Australian Politics: The Role of the Multicultural Left 1945–1975'. In *Reconciliation, Multiculturalism, Identities: Sensible Solutions*, edited by M. Kalantzis and B. Cope, 31–46. Australia: Common Ground Publishing.

Lloyd, C. 1993. 'Prime Ministers and the Media'. In *Menzies to Keating: The Development of the Australian Prime Ministership*, edited by P. Weller, 109–37. London: Hurst and Company.

MacCallum, M. 2013. *The Good, the Bad and the Unlikely: Australia's Prime Ministers*. Collingwood, VIC: Black Inc.

Macdonald, M. 2003. *Exploring Media Discourse*. London: Arnold.

Macintyre, S. and A. Clark. 2004. *The History Wars, 2nd Edition*. Melbourne, VIC: Melbourne University Press.

Maitland Daily Mercury. 1901. 'The Commonwealth Policy'. *Maitland Daily Mercury*, 18 January: 2.

Maddox, M. 2005. *God Under Howard: The Rise of the Religious Right in Australian Politics*. Crows Nest, NSW: Allen and Unwin.

Manne, R. 1994. *The Shadow of 1917: Cold War Conflict in Australia*. Melbourne, VIC: Text Publishing.

———. 2004. 'The Howard Years: A Political Interpretation'. In *The Howard Years*, edited by R. Manne, 3–53. Melbourne, VIC: Black Inc.

Marr, D. 2010. *Power Trip: The Political Journey of Kevin Rudd*, Quarterly Essay 38. Melbourne, VIC: Black Inc.

———. 2015. *Faction Man: Bill Shorten's Path to Power*, Quarterly Essay 59. Melbourne, VIC: Black Inc.

Marr, D. and M. Wilkinson. 2002. *Dark Victory*. Crows Nest, NSW: Allen and Unwin.

Masters, C. 2006. *Jonestown: The Power and Myth of Alan Jones*. Crows Nest, NSW: Allen and Unwin.

McAllister, I. 2014. 'The Personalisation of Politics in Australia'. *Party Politics* 21(3): 337–45.

McAllister, I. and R. Moore (Eds). 1991. *Party Strategy and Change: Australian Political Leaders' Policy Speeches since 1946*. Melbourne, VIC: Longman Cheshire.

McCombs, M. E. and D. L. Shaw. 1993. 'The Evolution of Agenda-Setting Research: Twenty-Five Years in the Marketplace of Ideas'. *Journal of Communication* 43: 58–67.

McDougall, D. 2014. 'The Australian Federal Election of 7 September 2013: A Watershed?' *The Round Table* 10(3): 289–99.

McKee, A. 2002. 'Textual Analysis'. In *The Media and Communications in Australia*, edited by S. Cunningham and G. Turner, 62–71. Crows Nest, NSW: Allen and Unwin.

McKenna, M. 2003. 'Howard's Warriors'. In *Why The War Was Wrong*, edited by R. Gaita, 167–200. Melbourne, VIC: Text Publishing.

McLachlan, N. 1989. *Waiting for the Revolution: A History of Australian Nationalism*. Ringwood, VIC: Penguin.

McLean, D. 2003. *The Prickly Pair: Making Nationalism in Australia and New Zealand*. Dunedin: University of Otago Press.

McNair, B. 2000. *Journalism and Democracy: An Evaluation of the Political Public Sphere*. New York, NY: Routledge.

McQuail, D. 2000. *McQuail's Mass Media Theory, 4th Edition*. London: Sage.

Megalogenis, G. 2003. *Faultlines: Race, Work and the Politics of Changing Australia*. Melbourne, VIC: Scribe.

———. 2010a. *Trivial Pursuit: Leadership and the End of the Reform Era*. Collingwood, VIC: Black Inc.

———. 2010b. 'Rudd Rides the Digital Age to Dominance'. *Australian*, 9 January. http://www.theaustralian.com.au/archive/opinion2013/rudd-rides-the-digital-age-to-dominance/news-story/9300d3866c99b7d045c686ddac63cca4.

Melbourne Herald. 1940a. 'Points from Labor's Policy Speech: War Effort and Finance'. *The Melbourne Herald*, 29 August: 8.

———. 1940b. 'Every Ounce Behind War Effort: Government Policy'. *The Melbourne Herald*, 3 September: 8.

Menzies, R. 1948. 'Politics as an Art'. *New York Times Magazine*, 28 November. Text at *Menzies Virtual Museum*, Menzies Foundation, accessed 30 June 2016. http://menziesvirtualmuseum.org.au/19-speech-is-of-time/112-politics-as-an-art.

———. 1967. *Afternoon Light: Some Memories of Men and Events*. Melbourne, VIC: Cassell Australia.

———. 1970. *The Measure of the Years*. Melbourne, VIC: Cassell Australia.

Meyer, M. 2001. 'Between Theory, Method and Politics: Positioning of the Approaches to CDA'. In *Methods of Critical Discourse Analysis*, edited by R. Wodak and M. Meyer, 14–31. London: Sage Publications.

Moran, A. 2005. *Australia: Nation, Belonging and Globalisation*. New York, NY: Routledge.

Mouffe, C. 2005. *On the Political*. New York, NY: Routledge.

Muir, K. 2008. *Worth Fighting For: Inside the Your Rights at Work Campaign*. Sydney, NSW: University of NSW Press.

Murdoch, W. 1999. *Alfred Deakin: A Sketch*. Melbourne, VIC: Bookman Press.

Murphy, K. 2016. 'Lucky Man: Has Bill Shorten Got What it Takes?'. *The Guardian Australia*, 9 May. http://www.theguardian.com/australia-news/2016/may/09/bill-shorten-election-2016-labor-alp-essay.

National Archives of Australia [NAA] (Undated) 'Gough Whitlam', *Australia's Prime Minsters Website*, accessed 8 May 2008. http://primeministers.naa.gov.au/meetpm.asp?pmId=21&pageName=before.

News, The 1925a. '"I am delighted": Mr M. Charlton Here'. *The News*, 2 November: 1.

———. 1925b. 'Case for Labor; Mr Charlton in Adelaide; No Fireworks'. *The News*, 3 November: 7.

Nicoll, F. 2001. *From Diggers to Drag Queens: Configurations of Australian National Identity*. Annandale, NSW: Pluto Press.

Noonan, P. 1990. *What I Saw At the Revolution: A Political Life in the Reagan Era*. New York, NY: Random House.

Norris, P. 2000. *A Virtuous Circle: Political Communication in Postindustrial Societies*. Cambridge: Cambridge University Press.

Norris, P., J. Curtice, D. Sanders, M. Scammell, and H. A. Semetko. 1999. *On Message: Communicating the Campaign*. London: Sage Publications.

Nussbaum, M. (Ed.). 2002. *For Love of Country? The Limits of Patriotism*. Boston, MA: Beacon Press.

Oakes, L. and D. Solomon. 1973. *The Making of An Australian Prime Minister*. Melbourne, VIC: Cheshire.

O'Shaugnessy, N. 1990. *The Phenomenon of Political Marketing*. New York, NY: St Martin's Press.

Overington, C. 2007. 'Campaign Trail, Election 2007: Oh Please, Let Me Stay Just A Little Bit Longer'. *Australian*, 13 November: 4.

Palfreeman, A. C. 1967. *The Administration of the White Australia Policy*. Melbourne, VIC: Melbourne University Press.

Papacharissi, Z. 2016. 'Affective Publics and Structures of Storytelling: Sentiment, Events and Mediality'. *Information, Communication & Society* 19(3): 307–24.

Partington, G. 1994. *The Australian Nation: Its British and Irish Roots*. Melbourne, VIC: Australian Scholarly Publishing.

Payne, T. 2007. *War and Words: The Australian Press and the Vietnam War*. Carlton, VIC: Melbourne University Press.

Peake, R. 2007. 'Kokoda Detour "Stinks": Rudd'. *Canberra Times*, 2 November: 3.

Pearlman, J. 2007. 'Rudd Slams Kokoda Mining Plans'. *Sydney Morning Herald*, 2 November: 10.

Pilger, J. 2014. 'The British-American Coup that Ended Australian Independence'. *The Guardian*, 23 October. http://www.theguardian.com/commentisfree/2014/oct/23/gough-whitlam-1975-coup-ended-australian-independence.

Pocock, B. 2009. 'The Best of Times, The Worst of Times: The Hawke and Rudd Governments, Employment, and Industrial Relations'. In *The Hawke Legacy*, edited by G. Bloustien, B. Comber and A. Mackinnon, 180–97. Kent Town, SA: Wakefield Press.

Pryor, D. 1987. 'As Television, This Made Good Wireless'. *Age*, 26 June: 18.

Puri, J. 2004. *Encountering Nationalism*. Malden, MA: Blackwell.

Purvis, T. and A. Hunt. 1993. 'Discourse, Ideology, Discourse, Ideology, Discourse, Ideology...'. *The British Journal of Sociology* 44(3): 473–99.

Reed, L. 2004. *Bigger Than Gallipoli: War, History and Memory in Australia*. Crawley, WA: University of Western Australia Press.

Rehn, A. 2010. 'Julia Gillard Says Her Campaign Launch Speech Was From the Heart'. *Daily Telegraph*, 17 August. http://www.dailytelegraph.com.au/julia-gillard-says-her-campaign-launch-speech-was-from-the-heart/story-fn5zm695-1225906476037.

Reynaud, D. 2007. *Celluloid Anzacs: The Great War Through Australian Cinema*. North Melbourne, VIC: Australian Scholarly Publishing.

Reynolds, H. 1996. *Aboriginal Sovereignty: Reflections on Race, State and Nation*. St Leonards, NSW: Allen and Unwin.

———. 2001. *An Indelible Stain? The Question of Genocide in Australia's History*. Ringwood, VIC: Penguin.

———. 2005. *Nowhere People*. Camberwell, VIC: Penguin.

Robertson, J. 1990. *Anzac and Empire: The Tragedy and Glory of Gallipoli*. Port Melbourne, VIC: Hamlyn Australia.

Ross, J. 1985. *The Myth of the Digger: The Australian Soldier in Two World Wars*. Marrickville, NSW: Hale and Iremonger.

Ross, L. 1996 [1977]. *John Curtin: A Biography*. Carlton South, VIC: Melbourne University Press.

Rowley, C. D. 1971. *Outcasts in White Australia*. Canberra, ACT: Australian National University Press.

———. 1972. *The Destruction of Aboriginal Society*. Ringwood, VIC: Penguin Books.

Rundle, G. 2006. 'Flagging passions'. *Age*, 1 April: 11–13.

Sawer, M. 1990. *Sisters in Suits: Women in Public Policy in Australia*. Sydney, NSW: Allen and Unwin.

Sawer, M., M. Tremblay and L. Trimble (Eds). 2006. *Representing Women in Parliament; A Comparative Study*. New York, NY: Routledge.

Special Broadcasting Service [SBS]. 2007. 'Sacrifice in War Is Ageless: Howard'. *World News*, SBS Television, broadcast 11 November.

———. 2016. 'Turnbull First PM to Host Iftar for Ramadan'. *SBS News Online*, 17 June. http://www.sbs.com.au/news/article/2016/06/16/turnbull-first-pm-host-iftar-ramadan.

Scammell, M. 1995. *Designer Politics: How Elections are Won*. New York, NY: St Martins Press.

Schultz, D. (Ed.). 2004. *Lights, Camera, Campaign! Media, Politics and Political Advertising*. New York, NY: Peter Lang Publishing.

Shanahan, D. 2007. 'Rudd's Walk into Vietnam Minefield'. *Australian Online*, 14 April. http://www.theaustralian.news.com.au/story/0,20867,21554452-2702,00.html.

———. 2016. 'Federal Election 2016: You Can Trust Them – To Dish Up Set Lines'. *Australian*, 30 May. http://www.theaustralian.com.au/opinion/columnists/dennis-shanahan/federal-election-2016-you-can-trust-them–to-dish-up-set-lines/news-story/7e50692fa75bdb9a71c321cdb610b9be.

Shanahan, D. and M. Franklin. 2012. 'Kevin Rudd ALP's Best Hope: Newspoll'. *Australian*, 25 February.

Shanahan, L. 2008. 'Keating's Gallipoli Campaign Targets PM and Premier'. *Age Online*, 3 November. http://www.theage.com.au/national/keatings-gallipoli-campaigntargets-pm-and-premier-20081102-5gas.html, accessed 3 November 2008.

Shea, D. 1996. *Campaign Craft: The Strategies, Tactics and Art of Political Campaign Management*. Westport, CT: Praeger.

Simms, M. 2001. 'Election Days: Overview of the 1901 Election'. In *1901: The Forgotten Election*, edited by M. Simms, 1–20. St. Lucia, QLD: University of Queensland Press.

Simms, M. and J. Warhurst (Eds). 2002. *2001: The Centenary Election*. St Lucia, QLD: University of Queensland Press.

Solomon, D. (Ed.). 2002. *Howard's Race: Winning the Unwinnable Election*. Pymble, NSW: Harper Collins.

Souter, G. 2000. *Lion and Kangaroo: The Initiation of Australia*. Melbourne, VIC: Text Publishing.

Sorensen, T. C. 1965. *Kennedy*. New York, NY: Harper and Row.

———. 2005. *Decision Making in the White House: The Olive Branch or the Arrow?* New York, NY: Columbia University Press.

Stapleton, J. and P. Maley. 2007. 'Nation Unites in Remembrance'. *Australian*, 12 November: 2.

Stratton, J. 1998. *Race Daze: Australia in Identity Crisis*. Sydney, NSW: Pluto Press.

Stockwell, S. 2005. *Political Campaign Strategy: Doing Democracy in the 21st Century*. Melbourne, VIC: Australian Scholarly Publishing.

Stokes, G. (Ed.). 1997. *The Politics of Identity in Australia*. Melbourne, VIC: Cambridge University Press.

Summers, A. 2002 [1975]. *Damned Whores and God's Police*. Camberwell, VIC: Penguin.

Swan, W. 2012. 'Wayne Swan's Statement on Rudd's Resignation'. *ABC News Online*, 22 February. http://www.abc.net.au/news/2012-02-22/wayne-swan-statement-on-rudd27s-resignation/3846188.

Sydney Morning Herald. 1901. 'Federal Policy Declared – Mr. Barton at Maitland'. *Sydney Morning Herald*, 18 January: 7–8.

———. 1903. 'Federal Campaign; The Ministerial Cause'. *Sydney Morning Herald*, 30 October: 7.

———. 1913. 'Liberalism; "Cult of Progress"; Mr Cook's Speech'. *Sydney Morning Herald*, 4 April: 6.

———. 1914. 'For Freedom: The Liberals' Policy'. *Sydney Morning Herald*, 16 July: 9.

———. 1917. 'Mr Hughes' Policy Speech; The Empire's Struggle'. *Sydney Morning Herald*, 28 March: 11–12.

———. 1925. 'Federal Campaign Opens; Mr Bruce's Policy Speech'. *Sydney Morning Herald*, 6 October: 9–10.

———. 1940. 'Federal Labor Policy Announced'. *Sydney Morning Herald*, 29 August: 7–8.

———. 1949a. 'Menzies Gives Policy; Trenchant Attack on Socialism'. *Sydney Morning Herald*, 11 November: 4.

———. 1949b. '"No Glittering Promises": Chifley Gives Policy'. *Sydney Morning Herald*, 15 November: 1.

———. 1961. 'Police Hustle Students From Rowdy Menzies Election Meeting'. *Sydney Morning Herald*, 16 November: 1.

———. 1972. 'McMahon Aims for the Young'. *Sydney Morning Herald*, 15 November: 1.

———. 2003. 'Bush Lauds Howard as "Man of Steel"'. *Sydney Morning Herald*, 3 May. http://www.smh.com.au/articles/2003/05/04/1051987592763.html.

———. 2007a. 'Sun Sets on Rudd and Hockey's Sunrise'. AAP Story. *Sydney Morning Herald*, 16 April. http://www.smh.com.au/news/National/Rudd-Hockey-leave-Sunrise/2007/04/16/1176575720572.html.

———. 2007b. 'The White Picket Fence Gets A Me-Too Makeover'. *Sydney Morning Herald*, 13 November: 12.

Tanner, L. 2011. *Sideshow: Dumbing Down Democracy*. Carlton North, VIC: Scribe.

Tavan, G. 2005. *The Long, Slow Death of White Australia*. Carlton North, VIC: Scribe.

Taylor, L. 2013. 'Coalition Digital Campaign "Slick" but Rudd Selfies More Engaging'. *The Guardian*, 11 September. http://www.theguardian.com/world/2013/sep/11/digital-campaigns-coalition-and-labor.

———. 2016a. 'The Long Game: Will Malcolm Turnbull's Gamble Pay Off?'. *The Guardian Australia*, 17 May. http://www.theguardian.com/australia-news/2016/may/17/election-2016-malcolm-turnbull-liberal-party-coalition-profile.

———. 2016b. 'No Winners on Election Debate Night When Answers Were Scripted and Ideas Untested'. *The Guardian Australia*, 29 May. http://www.theguardian.com/australia-news/2016/may/29/no-winners-election-debate-night-answers-scripted-ideas-untested.

Tlozek, E. and S. Anderson. 2016. 'PNG's Supreme Court Rules Detention of Asylum Seekers on Manus Island is Illegal'. *ABC News Online*, 27 April. http://www.abc.net.au/news/2016-04-26/png-court-rules-asylum-seeker-detention-manus-island-illegal/7360078.

Trent, J. S. and R. V. Friedenberg. 2004. *Political Campaign Communications: Principles and Practices*. Oxford: Rowman and Littlefield Publishers.

Trippi, J. 2004. *The Revolution Will Not Be Televised: Democracy, the Internet, and the Overthrow of Everything*. E-Book Publication: Harper Collins.

Tsokhas, K. 2001. *Making a Nation State: Cultural Identity, Economic Nationalism and Sexuality in Australia*. Carlton South, VIC: Melbourne University Press.

Turner, G. 2009. 'Politics, Radio and Journalism in Australia: The Influence of "Talkback"'. *Journalism* 10(4): 411–30.

Van Onselen, P. 2010. 'Politics Trumps a Moral Challenge'. *Australian*, 29 April. http://www.theaustralian.com.au/news/inquirer/politics-trumps-a-moral-challenge/story-e6frg6z6-1225859592923.

van Dijk, T. A. 1985. 'Preface'. In *Discourse and Communication: New Approaches to the Analysis of Mass Media Discourse and Communication*, edited by T. A. van Dijk, v–vi. New York: de Gruyter.

———. 1991. *Racism and the Press*. London: Routledge.

Vanstone, A. 2013. 'Rudd's Mission Is To Show Us That We Were Wrong'. *Age*, 19 August. http://www.theage.com.au/comment/rudds-mission-is-to-show-us-that-we-were-wrong-20130818-2s4uj.html.

Vromen, A. and W. Coleman. 2013. 'Online Campaigning Organisations and Storytelling Strategies: GetUp! In Australia'. *Policy and Internet* 5(1): 76–100.

Walker, D. 1999. *Anxious Nation: Australia and the Rise of Asia, 1850–1939*. St Lucia, QLD: University of Queensland Press.

———. 2010. 'The "Flow of Asia" – Vocabularies of Engagement: A Cultural History'. *Australian Journal of Political Science* 45(1): 45–58.

Walliker, A. 2007. 'Aussies Hooked on Facebook, MySpace and YouTube'. *Herald Sun*, 31 December.

Walter, J. 1980. *The Leader: A Political Biography of Gough Whitlam*. St Lucia, QLD: University of Queensland Press.

Ward, I. 1995. *Politics of the Media*. South Melbourne, VIC: Macmillan.

———. 2002. 'Talkback Radio, Political Communication and Australian Politics'. *Australian Journal of Communication* 29(1): 21–38.

Ward, T. 2010. *Sport in Australian National Identity: Kicking Goals*. Abingdon, Oxon: Routledge.

Ward, R. 1967. *The Australian Legend*. Melbourne, VIC: Oxford University Press.

———. 1988. *A Nation for A Continent: The History of Australia, 1901–1975*. Richmond, VIC: Heinemann Educational Australia.

Warhaft, S. (Ed.). 2004. *Well May We Say: The Speeches that Made Australia*. Melbourne, VIC: Black Inc.

Warren, I. (Ed.). 2004. *Buoyant Nationalism: Australian Identity, Sport and the World Stage* 1982–1983. Balaclava, VIC: Australian Society for Sports History.

Watson, D. 1995. 'Foreword'. In *Advancing Australia: The Speeches of Paul Keating, Prime Minister*, edited by M. Ryan, xiii–xvi. Sydney, NSW: Big Picture Publications.

———. 2001. *Rabbit Syndrome: Australia and America*. Quarterly Essay #4. Melbourne, VIC: Black Inc.

———. 2002. *Recollections of a Bleeding Heart: A Portrait of Paul Keating P.M.* Milsons Point, NSW: Random House.

———. 2003. *Death Sentence: The Decay of Public Language*. Milsons Point, NSW: Random House Australia.

Wesley, M. 2007. *The Howard Paradox: Australian Diplomacy in Asia, 1996–2006*. Sydney, NSW: ABC Books.

West, A. 2010. 'Keating Speech to be Honoured'. *Sydney Morning Herald*, 25 August. http://www.smh.com.au/national/keating-speech-to-be-honoured-20100824-13qkg.html.

West, A. 2006. *Now Australia: Inside the Lifestyles of the Rich and Tasteful*. North Melbourne, VIC: Pluto Press.

West, D. M., L. S. Maisel and B. M. Clifton. 2005. 'The Impact of Campaign Reform on Political Discourse'. *Political Science Quarterly* 120(4): 637–51.

White, L. 2011. 'The Role of the Horse in Australian Tourism and National Identity'. In *Tourism and National Identities: An International Perspective*, edited by E. Frew and L. White, 65–76. Abingdon, Oxon: Routledge.

White, R. 1981. *Inventing Australia: Images and Identity 1688–1980*. Crows Nest, NSW: Allen and Unwin.

———. 1997. 'Inventing Australia Revisited'. In *Creating Australia: Changing Australian History*, edited by W. Hudson and G. Bolton, 12–22. St Leonards, NSW: Allen and Unwin.

Whitington, D. 1964. *The Rulers: Fifteen Years of the Liberals*. Melbourne, VIC: Lansdowne Press.

Willard, M. 1923. *History of the White Australia Policy to 1920*. Melbourne, VIC: Melbourne University Press.

Williams, P. 1997. *The Victory: The Inside Story of the Takeover of Australia*. St. Leonards, NSW: Allen and Unwin.

Wills, A. 1993. *Illusions of Identity: The Art of Nation*. Sydney, NSW: Hale and Iremonger.

Wilson, J. 2001. 'Political Discourse'. In *The Handbook of Discourse Analysis*, edited by D. Schiffrin, D. Tannen and H. Hamilton, 398–415. Oxford: Blackwell.

———. 2014. 'Kevin Rudd, Celebrity and Audience Democracy in Australia'. *Journalism* 15(2): 202–17.

Windschuttle, K. 2004. *The White Australia Policy*. Paddington, NSW: Macleay Press.

Winter, C. 2011. 'Battlefield Tourism and Australian Identity: Gallipoli and the Western Front'. In *Tourism and National Identities: An International Perspective*, edited by E. Frew and L. White, 176–89. Abingdon, Oxon: Routledge.

Wodak, R. 2002. 'Discourse and Politics: The Rhetoric of Exclusion'. In *The Haider Phenomenon*, edited by R. Wodak and A. Pelinka, 33–60. London: Transaction Publishers.

Wolin. S. 1996. 'Fugitive Democracy'. In *Democracy and Difference: Contesting the Boundaries of the Political*, edited by S. Benhabib, 31–45. Princeton, NJ: Princeton University Press.

Wright, T. 2007. 'Election 2007 On the Road: Fans Hail Scrooge the Messiah as Technocrat Kevin Works His Mojo'. *Age*, 15 November: 1.

———. 2010a. 'Abbott and Gillard as Packaged as Plastic-wrapped Cheese'. *Age*, 26 July.

———. 2010b. 'The Hidden Truth Behind the PM's "Impromptu" Speech'. *Sydney Morning Herald*, 17 August. http://m.smh.com.au/federal-election/the-hidden-truth-behind-the-pms-impromptu-speech-20100817-127hr.html.

———. 2010c. 'Did We Get to See The Real Julia? Perhaps We Did'. *Sydney Morning Herald*, 17 August. http://www.smh.com.au/federal-politics/did-we-get-to-see-the-real-julia-perhaps-we-did-20100816-126xl.html.

Younane, S. 2008. '"Working Families" and the "Opportunity Society": Political Rhetoric in the 2007 Australian Federal Election Campaign'. *Communication, Politics and Culture* 41(2): 62–83.

Young, S. 2008. 'Political Discourse in the Age of the Soundbite: The Election Campaign Soundbite on Australian Television News'. Refereed paper presented to the *Australasian Political Studies Conference*, University of Queensland, Brisbane, 6–9 July.

———. 2011. *How Australia Decides: Election Reporting and the Media*. Port Melbourne, VIC: Cambridge University Press.

Yuval-Davis, N. 2004. 'Borders, Boundaries and the Politics of Belonging'. In *Ethnicity, Nationalism and Minority Rights*, edited by S. May, T. Modood and J. Squires, 214–29. New York, NY: Cambridge University Press.

REFERENCES

Campaign Speech and Archival Sources

Abbott, T. 2010a. Leaders' Debate. National Press Club, Canberra, ACT. 25 July. Transcript from the *Liberal Party of Australia* 2010 Election Website, archived by the National Library of Australia [NLA] *Pandora Web Archive*. http://pandora.nla.gov.au/pan/22107/20100826-0009/www.liberal.org.au/index.html.

———. 2010b. Press Conference with Julie Bishop and Scott Morrison. Brisbane, QLD. 7 August. Transcript from the *Liberal Party of Australia* 2010 Election Website, archived by the NLA *Pandora Web Archive*. http://pandora.nla.gov.au/pan/22107/20100826-0009/www.liberal.org.au/index.html.

———. 2013a. Press Conference. Parliament House, Canberra, ACT. 4 August. Transcript from the *Liberal Party of Australia* 2013 Election Website, archived by the NLA *Pandora Web Archive*. http://pandora.nla.gov.au/pan/22107/20130918-1400/www.liberal.org.au/index.html.

———.2013b. Interview with Sabra Lane. AM, ABC Radio. 5 August. Transcript from the *Liberal Party of Australia* 2013 Election Website, archived by the NLA *Pandora Web Archive*. http://pandora.nla.gov.au/pan/22107/20130918-1400/www.liberal.org.au/index.html.

———. 2013c. Doorstop Interview. Launceston, TAS. 7 August. Transcript from the *Liberal Party of Australia* 2013 Election Website, archived by the NLA *Pandora Web Archive*. http://pandora.nla.gov.au/pan/22107/20130918-1400/www.liberal.org.au/index.html.

———. 2013d. Speech. Garma Festival, Northern Territory. 10 August. Transcript from the *Liberal Party of Australia* 2013 Election Website, archived by the NLA *Pandora Web Archive*. http://pandora.nla.gov.au/pan/22107/20130918-1400/www.liberal.org.au/index.html.

———. 2013e. Press Conference with Nigel Scullion and Warren Mundine. Garma Festival, Northern Territory, 10 August. Transcript from the *Liberal Party of Australia* 2013 Election Website, archived by the NLA *Pandora Web Archive*. http://pandora.nla.gov.au/pan/22107/20130918-1400/www.liberal.org.au/index.html.

———. 2013f. Interview with Cameron Williams. *Today*, Channel Nine. 11 August. Transcript from the *Liberal Party of Australia* 2013 Election Website, archived by the NLA *Pandora Web Archive*. http://pandora.nla.gov.au/pan/22107/20130918-1400/www.liberal.org.au/index.html.

———. 2013g. People's Forum. Brisbane Broncos Leagues Club, Brisbane QLD. 21 August. Transcript from the *Liberal Party of Australia* 2013 Election Website, archived by the NLA *Pandora Web Archive*. http://pandora.nla.gov.au/pan/22107/20130918-1400/www.liberal.org.au/index.html.

———. 2013h. Speech. Robertson Barracks, Darwin NT. 23 August. Transcript from the *Liberal Party of Australia* 2013 Election Website, archived by the NLA *Pandora Web Archive*. http://pandora.nla.gov.au/pan/22107/20130918-1400/www.liberal.org.au/index.html.

———. 2013i. Press Conference. Darwin, NT. 23 August. Transcript from the *Liberal Party of Australia* 2013 Election Website, archived by the NLA *Pandora Web Archive*. http://pandora.nla.gov.au/pan/22107/20130918-1400/www.liberal.org.au/index.html.

———. 2013j. Policy Launch Speech. Four Seasons Hotel, Sydney, NSW. 25 August. Transcript from the *Liberal Party of Australia* 2013 Election Website, archived by the NLA *Pandora Web Archive*. http://pandora.nla.gov.au/pan/22107/20130918-1400/www.liberal.org.au/index.html.

———. 2013k. Speech. National Press Club, Canberra, ACT. 2 September. Transcript from the *Liberal Party of Australia* 2013 Election Website, archived by the NLA *Pandora Web Archive*. http://pandora.nla.gov.au/pan/22107/20130918-1400/www.liberal.org.au/index.html.

Barton, E. 1901. Policy Launch Speech. Maitland Town Hall, Sydney NSW. 17 October. *Age*, 18 January: 4–6.

Beazley, K. 2001. Policy Launch Speech. 31 October. Transcript from *Museum of Australian Democracy*, Election speeches online. http://electionspeeches.moadoph.gov.au/speeches/2001-kim-beazley.

Bruce, S. 1925. Policy Launch Speech. Shire Hall, Dandenong, VIC. 5 October. *Age*, 6 October: 11.

———. 1928. Policy Launch Speech. Shire Hall, Dandenong, VIC. 8 October. NLA Np 329.994 NAT (2314682).

Calwell, A. 1963. Policy Launch Speech. Royal Ballroom, Melbourne, VIC. 6 November. *Age*, 7 November: 12–13.

———. 1966. Policy Launch Speech. St Kilda Town Hall, Melbourne, VIC. 10 November. *Canberra Times*, 11 November: 14.

Charlton, M. 1925. Policy Launch Speech. Sydney Town Hall, Sydney, NSW. 9 October. *Age*, 10 October: 17.

Chifley, J. 1946. Policy Launch Speech. Live radio address, Canberra, ACT. 2 September. Parliamentary record copy, National Archives of Australia [NAA] B5459/4 Book 119.

———. 1949. Policy Launch Speech. Pre-recorded radio address, broadcast from Canberra, ACT. 14 November. Parliamentary Record Copy, NAA B5459/4, Book 148.

Cook, J. 1913. Policy Launch Speech. Parramatta Town Hall, Sydney, NSW. 3 April. *Age*, 4 April: 7.

Curtin, J. 1940. Policy Launch Speech. Radio broadcast from Perth, WA. 28 August. John Curtin Prime Ministerial Library, Records of the Australian Labor Party National Branch, John Curtin Prime Ministerial Library 00421/2.

Deakin, A. 1903. Policy Launch Speech. Her Majesty's Theatre, Ballarat, VIC. 29 October. *Age*, 30 October.

———. 1906. Policy Launch Speech. Alfred Hall, Ballarat, VIC. 17 October. *Sydney Morning Herald*, 18 October: 7–8.

———. 1910. Policy Launch Speech. The Coliseum, Ballarat, VIC. 7 February. *Sydney Morning Herald*, 8 February, p. 7–8.

Evatt, H. V. 1954. Policy Launch Speech. Rivoli Hall, Hurstville, NSW. 10 November. *Sydney Morning Herald*, 7 May: 4–5.

Fisher, A. 1910. Policy Launch Speech. Maryborough Town Hall, Maryborough, QLD. 9 February. *Maryborough Chronicle*, 10 February: 3.

Fisher, A. 1913. Policy Launch Speech. 'The Bungalow', Maryborough. 31 March. *Age*, 1 April: 9.

———. 1914. Policy Launch Speech. Bundaberg, QLD. 6 July. *Sydney Morning Herald*, 7 July: 7.

Fraser, M. 1975. Policy Launch Speech. 27 November. Liberal Party Pamphlet, NAA M1277 Item 59.

———. 1977a. Policy Launch Speech. Malvern Town Hall, Melbourne, VIC. 27 November. Liberal Party Pamphlet 'Doing the Job', NAA M1263 Item 558.

———. 1977b. Election Speech: National Press Club Address. Canberra, ACT. 7 December. NLA Oral TRC 588/B (1670883).

———. 1980. Policy Launch Speech. Moorabbin Town Hall, Melbourne, VIC. 30 September. *Age*, 1 October: 18.

———. 1983. Policy Launch Speech. 15 February. *Canberra Times*, 16 February: 12–13.

Gillard, J. 2010a. Press conference. Parliament House, Canberra, ACT. 17 July. Transcript from the *Australian Labor Party* 2010 Election Website, archived by the NLA *Pandora Web Archive*. http://pandora.nla.gov.au/pan/22093/20100823-0245/alp.org.au/index0767.html?400;http://alp.org.au:80/%2a.aspx/.

———. 2010b. Leaders' debate. National Press Club, Canberra ACT. 25 July. Transcript from the *Australian Labor Party* 2010 Election Website, archived by the NLA *Pandora Web Archive*. http://pandora.nla.gov.au/pan/22093/20100823-0245/alp.org.au/index0767.html?400;http://alp.org.au:80/%2a.aspx/.

———. 2012. ABC News interview footage, 'This is not celebrity Big Brother: Gillard'. 24 February. http://www.abc.net.au/news/2012-02-24/this-is-not-celebrity-big-brother-gillard/3850384.

Hawke, B. 1983. Policy Launch Speech. Opera Theatre, Sydney Opera House, Sydney, NSW. 16 February. *Canberra Times*, 17 February: 10–11.

———. 1984. Election Debate. *ABC* Television Broadcast; National Press Club, Canberra, ACT. 26 November. Transcribed by the author from original broadcast.

———.1987. Policy Launch Speech. Sydney Opera House, Sydney, NSW. 23 June. Bob Hawke Prime Ministerial Library [BHPML]. http://www.library.unisa.edu.au/BHPML/.

———. 1990a. Election Speech: SA Launch of Women's Policy. Adelaide, SA. 4 March. BHPML. http://www.library.unisa.edu.au/BHPML/.

———. 1990b. Address to Farewell the HMAS Sydney, Tobruk and Oxley. Fremantle, WA. 14 March. BHMPL, http://www.library.unisa.edu.au/BHPML/.

———. 2012. Interview with Naomi Woodley. *AM Program*, ABC Radio. 2 January. Transcript from http://www.abc.net.au/am/content/2011/s3400566.htm.

Holt, H. 1966. Policy Launch Speech. Television broadcast. 8 November. NAA Item 4340109.

Howard, J. 1987. Election Speech: Address to the National Press Club. Canberra, ACT, 7 July. NLA Oral TRC 4031 Recording; NLA Oral TRC 4031 Transcript.

———. 1996a. Policy Launch Speech. Ryde Civic Centre, Sydney, NSW. 18 February. *Canberra Times*, 19 February: 6.

———. 1996b. Election Speech: Address to the National Press Club. Canberra, ACT. 28 February. NLA Oral TRC 4537.

———. 2001a. Election Speech: Address at Launch of Multicultural Policy 'Strength through Diversity'. Hindmarsh Electorate, Wellend, Adelaide, SA. 16 October. Transcript from the *Prime Minister of Australia* website archived on the NLA *Pandora Web Archive*. http://pandora.nla.gov.au/tep/10052.

———. 2001b. Election Speech: Address to the Australian Defence Association. Melbourne, VIC. 25 October. Transcript from *Australian Politics Online*. http://www.australianpolitics.com.au.

———. 2001c. Liberal Party Campaign Launch, Sydney, NSW. 28 October. Transcript from the *Prime Minister of Australia* website archived on the *NLA Pandora Web Archive*, http://pandora.nla.gov.au/tep/10052.

———. 2001d. Interview with Tony Jones. *Lateline*, ABC Television. 8 November. Transcript from the *Prime Minister of Australia* website archived on the NLA *Pandora Web Archive*. http://pandora.nla.gov.au/tep/10052.

———. 2002. Keynote Speech to the International Democratic Union Luncheon. Ronald Reagan Building, Washington DC. 10 June. Archived at *PM Transcripts: Transcripts from the Prime Ministers of Australia*, Department of the Prime Minister and Cabinet. https://pmtranscripts.dpmc.gov.au/release/transcript-12891.

———. 2006. Address at the Launch of 'The Howard Factor'. Parliament House, Canberra, ACT. 2 March. Archived at *PM Transcripts: Transcripts from the Prime Ministers of Australia*, Department of the Prime Minister and Cabinet. https://pmtranscripts.dpmc.gov.au/release/transcript-22148.

———. 2007a. Interview with Phillip Clark. Radio 2GB, Sydney, NSW. 23 October. Transcript from the *Liberal Party of Australia* website archived on the NLA *Pandora Web Archive*. http://pandora.nla.gov.au/pan/22107/20071126-0847/www.liberal.org.au/index.html.

———. 2007b. Address at Remembrance Day Ceremony. Canberra, ACT. 11 November. Transcript from the *Liberal Party of Australia* website archived on the NLA *Pandora Web Archive*. http://pandora.nla.gov.au/pan/22107/20071126-0847/www.liberal.org.au/index.html.

———. 2007c. Policy Launch Speech. Queensland Performing Arts Centre, Brisbane, QLD. 12 November. Transcript from the *Liberal Party of Australia* website archived on the *NLA Pandora Web Archive*, http://pandora.nla.gov.au/pan/22107/20071126-0847/www.liberal.org.au/index.html.

———. 2007d. Press Conference. Our Lady of the Way School, Brisbane, QLD. 13 November. Transcript from the *Liberal Party of Australia* website archived on the NLA *Pandora Web Archive*. http://pandora.nla.gov.au/pan/22107/20071126-0847/www.liberal.org.au/index.html.

———. 2007e. Election Speech: 'Go for Growth' Corporate Function. Wentworth Hotel, Sydney, NSW. 21 November. Transcript from the *Liberal Party of Australia* website archived on the NLA *Pandora Web Archive*, http://pandora.nla.gov.au/pan/22107/20071126-0847/www.liberal.org.au/index.html.

———. 2007f. Election Speech: National Press Club Address. National Press Club, Canberra, ACT. 22 November. Transcript from the *Liberal Party of Australia* website archived on the NLA *Pandora Web Archive*, http://pandora.nla.gov.au/pan/22107/20071126-0847/www.liberal.org.au/index.html.

Hughes, W. 1917. Policy Launch Speech. Bendigo, VIC. 27 March. *Age*, 28 March: 9.

Keating, P. 1993. Election Speech: National Press Club Address. National Press Club, Canberra, ACT. 9 February. Transcript from *Australian Politics Online*. http://www.australianpolitics.com.

———. 1996a. Policy Launch Speech. World Congress Centre, Melbourne, VIC. 14 February. Transcript from *Australian Politics Online*. http://www.australianpolitics.com.au.

———. 1996b. Concession Speech. Bankstown Sports Club, Sydney, NSW. 2 March. Transcribed by the author from audio at *Australian Politics Online*. http://www.australianpolitics.com.

Koch, D. and M. Doyle. 2013. Interview with Tony Abbott. *Sunrise*, Channel 7 Television. 5 August. Transcript from the *Liberal Party of Australia* 2013 Election Website, archived by the NLA *Pandora Web Archive*. http://pandora.nla.gov.au/pan/22107/20130918-1400/www.liberal.org.au/index.html.

Latham, M. 2004. The Great Debate. *Sixty Minutes*, Channel Nine, Moderator: Laurie Oakes. 12 September. Transcript from *Sixty Minutes* website. http://sixtyminutes.ninemsn.com.au/article.aspx?id=259214.

REFERENCES

Lyons, J. 1931. Policy Launch Speech. Sydney Town Hall, Sydney, NSW. 2 December. *Sydney Morning Herald*, 3 December: 9.

McMahon, W. 1972. Policy Launch Speech. Sydney, NSW. 14 November. *Sydney Morning Herald*, 15 November: 13.

Menzies, R. 1940. Policy Launch Speech. Camberwell, VIC. 2 September. NLA Np 329.994 MEN (2784591).

———. 1946. Policy Launch Speech. Camberwell Town Hall, Melbourne, VIC. 20 August. NLA NL 329.994 MEN (2792786).

———. 1949. Policy Launch Speech. RSL Memorial Hall, Melbourne, VIC. 10 November. *Sydney Morning Herald*, 11 November: 4–5.

———. 1955. Policy Launch Speech. Canterbury Memorial Hall, Melbourne, VIC. 15 November. NAA Item 302696.

———. 1958. Policy Launch Speech. Canterbury Memorial Hall, Melbourne, VIC. 15 November. NAA M2606/6.

———. 1963. Policy Launch Speech. Melbourne, VIC. 12 November. NLA NLp 329.994 MEN (418097).

Peacock, A. 1990. Policy Launch Speech. National Gallery of Victoria, Melbourne, VIC. 5 March. *Canberra Times*, 6 March: 10.

Reid. G.H. 1901. Election Speech. Richmond Town Hall, Melbourne, VIC. 21 January. *Age*, 22 November: 6.

———. 1903. Policy Launch Speech. Melbourne Town Hall, Melbourne. 30 October. *Age*, 31 October: 14.

———. 1906. Policy Launch Speech. I.O.O.F. Temple, Elizabeth St, Sydney, NSW. 24 October. *Sydney Morning Herald*, 24 October: 9.

Rudd, K. 2007a. Press Conference with Jenny Macklin and Ross Daniels. QLD. 1 November. Transcript from the *Australian Labor Party* Election 2007 Website, archived at the NLA *Pandora Web Archive*. http://pandora.nla.gov.au/pan/22093/20071124-0102/www.alp.org.au/index.html.

———. 2007b. Press Conference. Lavarack Barracks, Townsville, QLD. 12 November. Transcript from the *Australian Labor Party* Election 2007 Website, archived at the NLA *Pandora Web Archive*. http://pandora.nla.gov.au/pan/22093/20071124-0102/www.alp.org.au/index.html

———. 2007c. Policy Launch Speech. Queensland Performing Arts Centre, Brisbane, QLD. 14 November. Transcript from the *Australian Labor Party* Election 2007 Website, archived at the NLA *Pandora Web Archive*. http://pandora.nla.gov.au/pan/22093/20071124-0102/www.alp.org.au/index.html

———. 2007d. National Press Club Address. Canberra, ACT. 21 November. Transcript from the *Australian Labor Party* Election 2007 Website, archived at the NLA *Pandora Web Archive*. http://pandora.nla.gov.au/pan/22093/20071124-0102/www.alp.org.au/index.html

———. 2007e. Victory Speech. Members' Dining Room, Suncorp Stadium, Brisbane QLD. 24 November. Transcript from the *Australian Labor Party* Election 2007 Website, archived at the NLA *Pandora Web Archive*. http://pandora.nla.gov.au/pan/22093/20071124-0102/www.alp.org.au/index.html

———. 2009. Interview with Kerry O'Brien, *7:30 Report* ABC Television. 22 October. http://www.abc.net.au/7.30/content/2009/s2721817.htm.

———. 2012. Transcript of Press Conference, Brisbane Airport, QLD. 24 February. Kevin Rudd MP Website. http://www.kevinruddmp.com/2012/02/transcript-of-press-conference-brisbane.html.

———. 2013a. Press Conference: Campaign Announcement, Parliament House, Canberra. 4 August. Transcript from the *Australian Labor Party* Election 2013 Website, archived at the NLA *Pandora Web Archive*. http://pandora.nla.gov.au/pan/22093/20130918-1637/www.alp.org.au/index.html.

———.2013b. Election Speech: Launch of 'Afghanistan: The Story'. Australian War Memorial, Canberra, ACT. 6 August. Transcript from the *Australian Labor Party* Election 2013 Website, archived at the NLA *Pandora Web Archive*. http://pandora.nla.gov.au/pan/22093/20130918-1637/www.alp.org.au/index.html.

———. 2013c. Election Speech: Launch of Bronwyn Taha's Campaign for Dawson. Mackay, QLD:.12 August. Transcript from the *Australian Labor Party* Election 2013 Website, archived at the NLA *Pandora Web Archive*. http://pandora.nla.gov.au/pan/22093/20130918-1637/www.alp.org.au/index.html.

———. 2013d. Doorstop Interview. Darwin Cenotaph, NT. 15 August. Transcript from the *Australian Labor Party* Election 2013 Website, archived at the NLA *Pandora Web Archive*. http://pandora.nla.gov.au/pan/22093/20130918-1637/www.alp.org.au/index.html.

———. 2013e. Election Speech: Roberston Barracks. Darwin, NT. 15 August. Transcript from the *Australian Labor Party* Election 2013 Website, archived at the NLA *Pandora Web Archive*.   http://pandora.nla.gov.au/pan/22093/20130918-1637/www.alp.org.au/index.html.

———.2013f. People's Forum. Brisbane Broncos Leagues Club, Brisbane QLD. 21 August. Transcript from the *Australian Labor Party* Election 2013 Website, archived at the NLA *Pandora Web Archive*. http://pandora.nla.gov.au/pan/22093/20130918-1637/www.alp.org.au/index.html.

———. 2013g. Question and Answer Session. Lowy Institute for International Policy, Sydney, NSW. 27 August. Transcript from the *Australian Labor Party* Election 2013 Website, archived at the NLA *Pandora Web Archive*. http://pandora.nla.gov.au/pan/22093/20130918-1637/www.alp.org.au/index.html.

———. 2013h. Election Speech: National Press Club Address. National Press Club, Canberra, ACT. 5 September. Transcript from the *Australian Labor Party* Election 2013 Website, archived at the NLA *Pandora Web Archive*. http://pandora.nla.gov.au/pan/22093/20130918-1637/www.alp.org.au/index.html.

Shirley, M., P. Jones, W. Young, P. Shenstone and T. Stevenson. 1971. *It's Time*. Full Proposal for the 1972 election campaign. Papers of Graham Freudenberg, Record number 000043259, Whitlam Institute Digital Records, University of Western Sydney, NSW.

Shorten, B. 2016a. Address on National Sorry Day. Darwin, NT. 26 May. Transcript from *Bill Shorten Website*. http://www.billshorten.com.au/address_on_national_sorry_day_darwin_thursday_26_may_2016.

———. 2016b. Address to the Reconciliation Australia Dinner. Melbourne, VIC. 27 June. Transcript from *Bill Shorten Website*. http://www.billshorten.com.au/address_to_the_reconciliation_australia_dinner_melbourne_friday_27_may_2016.

———. 2016c. Address to the Long Walk. Melbourne, VIC. 28 May. Transcript from *Bill Shorten Website*. http://www.billshorten.com.au/address_to_the_long_walk_melbourne.

———. 2016d. Doorstop Interview with Matt Thistlethwaite and Anthony Albanese. Sydney, NSW. 18 May. Transcript from the *Australian Labor Party* Election 2016 Website. http://www.alp.org.au.

———. 2016e. Leaders' debate. National Press Club, Canberra ACT. 29 May. Transcript from the *Liberal Party of Australia* 2016 Election website. http://www.malcolmturnbull.com.au/media/leaders-debate-at-the-national-press-club-canberra

———. 2016f. Address to Labor's Queensland Campaign Launch. Brisbane, QLD. 26 June. Transcript at *Bill Shorten Website*. http://www.billshorten.com.au/address_to_labor_s_queensland_campaign_launch_brisbane_sunday_26_june_2016.

Stefanovic, K. 2010. Interview with Tony Abbott, *Today*, Channel Nine. 9 August. Transcript from the *Liberal Party of Australia* 2010 Election website, archived by the National Library of Australia [NLA] *Pandora Web Archive*. http://pandora.nla.gov.au/pan/22107/20100826-0009/www.liberal.org.au/index.html.

Turnbull, M. 2016a. Doorstop Interview. Townsville QLD. 18 May. Transcript from *Liberal Party of Australia* 2016 Election website. https://www.liberal.org.au.

———. 2016b. 'The Truth is Our Successful Multicultural Society is Built on Secure Borders'. *Sydney Morning Herald*, 20 May. http://www.smh.com.au/comment/the-truth-is-our-successful-multicultural-society-is-built-on-secure-borders-20160519-goz3ro.html.

———. 2016c. Speech at Iftar Dinner. Kirribilli House, Sydney, NSW. 16 June. Transcript from *Malcolm Turnbull Website*. http://www.malcolmturnbull.com.au/media/speech-at-kirribilli-house-sydney.

———. 2016d. Leaders' Debate. National Press Club, Canberra, ACT. 29 May. Transcript from the *Liberal Party of Australia* 2016 Election website. http://www.malcolmturnbull.com.au/media/leaders-debate-at-the-national-press-club-canberra.

Whitlam, E. G. 1971. Speech to the ALP Federal Conference. Launceston, TAS. 20 June. Whitlam Institute Digital Records, University of Western Sydney, Record Number 19710620.

———. 1972. Policy Launch Speech. Blacktown Civic Centre, Sydney, NSW. 13 November. Transcript from *Australian Politics Online*, http://australianpolitics.com.au.

———. 1974. Policy Launch Speech. Blacktown Civic Centre, Sydney, NSW. 29 April. *Australian*, 30 April: 4–5.

———. 1975. Policy Launch Speech. Festival Hall, Melbourne, VIC. 24 November. NAA M533 Item 59.

———. 1977. Policy Launch Speech. Sydney Opera House, Sydney, NSW. 17 November. Transcript from *Australian Politics Online*. http://www.australianpolitics.com.au.

INDEX

Abbott, Tony 29–30, 107, 109–12, 124, 133–35, 137, 146, 147, 153, 172
'Accord' (trade union agreement) 66–67
Afghanistan War (2001) 117, 133
al-Qaeda 119
Althusser, Louis 27–28
Anderson, Benedict 8, 19
Andrews, Kevin 102
Anzac myth 62, 80–85, 117, 118, 131
ANZUS. 50, 52
asylum seekers. *See under* immigration
Australian Council of Trade Unions (ACTU) 64, 66, 127, 140, 150
Australian Workers' Union 173
authenticity 28, 31–32, 34, 38, 63, 70

Barton, Edmund 41, 42, 91–93
Beazley, Kim 75, 148
bin Laden, Osama 119
Boer War 119
Brett, Judith 69, 73, 82, 94, 125
Bruce, Stanley 36, 125, 126–28, 164, 165, 166
Bush, George W. 73
Button, James 36, 38

Calwell, Arthur 67 n. 3, 75, 98n. 9, 101, 102, 139, 141, 142
Cassidy, Barrie 153
Catholic Social Studies Movement 139
Charlton, Matthew 125–26, 128–31, 164
Chifley, Joseph 6, 35, 97–100, 135, 165
China 140, 151
climate change 19, 57, 138, 146, 151, 156, 166
Cold War 47, 49, 118, 122
Coleman, Stephen 17–18

communism 116, 118–19, 123, 124, 140, 141, 163, 166, 169
Cook, Joseph 44, 119, 120, 162
Copenhagen Conference of the Parties 156
corporatisation of campaign language 164
Cottle, Simon 12–13, 26
Curtin, John 35, 37, 48, 81, 117, 121, 133, 144

Deakin, Alfred 5, 9, 41, 42, 43, 44, 45–46, 92, 93–97, 100–01, 102, 166, 175
Democratic Labor Party 139
digger myth 80–81, 84, 117, 120, 121, 124
Downer, Alexander 71
Dutton, Peter 174–75

Edwards, Cecil 36
Eggleton, Tony 36
Ellis, Bob 36, 64
Emissions Trading Scheme 146, 156
European Economic Community 49, 117
Evatt, H. V. 49, 50, 67n. 3, 118

federal election
    1901 42–43, 91–93
    1903 43, 44–47, 93–97, 118
    1906 5, 43, 44–47, 100–01
    1913 162
    1914 119, 162
    1917 122
    1919 164
    1925 36, 125, 128–31, 164
    1928 127–28
    1931 118
    1937 37
    1949 98–100, 137, 142, 144
    1955 49, 163

1958 50
1961 162
1963 123–24, 142, 143
1966 75, 139, 165
1969 139
1972 101–02, 132, 139–45, 150
1975 104–05
1977 105–06, 111
1983 64–66, 137, 165, 166
1984 67
1987 68–69
1990 81
1993 154
1996 21–22, 53–56, 132, 137, 154, 165, 166, 169, 170
2001 74–76, 87–88, 170
2004 131
2007 1, 57–58, 106–07, 131, 132–33, 145–55, 160, 166
2010 28, 31–32, 34–35, 108, 133, 144, 146, 147, 153
2013 18–19, 109–12, 124, 133–36, 137, 146, 152, 153, 156–57, 162
2016 112, 153, 162, 163, 164, 171–78
Fisher, Andrew 6, 73, 101, 119, 161
Fraser, Malcolm 6, 24, 64, 65, 66, 102–06, 111
Free Trade Party 41, 91
Freudenberg, Graham 16, 32, 35–36, 37, 65, 83, 145, 159

Gallipoli 81, 82, 83, 84, 121, 123, 125
Gillard, Julia 28, 31–32, 34–35, 107, 108, 133, 146, 147, 153
globalisation 19, 52, 56, 82, 88, 89, 168, 169
Glover, Dennis 33, 36
Gorton, John 21, 139
Green Party 133, 173n. 2, 174

Hage, Ghassan 4, 46, 58, 76, 94, 96, 106
Hanson, Pauline 22, 55, 88, 102
Hawke, Bob 2, 6, 9, 21, 38, 52, 120n. 1, 137, 164, 165, 166
   ACTU leadership 64, 66, 140
   Anzac myth 81–82
   indigenous Australians 111
   National Press Club debate (1984) 67
   policy launch speech (1983) 64–66

policy launch speech (1987) 68
polling popularity 29
television performance 65
Hayden, Bill 64
Hockey, Joe 148
Holt, Harold 51, 67n. 3, 165
Horne, Donald 20, 36, 122
Howard, John 7, 21–22, 55–56, 68–80, 106–07, 119, 120n. 1, 132, 137, 151, 152, 154, 160, 164, 166, 170, 172, 175, 176
   Anzac myth 82–84
   'Howard's battlers' 9, 55, 107, 170
   immigration 6, 22, 74–76, 87–88, 106–07
   Lazarus Rising. 70
   National Press Club speech (1987) 68–69
   National Press Club speech (2007) 1–2, 4, 9, 78
   policy launch speech (2007) 77–78
   Remembrance Day speech (2007) 83–84
   speechwriting 37
   talkback radio 70–71, 148, 152, 165
   US alliance 51, 72–73, 119
Hughes, William 36, 83, 119–23, 124, 164

identity security 4–6, 7, 15, 58–59, 85, 138, 159–60, 166–71, 178, *and passim*
Ilhan, John 106
'imagined community' 8, 22
immigration 4, 5, 6, 74–76, 78, 87–110, 166, 168, *See also* White Australia policy; 'Yellow Peril'
   Asian 56
   assimilation 101–02
   asylum seekers 4, 5, 75, 76, 87, 130n. 5, 168, 173–78
   'big Australia' 107–08
   British 43
   Pacific Islanders 5, 92, 93, 96
   Pacific Solution 74
   skills and usefulness 97–101, 108–10
   'special needs' group 102–06
   'success stories' 106–07
   white commonwealth 43, 44
Imperial War Conference 123
indigenous Australians 168, 174n. 3

absence from electoral discourse 23–24, 45, 92, 96
acknowledgement in recent elections 110–12
'special needs' group 104–05
Stolen Generations 155
Institute of Multicultural Affairs 103
'interpellation' 27–28
Iraq War (2003) 117
Islam 115, 119
It's Time 140–45

Jones, Alan 36
Jones, Tony 75–76

Keating, Paul v, 2, 9, 21–22, 35–36, 39–40, 52, 53–56, 81n. 7, 132, 136, 154, 164, 165, 169
  'Redfern Park' speech 23, 38
Kemp, David 36
Kissinger, Henry 140
Koch, David 31n. 3
Kokoda 83, 84, 117
Kyoto protocol 155

Labor
  trade union movement 123, 125
Labor Party. *Passim*
  conservative portrayal as unpatriotic 120–24, 127–28
    Labor rebuttal 128–33
  Federal Conference (1971) 141
  trade union movement 122, 139
Latham, Mark 131
Liberal Party. *Passim*
  attacks on Labor's patriotism 123–24
  conservative immigration policies 101–02
  family values 78
  founding by Menzies 47
  free enterprise 78, 106
  politicisation of Anzac myth 83
  promotion of US alliance 49–51
  scare tactics 177
Lyons, Joseph 118

MacCallum, Alison 141
Maddox, Marion 70
Manus Island 174
Marr, David 156, 173

McKew, Maxine 154
McMahon, Sonia 142
McMahon, William 67n. 3, 101–02, 139, 140, 143, 165
Menzies, Robert 9, 21, 39–40, 78, 81, 100, 121, 137, 139, 140, 142, 162
  anti-communism 49, 50, 118
  radio performance 70, 99, 163, 165
  speechwriting 3, 35, 37, 159
  television performance 48, 123–24, 143
  US alliance 47–50, 51
Mouffe, Chantal 25
multiculturalism 6, 70, 72, 88, 89, 102–06, 176, 177, 178

National Economic Summit (1983) 67
National Labor Party 120
National Press Club 1, 4, 9, 67, 134, 135, 136, 155, 163, 164, 177
nationalism. *See also* identity security
  culture of worrying 4, 22
  Imperial 21, 39, 40–41, 42–47, 48–49, 50, 96, 97, 116, 117, 120–22, 128–30
  'new nationalism' 21
  parochial 73
  racial 44, 48, 51, 89, 91–97, 98, 103, 120, 170
Nationalist Party 120
Nauru 174
New Zealand 20
Nixon, Richard 140

Obama, Barack 18, 29, 153, 166
O'Brien, Kerry 29–30, 53n. 6, 108
One Nation Party 55, 102

Peacock, Andrew 67, 70
'Petrov Affair' 49, 50
policy launch speech 16, 36, 94, 143, 161–62
'presidentialisation' of elections 8, 28
professionalisation of politics 32, 34, 35, 161, 162, 164
Protectionist Party 41, 91

Reagan, Ronald 18n. 1
refugees. *See* immigration, asylum seekers
regional engagement 52–58

Reid, George Houston 39–40, 41–45, 46–47, 100–01, 118
Rodgers, Don 35
Royal Commission into espionage 49
Rudd, Kevin 1, 18–19, 29, 36, 76, 79–80, 107, 133, 135–36, 145–57, 160, 162, 166
   Anzac myth 83, 84
   Apology to Australia's Indigenous Peoples 23
   celebrity media 71
   immigration 108–09
   indigenous Australians 23, 24
   National Press Club speech (2013) 135, 136
   policy launch speech (2007) 77, 150–52
   regional competition 57–58
   speechwriting 37–38
   US alliance 51–52, 131, 132–33
Russell, Don 55n. 8

Santamaria, B.A. 139
Seamen's Union 125
SEATO 52
September 11 attack 72–73, 74, 119, 168, 169, 170
Shorten, Bill 112, 130n. 5, 163, 164, 172–73, 176–77
socialism 115, 116, 118, 122, 123, 124, 169
Special Broadcasting Service (SBS) 78, 103
speechwriting 34–38, 165
Sudan 119
Sunrise 148, 156
Syrian civil war 136

talkback radio 70–71
Tampa 74, 170
Tanner, Lindsay 32
Tempest, Kate 174n. 3
terra nullius 2, 23, 112
terrorism 4, 19, 72, 74, 75, 87, 115, 119, 124, 133, 138, 166, 168, 174
Trippi, Joe 152
Turnbull, Malcolm 155, 163, 164, 171, 172, 175–76, 177–78
Turner, Graeme 20

United Australia Party 118
United Nations 51, 52, 159
US alliance 49, 50–52, 72–73, 116, 117, 131–32, 133

Vietnam War 51, 84, 89, 118–19

Walsh, Thomas 125n. 4
Ward, Russel 20, 97, 102, 117
Watson, Don v, 9, 22, 33, 35–36, 38, 55n. 8, 164, 165
Watson, John 41
White Australia policy 5, 44n. 2, 46, 78, 88, 91–97, 101, 103, 123, 127, 162
Whitlam, Gough 6, 23, 35–36, 87, 101, 102, 132, 139, 140–41, 142, 144–45, 150, 155–56, 165
Whitlam, Margaret 142
WorkChoices legislation 80, 149–50, 151
World War I 6, 73, 117, 119–23
World War II 47, 48–49, 73, 81, 84, 116, 121

'Yellow Peril' 4, 47n. 3, 73, 128, 175

Zhou En-Lai 140

www.ingramcontent.com/pod-product-compliance
Lightning Source LLC
Chambersburg PA
CBHW021826300426
44114CB00009BA/338